THE SYNAGOGUE OF SATAN

Other Books By RiverCrest Publishing

Codex Magica: Secret Signs, Mysterious Symbols and Hidden Codes of the Illuminati, *by Texe Marrs*

Gladiator: Witchcraft, Propaganda, and the Rise of the World Hero, *by John D. Christian*

Letters on Freemasonry, *by John Quincy Adams*

Honoring the King James Bible, *by Dr. Solomon Aordkian*

Days of Hunger, Days of Chaos, *by Texe Marrs*

Project L.U.C.I.D.: The Beast 666 Universal Human Control System, *by Texe Marrs*

Circle of Intrigue: The Hidden Inner Circle of the Global Illuminati Conspiracy, *by Texe Marrs*

Dark Majesty: The Secret Brotherhood and the Magic of A Thousand Points of Light, *by Texe Marrs*

Mystery Mark of the New Age, *by Texe Marrs*

Dark Secrets of the New Age, *by Texe Marrs*

New Age Lies to Women, *by Wanda Marrs*

THE SYNAGOGUE OF SATAN

Andrew Carrington Hitchcock

RCP RiverCrest Publishing
1708 Patterson Road • Austin, Texas 78733

The Synagogue of Satan

Second Printing, 2007

All scriptures quoted in this book are from the
Authorized King James Version.

Printed in the United States of America

Library of Congress Catalog Card Number 2007921556
Categories: 1. Religion-Bible Prophecy 2. Politics
3. Current Affairs 4. World History

ISBN 978-1-930004-45-0

To contact the author:
Andrew Carrington Hitchcock invites you to contact him at: *andrewcarringtonhitchcock@hotmail.com*, or go to his website: *www.thesynagogueofsatan.com*

Dedicated to the millions of men, women, and children who, throughout the centuries, have suffered at the behest of this "synagogue of Satan."

You are **not** forgotten.

"Ye are of your father, the devil..."

"Jesus said unto them, If God were your father, ye would love me: for I proceeded forth and came from God; neither came I of myself, but he sent me.

Why do ye not understand my speech? *even* because ye cannot hear my word.

Ye are of *your* father the devil, and the lusts of your father ye will do. He was a murderer from the beginning, and abode not in the truth, because there is no truth in him. When he speaketh a lie, he speaketh of his own: for he is a liar, and the father of it.

And because I tell *you* the truth, ye believe me not.

Which of you convinceth me of sin? And if I say the truth, why do ye not believe me?

He that is of God heareth God's words: ye therefore hear *them* not, because ye are not of God.

Then answered the Jews..."

John 8:42 - 8:48

Blood Secrets of the Synagogue of Satan

One group and one group alone is responsible for virtually all wars and bloodshed on the face of this planet. This evil cabal is few in numbers but, like a deadly octopus, its tentacles reach out to grip and strangle untold multitudes of innocent victims. The initiates of every secret society and internationalist organization, from the Council on Foreign Relations and the Jesuits to the Bilderbergers and the Order of Skull & Bones, obey the dictates of this sinister group and tremble when standing before its leaders.

The cabalist group I refer to is the *Synagogue of Satan*, an ancient, yet modern elite so politically powerful and so fabulously wealthy that even past history has been twisted, reshaped, and revised to meet its preferred version of humanity's gloomy, totalitarian future.

Religious and racial in nature, the Synagogue of Satan is, at its essence, a grotesque, satanic cult. Its high council is composed of High Priests of Lucifer; these are men who literally worship death while practicing sexual magick and occult rituals of the blackest nature.

Regrettably, this Luciferian cabal of high priests is supported by over eighteen million people around the globe who call themselves "Jews." Some of these people, a great many, are fanatical in their support of the Synagogue of Satan. They go by the name, "Zionists." Others provide the Cabal with only token, often nominal, support.

These eighteen million Jews are joined in their often zealous embrace by a great number of Gentiles who are also boastful of being Zionists. While these Gentile supporters are, on the whole, woefully ignorant of the horrific, ultimate goal of the Synagogue of Satan, their support and service to the cause of Lucifer helps drive the global Synagogue of Satan's never-ending successful campaigns of revolution, war, famine, financial calamity, and bloodshed.

Given the proven fact that the elitist High Priests of Lucifer who comprise the Synagogue of Satan and their servants possess ownership of almost every major book publishing firm in the world, rarely is a book or volume ever printed that has the courage and audacity requisite to expose the ongoing conspiracy of this monstrous group.

I am, therefore, extremely pleased to recommend to thinking men and women this excellent volume, The *Synagogue of Satan*, by Britain's Andrew Hitchcock. You will find it to be a useful, revealing, and accurate historical guide to the sinister crimes and dark events that have propelled the Synagogue of Satan to the precipice of world power.

The term *Synagogue of Satan* is biblical in origin. As Mr. Hitchcock notes, the book of Revelation in the Holy Bible minces no words. God warns us of the horrendous and diabolical power to be wielded in the last days by the entity identified as the "Synagogue of Satan."

What is most fascinating, however, is that the scriptures clearly tell us that the evil leaders of this entity are *not* Jews! Yes, they say they are Jews, and the world recognizes them as Jews, even as "Israel," but they lie! Listen to what God's Word reveals:

> *"I know the blasphemy of them which say they are Jews, and are not, but are the Synagogue of Satan." (Revelation 2:9)*

Mind-boggling, isn't it? These wicked, world power-brokers want us to believe they are Jews; they boastfully lay claim to Israel as their heritage. But, in reality, they are blasphemous liars. What is going on here?

Given the fact that the masters of the Synagogue of Satan today possess such incredible and extraordinary influence over the media, it stands to reason that the average world citizen easily falls for the Lie. People everywhere trust these great and beneficent leaders who say, *"We are Jews"* to be exactly that: Jews. No wonder the Apostle Paul warned that Satan's disciples come disguised as "ministers of righteousness" and as "angels of light."

In the case of the minions of the Synagogue of Satan, they come to us disguised as "God's Chosen," as "Israel," as the One Race selected by God to produce in the future a Messiah (not Jesus!) for eternity. We are Jews, they proudly boast while, at the same time they suggest that others—that is, the defective lower and inferior races—are obligated by God to bless them, to follow the "Jews" lead, to bow down and serve them as "God's Chosen."

"Yes," they arrogantly explain, "we are Jews, and you are *goyim* (cattle), and we have been chosen by divine edict to rule over you and over the entire planet."

Shocking as it is, these claims by the Jewish pretenders of racial superiority, even Super Race consciousness, have for the most part been accepted by Christian evangelicals as legitimate, authoritative, and coming direct from God. Christian evangelicals say it is the lot of the Gentiles to bow down and accord virtual god-like status to the "Jews" and to their newly formed political entity, Israel, lest God be angered and curse and punish those who resist the Jews and their artificially created nation, "Israel."

Sadly, nowhere in the established Christian Church can be found a pastor or evangelist today who has the spiritual wisdom, or even the common sense, to ask the cardinal question, *"Who is this Synagogue of Satan that God warns about in the book of Revelation?"* And nary a soul seems to ask the correlating question, *"Just who are these wicked imposters of whom God warns will say they are "Jews" and are not, but do lie?*

One thing is for sure—the Bible regards these false, lying Jewish imposters as dangerous, murderous vessels in the hands of their infernal lord, Satan. Revelation 2:10

says the Synagogue of Satan will cast some Christians into prison and kill many others. Their evil plot to conquer the world by stealth and deceit will finally bring about a precarious *Hour of Temptation* for all mankind (Revelation 3:10). So, why aren't pastors and evangelists today warning us to watch out for and beware of these imposter Jews of the Synagogue of Satan?

The riddle of those who say they are Jews but are not, and do lie may be explained by the fact that the men at the top tier of power in the Synagogue of Satan organization have been proven by many respected researchers to be *"Khazar Jews,"* also called *"Ashkenazi Jews."* The Khazars were a Turk-Mongol people who lived centuries ago in the Kingdom of Khazaria, eventually to be integrated into the Russian Empire by the Czars. The King of the Khazars forced his citizens, upon penalty of death, to convert to Judaism. Later, after their takeover by hostile enemies, demographers and historians say that the Khazars migrated into Eastern Europe, especially to Poland, France, Romania, Hungary, and to Germany.

There, in Europe, the Khazars—who *said* they were Jews and practiced a mystical and pagan form of Judaism—gathered in their own communities, keeping separate from those around them whom they classified as "Gentiles." The Khazar "Jews" considered the Gentiles to be racial inferiors. In fact, the racial inferiority of Gentiles was taught to them in their Talmud.

Europe soon became populated by peoples who said

they were Jews, who acculturated as Jews, who adopted and practiced the Babylonian Judaic Pharisaic Religion, but who *were not* real Jews. Most of these people have not a drop of Jewish blood in their bodies, yet they pretend to be "Jews." Many no doubt have bought into their own historical lie. Others know the truth, but attempt to conceal their true, non-Jew heritage to gain advantage since it pays to be a Jew.

To this day, the Ashkenazi Jews, the heirs of the Khazar genealogical lineage, shun DNA tests. They want no evidence produced that will prove they arc *not* Jews. They continue to lie and *say* they are Jews.

In fact, an increasing number of DNA studies and analyses have been published over the past decade. In every case, it was scientifically established that a vast majority of the people alive today who say they are Jews have little or no DNA relationship to the ancient bloodline of the Israelites. One researcher has even reported that Arabs and Palestinians probably have a greater percentage of ancient Israelite blood flowing through *their* veins than today's modern-day "Jew."

It is as if the modern-day descendants of Attila the Hun, Genghis Khan, or Japan's World War II Emperor Hirohito were to falsely declare, with absolutely no proof or evidence to back up their contention, that they are "Jews", and the whole world were to foolishly accept their preposterous, juvenile and unscientific bloodline claims.

Why do these Jewish imposters insist, in the face of overwhelming evidence to the contrary, that they are

"Jews?" Why do they falsely lay claim to being in the direct lineage of Israel's patriarchs, Abraham, Moses, Elijah, and others?

The reason is clear: FOR ADVANTAGE. When modern-day Israel was formed in 1948, the Khazar/Ashkenazi Jews took all the leadership roles in that fledgling nation. Men who lied and said they were Jews, but were not, soon were receiving billions of dollars in free foreign aid money from U.S.A. taxpayers and hundreds of millions more in reparations from a defeated German nation.

These Jewish imposters, moreover, garnered the sympathy and support of billions of deceived dupes around the world who feel guilty or who want to help Jewish *holocaust* victims—though few of the Khazars really ever were victims.

In effect, what we have here is a massive *Personality and Race Cult,* made up of false "Jews" who enthusiastically pretend they are God's Chosen People, the "apple" of His eye, but in reality are blasphemers of God, liars extraordinaire, and global scam artists! These, then, are the denizens of the hellish Synagogue of Satan, who are exposed so well in this book by Andrew Hitchcock.

Wherever those who say they are Jews have chosen to reside in the world today, they prosper and thrive.

In America this is doubly true. In his insightful book, *The Power of Israel in the United States*, Professor James Petras documents the overwhelming control exercised over U.S. foreign and domestic policy by the Jewish Lobby and by Israel. Jews represent only about 2.2% of America's voter-age demographics. The basis for their power, says Petras, is Jewish wealth. In other words—*Money*.

> "The basis of the (Jewish) Lobby's PAC power is rooted in the high proportion of Jewish families among the wealthiest families in the United States. According to *Forbes*, 25 to 30 percent of U.S. multimillionaires and billionaires are Jewish."

Due to their willingness to exercise this Money Power to advance their own race and its prospects, Petras writes, the Jews have established a "tyranny over the U.S."—a tyranny that, Petras warns, *"has grave consequences for world peace and war, the stability and unstability of the world economy, and for the future of democracy in the U.S."*

Petras, in his book, convincingly demonstrates the vile nature of the unseemly Jewish influence over the U.S. political establishment. The United States, because of unrelenting Jewish demands, has become the military and economic proxy of Israel in the Middle East and the globe, committing violence, torture, assassination, terrorism, robbery of resources, and thuggery on a grand scale. When the Jewish Power tell us to do it, we jump to go and do it. Even the horror of genocide is perpetrated if it is to the advantage of the Jews.

In effect, the United States has become a colony of Greater Israel. We, the people of America, act as the

Jews' global bodyguard, fixer, and hit man. We, led by the Gentile puppets who slavishly do the bidding of the Jewish Money Masters, are global capos. On behalf of Jewish interests we are busy converting the entire world into one, giant concentration camp. We are the camp's guards and its executioners; the "Jews" are its commandants, and the people of planet earth are its inmates. At the mere whim of the Synagogue of Satan, the inmates are starved, worked to death, and discarded.

The best and brightest of the Gentiles are rewarded with grotesque entertainments and lustful transient pleasures. Until their usefulness is exhausted and then, they, too, are thrown off the deep end of a pier, dying of alcoholism, clogged arteries, Alzheimer's, and other diseases brought on by the debilitating pharmaceuticals sold by Jewish-owned corporate drug giants.

What of the *real* Jews? Here, we refer to the Sephardic Jews, some of whom are actually able to trace their heritage back to ancient Israel.

Please keep in mind that God is no respecter of persons, and that racial advantage has no part to play in God's heavenly Jerusalem. Indeed, contrary to the doctrines of devils spread by lying evangelicals, God does not distinguish between races in choosing a people for His name. *Galatians 3:28-29* is marvelous in dispelling satanic notions of racial superiority. God does not favor those who are "Jew" or those of any one race or ethnic heritage. Instead, the Bible invites men and women of every nation and race on earth to come and drink of Jesus' living water: *"And if ye be Christ's, then are ye Abraham's seed and heirs according to the promise."*

Paul perfectly explains the spiritual applications of this life-giving principle when he states that according to the Word of God, *"They which are the children of the flesh, these are not the children of God: but the children of the promise are counted for the seed." (Romans 9:8)*

What a wonderful thing! Regardless of a person's race or bloodline, and in spite of lowly physical or geographical origins, any man or woman can be elevated to the high and eternal status of God's Chosen. How is this amazing feat accomplished? Through faith in Jesus Christ alone, for it is the gift of God, a gift awarded not based on a man's racial heritage, but on the spiritual treasure that resides in his heart.

Tragically, today I find that many, indeed, almost the whole majority of Jews, have bought into the lies of the Synagogue of Satan. Their xenophobic racial and national pride has overcome far too many Jews. Secular Jews and religious "Jews" alike, Ashkenazi and Sephardic Jews, have fallen in the trap. Believing the rabbis' lying doctrines, as elaborated in the poisonous, racially infused holy books of Judaism, the Talmud and the texts of the Kaballah, those who identify themselves as Jews often love to presume they are smarter, better, more spiritual, more divine than their fellows who are Gentiles.

These "Jews" may be privy to or may not even remotely understand the heinous plan and designs of the Sabbatian, satanic "Jews" of the Synagogue of Satan. Nevertheless, by flattery they have been deceived. So, they sit back and luxuriate and bask in the glow of their supposed racial blood superiority. They also acquiesce in the imperial designs of the butchers who run the fascist government of today's physical nation of Israel. They believe it when their rabbis tell them that as God's Chosen, their destiny is to rule the world and acquire all its wealth. They give monies to politicians and to Jewish causes that lead to violence and bloodshed for the beleaguered Palestinians and Arabs. After all, Arabs are thought to be inferior people. Many rabbis eagerly classify Arabs and other Gentiles as like unto insects, Goyim (cattle) at best, destined for the dung heap of history. *Long live the Jewish Super race!*

It is true that not every Jew expresses such deviant views. Yet, many "Jews" are silent. Inwardly, they crave the rabbinical and talmudic flattery heaped on them. They also realize that they gain advantage because they are "Jews," so they say and do nothing to prevent the Synagogue of Satan from advancing its goals. In truth, the silent are themselves complicit. Omission and commission are one and the same. And "not to decide" to do what is right *is* to decide to do what is wrong.

It has always been the case that the cowardly inactions of the "Silent Majority" lend power and credentials to the active Minority who rule. In the ongoing American war against the hapless, suffering citizens of Iraq, the U.S. Armed Forces have, according to a Johns Hopkins Medical University Study published in the respected *Lancet* medical journal, now massacred over 655,000 Iraqis. This gruesome statistic is of non-combatant, innocent men, women and children.

But watch out!—It is not only the military brass and the leaders in the Bush Administration who are culpable in this genocidal crime. Every American citizen, by his inaction and failure to protest, is guilty of this mayhem and murder.

Likewise, every person who says, "I am a Jew" and who, being racially prejudiced and bigoted, tends to prefer his or her racial tribe (Jew) to all others and proceeds to discriminate and mistreat the so-called inferior Gentiles (Goyim) is guilty of satanic crimes. This is especially the case for all those who are Zionists; all such people are guilty of membership in, and support for, the Synagogue of Satan. This includes Jewish bankers, corporate CEOs, educators, teachers, broadcasters—the whole kit and caboodle of people who say they are "Jews."

Virtually all Jews, by extension, are of the Synagogue of Satan. A Jew may say, "No, that cannot be. I did not vote for these evil men. I do not approve of their monstrous deeds. I just live my daily life in the pursuit of happiness and prosperity."

Do not be deceived. You are wrong. You *are* guilty. You may be silent, yet your inaction makes you as a willing accomplice in the crimes and designs of the Synagogue of Satan. You are a co-conspirator, and you *will* someday pay the full price for your heinous crimes, whether of omission or commission.

Is this a "collective guilt?" Yes, indeed it is and while man may frown on it, God has ordained it. Truly, all of mankind is under a collective curse due to the fall of Adam and Eve in the Garden. That is why man needs a redeemer, to redeem and deliver him from this curse. As for the Jews, Jesus Himself solemnly declared this prophecy.

> *"Fill ye up then the measure of your fathers.*
>
> *Ye serpents, ye generation (race) of vipers, how can ye escape the damnation of hell?...*
>
> *That upon you may come all the righteous blood shed upon the earth...*
>
> *Behold, your house is left unto you desolate."*
> *—Matthew 23: 32-38*

Whether man likes it or not, Jesus Christ has placed a terrible, collective curse on the Jews. If a man, by his own tongue, identifies himself as a Jew, even if he lies in doing so, he unwisely places himself under this horrendous curse. He becomes, then, a cog in the terrible inhuman machine called the Synagogue of Satan. Yet, let it be known by all that every man and woman, Jew and Gentile, is offered liberty and a means of escape from the curse through faith in Jesus Christ our Lord. A curse may be collective or individual, but the blessings of salvation and deliverance are always tendered to individuals.

So as not to be misconstrued, I level this same warning and accusation against Gentiles. You Gentiles who suspect or know of the evil ways of the elite leaders of the Synagogue of Satan and do nothing to stop them—or worse, act as their accomplice—are equally guilty of their crimes. Thus, the Synagogue of Satan is made up not only of lying, blasphemous men and women who say they are Jews and are not, but also of Gentiles who collaborate with them. All are complicit and are serving Lucifer.

What is the ultimate goal of the Synagogue of Satan? Its goal is to corrupt mens' souls, destroy every independent government and enslave the world in a Luciferian dictatorship led by their own Despot King. The method they employ as they proceed in this endeavor is to cause chaos, followed by their own well-designed establishment of order: *Order Ab Chao*. Cyclically, perpetually played out on the world scene, they cause wars and revolutions and foster economic chaos and social instability. Chaos is their engine of progress until, eventually, all of mankind is so exhausted people everywhere are expected to desperately cry out for a World Authority to finally bring in order and global peace. But for the evil-doers who say they are Jews there truly is no peace to be had. Only a police state with absolute slavery for all mankind will satisfy them.

Why are these evil-doers so determined to wreak havoc, to work bloodshed and to demolish the earth to bring about their long-sought, vain-glorious *"Jewish Utopia?"* I do not blink to state to you clearly and in no uncertain terms that the worst of these wicked perverts are Luciferians. The people at the very top of the Synagogue of Satan are possessed by devils. Their plot is of biblical proportions. It is also of intergenerational character. The same demons who yesterday infested Mayer Rothschild, Napoleon, Marx, and Lenin today work inside the human shells of 21st century disciples. Since the day of Luciferian deception in the Garden of Eden and the murder of righteous Abel by Satan's Cain, these partisans of hell have labored.

Their more recent incarnations have produced the *Protocols of the Learned Elders of Zion*, the horrors of World Wars I and II, and the so-called Cold War and its many conflicts. Now, through their aggression and wars in the Middle East, they threaten to annihilate and engulf the world in the nuclear nightmare of World War III. The death and misery will never stop until Christ returns again.

The Synagogue of Satan will steadily deceive, slander, kill and plot until the end comes. They have no other choice. The devil and his fallen angels eons ago rolled the dice, figuratively speaking, and lost. They foolishly rebelled and now must pay the full penalty. So, too, will all those who ally themselves with today's devil-led Synagogue of Satan.

Someday, all who ally themselves with the Synagogue of Satan, including those who attempt to remain aloof and choose to remain silent, will be forced to grovel at the very feet of those whom the Synagogue of Satan have so viciously and cruelly robbed, persecuted, and killed.

> *"Behold, I will make them of the synagogue of Satan, which say they are Jews, and are not, but do lie; behold, I will make them to come and worship before thy feet, and to know that I have loved thee." (Revelation 3:9)*

— Texe Marrs, author,
Codex Magica

"I know thy works, and tribulation and poverty, (but thou art rich) and *I know* the blasphemy of them which say they are Jews, and are not, but *are* the synagogue of Satan."

Revelation 2:9

The Synagogue of Satan—A Chronology of Its History and Agenda

740: In 740 A.D. in a land locked between the Black Sea and the Caspian Sea known as Khazaria, a land which today is predominantly occupied by Georgia, but also reaches into Russia, Poland, Lithuania, Hungary, and Romania, the modern Jewish race is born. A modern Jewish race that incidentally is not Jewish.

How can this be? The Khazarian people were a vulnerable people. They had Muslims one side of them and Christians the other side, and thus constantly feared attack from either side. The Khazarian people were of neither faith and instead practiced idol worship, which made them ripe for invasion by a people who wished to convert them to an established faith. The Khazarian King, King Bulan, decided in order to protect themselves against attack, the Khazarian people must convert to one of these faiths, but which one? If they converted to the Muslim faith they would risk attack by the Christians and if they converted to the Christian faith they would risk attack by the Muslims.

There was another religion that he was aware was able to deal with both the Muslims and the Christians. That race was the Jews. King Bulan decided if he instructed his people to convert to Judaism he could keep both the Muslims and the Christians happy, as they were both already willing to trade with the Jews, so this is what he did.

King Bulan was right. He would live to see his country unconquered, his people convert to Judaism and adopt the principles of the most holy Jewish book, the Talmud. There are many things the king would not live to see, however.

He would not live to see his nation's converts to Judaism one day represent 90% of all the Jews on the planet, and call themselves Ashkenazi Jews, when in fact they were not Jews, but an Asiatic race of people who converted to the Jewish religion, whilst still continuing to speak the Khazarian language of Yiddish, totally different to the language of Hebrew. He would not live to see his people turn to the descendants of a man, far more powerful than him, who would be born just over 1,000 years later in Germany, a man named Bauer, who would spawn the Rothschild dynasty.

He would not live to see this dynasty usurp the wealth of the world through deception and intrigue, which they would finance through the vast riches they accumulate as they usurp the wealth of the world by gaining control of the world's money supply.

He would not live to see his people demand a homeland for themselves in Palestine as their birthright, and ensure every Prime Minister there from its inception in 1948 is an Ashkenazi Jew, even though the true homeland of the Ashkenazi Jews, Khazaria, is a land some 800 miles away.

And he would not live to see his people fulfill bible prophecy, as the "synagogue of Satan."

1649: Oliver Cromwell obtains backing from the British parliament for the execution of King Charles I on a charge of treason. Afterwards, Cromwell permits the Jews to enter England again, effectively reversing the Edict of Expulsion issued by King Edward I in 1290, which expelled all Jews forever from England and made the provision that any who remained after November 1st 1290, were to be executed.

Indeed England is not the first country to expel the Jews. Here is a partial list of all the areas from which the Jews have been banished from, sometimes on numerous occasions, over the last thousand years.

Mainz, 1012
France, 1182
Upper Bavaria, 1276
England, 1290
France, 1306
France, 1322
Saxony, 1349
Hungary, 1360
Belgium, 1370
Slovakia, 1380
France, 1394
Austria, 1420
Lyons, 1420
Cologne, 1424
Mainz, 1438
Augsburg, 1438
Upper Bavaria, 1442
Netherlands, 1444
Brandenburg, 1446
Mainz, 1462
Lithuania, 1495
Portugal, 1496
Naples, 1496
Navarre, 1498
Nuremberg, 1498
Brandenburg, 1510
Prussia, 1510
Genoa, 1515
Naples, 1533
Italy, 1540
Naples, 1541
Prague, 1541
Genoa, 1550
Bavaria, 1551
Prague, 1557
Papal States, 1569
Hungary, 1582
Hamburg, 1649
Vienna, 1669
Slovakia, 1744

Mainz, 1483	Moravia, 1744
Warsaw, 1483	Bohemia, 1744
Spain, 1492	Moscow, 1891
Italy, 1492	

In his book, "L'antisémitisme son histoire et ses causes," published in 1894, noted Jewish author, Bernard Lazare, stated the following with regard to these expulsions of Jews,

> "If this hostility, even aversion, had only been shown towards the Jews at one period and in one country, it would be easy to unravel the limited causes of this anger, but this race has been on the contrary an object of hatred to all the peoples among whom it has established itself. It must be therefore, since the enemies of the Jews belonged to the most diverse races, since they lived in countries very distant from each other, since they were ruled by very different laws, governed by opposite principles, since they had neither the same morals, nor the same customs, since they were animated by unlike dispositions which did not permit them to judge of anything in the some way, it must be therefore that the general cause of anti-Semitism has always resided in Israel itself and not in those who have fought against Israel."

Professor Jesse H. Holmes, writing in, "The American Hebrew," expressed the following similar sentiments,

> "It can hardly be an accident that antag-

> onism directed against the Jews is to be found pretty much everywhere in the world where Jews and non-Jews are associated. And as the Jews are the common element of the situation it would seem probable, on the face of it, that the cause will be found in them rather than in the widely varying groups which feel this antagonism."

1688: A. N. Field, in his book, "All These Things," published in 1931, explains the situation in England this year, as a result of Cromwell's decision to ignore the law banning the Jews from entering England, and allowing them back in defiance of the law, only 33 years earlier, as follows,

> "Thirty-three years after Cromwell had let the Jews into Britain a Dutch Prince arrived from Amsterdam surrounded by a whole swarm of Jews from that Jewish financial centre. Driving his royal father-in-law out of the kingdom, he graciously consented to ascend the throne of Britain. A very natural result following on this event was the inauguration of the National Debt by the establishment six years later of the Bank of England for the purpose of lending money to the Crown. Britain had paid her way as she went until the Jew arrived."

1694: The deceptively named, "Bank of England," is founded. It is deceptively named as it gives the impression it is controlled by the Government of

England when in fact it is a private institution founded by Jews. In his book, "The Breakdown of Money," published in 1934, Christopher Hollis explains the formation of the Bank of England, as follows,

> "In 1694 the Government of William III (who had come in from Holland with the Jews) was in sore straits for money. A company of rich men under the leadership of one William Paterson offered to lend William £1,200,000 at 8 per cent on the condition that, 'the Governor and Company of the Bank of England,' as they called themselves, should have the right to issue notes to the full extent of its capital. That is to say, the Bank got the right to collect £1,200,000 in gold and silver and to turn it into £2,400,000 (that is, double it), lending £1,200,000, the gold and silver to the Government, and using the other £1,200,000, the banknotes, themselves.
>
> Paterson was quite right about it that this privilege which had been given to the Bank was a privilege to make money.... In practice they did not keep a cash reserve of nearly two or three hundred thousand pounds. By 1696 (ie. within two years) we find them circulating £1,750,000 worth of notes against a cash reserve of £36,000. That is with a, 'backing,' of only about 2 percent of what they issued and drew interest on."

The names of the Jewish controllers of the Bank of England are never revealed, but it is clear, as early as this year, through their control of the Bank of England, Jews had control over the British Royal family. However, whilst their identity is protected, they may have wished they picked a more discreet front man, after William Paterson states,

> "The Bank hath benefit of interest on all monies which it creates out of nothing."

The fact that Paterson chose to let the cat out of the bag in this manner may explain why he would go on to die a poor man, outcast by his associates, or maybe this "shabbez goy" (a non Jew who chose to clandestinely represent the interests of Jews) had merely outlived his usefulness to the Jews behind the scenes.

1698: Following four years of the Bank of England, the Jewish control of the British money supply had come on in leaps and bounds. They had flooded the country with so much money that the Government debt to the Bank had grown from its' initial £1,250,000, to £16,000,000, in only four years, an increase of 1,280%.

Why do they do it? Simple, if the money in circulation in a country is £5,000,000, and a central bank is set up and prints another £15,000,000, stage one of the plan, and sends that out into the economy through loans etc, then this will naturally reduce the value of the initial £5,000,000 that was in circulation before the bank was formed. This is because the initial £5,000,000 that was 100% of the economy is now only 25% of the economy. It will also give the bank control of 75% of the money in circulation with the £15,000,000 they sent out into the economy.

This causes inflation which is simply the reduction in worth of money borne by the common person, due to the economy being flooded with too much money, an economy which the Central Bank are responsible for. As the common person's money is worth less, he has to go to the bank to get a loan to help run his business and when the Central Bank is satisfied there are enough people with debt out there, the bank will tighten the supply of money by not offering loans. This is stage two of the plan.

Stage three, is sitting back and waiting for the people in debt to them to go bankrupt, allowing the bank to then seize from them real wealth, businesses and property etc, for pennies on the pound. Inflation never affects a central bank, in fact they are the only group who can benefit from it, as if they are ever short of money they can simply print more.

1744: On February 23rd, Mayer Amschel Bauer, an Ashkenazi Jew, is born in Frankfurt, Germany, the son of Moses Amschel Bauer, a money lender and the proprietor of a counting house.

Moses Amschel Bauer places a red sign above the entrance door to his counting house. This sign is a red hexagram (that geometrically and numerically translates into the number 666), which under Rothschild instruction will end up on the Israeli flag some two centuries later.

1753: Gutle Schnaper, an Ashkenazi Jew (future wife of

Mayer Amschel Bauer), is born to respected merchant, Wolf Salomon Schnaper.

1760: During this decade Mayer Amschel Bauer works for a bank owned by the Oppenheimers in Hanover, Germany. He is highly successful and becomes a junior partner. Whilst working at the bank he becomes acquainted with General von Estorff.

Following his father's death, Bauer returns to Frankfurt to take over his father's business. Bauer recognises the significance of the red hexagram and changes his name from Bauer to Rothschild after the red hexagram or sign signifying 666 hanging over the entrance door ("Rot," is German for "Red," "Schild" is German for "Shield," or "Sign").

Under his new identity of Mayer Amschel Rothschild, he discovers that General von Estorff is now attached to the court of Prince William IX of Hesse-Hanau, one of the richest royal houses in Europe, which gained its' wealth by the hiring out of Hessian soldiers to foreign countries for vast profits (a practice that continues today in the form of exporting United Nations' "peace-keeping" troops throughout the world).

He therefore makes the General's re-acquaintance on the pretext of selling him valuable coins and trinkets at discounted prices. As he plans, Rothschild is subsequently introduced to Prince William himself who is most pleased with the discounted prices he charges for his rare coins and trinkets, and Rothschild offers him a form of commission for any other business the Prince can direct his way.

Rothschild subsequently becomes close associates with Prince William, and ends up doing business with him and members of the court. He soon discovers that loaning money to governments and royalty is far more profitable than loaning to individuals, as the loans are bigger and they are secured by the nation's taxes.

1769: Mayer Amschel Rothschild becomes court agent for Prince William IX of Hesse-Cassel: the grandson of George II of England; cousin to George III; nephew to the King of Denmark; and brother-in-law to the King of Sweden. He is subsequently given permission by Prince William to hang a sign on the front of his business premises declaring that he is, "M. A. Rothschild, by appointment court factor to his serene highness, Prince William of Hanau."

1770: Mayer Amschel Rothschild draws up plans for the creation of the "Illuminati," and entrusts Ashkenazi Jew, Adam Weishaupt, a Crypto-Jew (a Jew who pretends he's not Jewish) who is outwardly Roman Catholic, with its organization and development. The "Illuminati" is to be based upon the teachings of the Talmud, which is in turn the teachings of Rabbinical Jews. It is to be called the "Illuminati," which is a Luciferian term which means "keepers of the light."

On August 29th, Mayer Amschel Rothschild marries Gutle Schnaper.

1771: On August 20th, Schönche Jeannette Rothschild is born, the first of Mayer Amschel Rothschild's five daughters. She goes on to marry Benedikt Moses Worms.

1773: On June 12th, Amschel Mayer Rothschild is born, the first of Mayer Amschel Rothschild's five sons. He, like all his brothers who follow him, will enter the family business at the age of twelve.

1774: On September 9th, Salomon Mayer Rothschild is born.

1776: Adam Weishaupt officially completes his organisation of the "Illuminati," on May 1st of this year. The purpose of the "Illuminati" is to divide the non-Jews through political, economic, social, and religious means. The plan is for the opposing sides of the goyim (non-Jews) to be armed whilst incidents are to be provided in order for them to fight amongst themselves; destroy national governments; destroy religious institutions; and eventually destroy each other.

Weishaupt soon infiltrates the Continental Order of Freemasons with this "Illuminati" doctrine and establishes lodges of the Grand Orient to be their secret headquarters. This is all under the orders and finance of Mayer Amschel Rothschild, and the concept subsequently spreads into Masonic Lodges worldwide to the present day.

Weishaupt also recruits 2,000 paid followers including

the most intelligent men in the field of arts and letters, education, science, finance, and industry. They are instructed to follow the following methods in order to control people:

> 1) Use monetary and sex bribery to obtain control of men already in high places, in the various levels of all governments and other fields of endeavour. Once influential persons have fallen for the lies, deceits, and temptations of the Illuminati they are to be held in bondage by application of political and other forms of blackmail, threats of financial ruin, public exposure, and fiscal harm, even death to themselves and members of their families.
>
> 2) The faculties of colleges and universities are to cultivate students possessing exceptional mental ability as well as belonging to well-bred families with international leanings, and recommend them for special training in internationalism, or rather the notion that only a one-world government can put an end to recurring war and strife. Such training is to be provided by granting scholarships to those selected by the "Illuminati."
>
> 3) All influential people trapped into coming under the control of the "Illuminati," plus the students who had been specially educated and trained, are to be used as agents and placed behind the scenes of all governments as experts and specialists. This is to ensure they advise the top executives to adopt policies which in the

long-run serve the secret plans of the "Illuminati" one-world conspiracy and bring about the destruction of the governments and religions they are elected or appointed to serve.

4) To obtain absolute control of the press, at that time the only mass-communications media which distributed information to the public, so that all news and information could be slanted in order to make the masses believe that a one-world government is the only solution to the world's many and varied problems.

1777: On September 16th, Nathan Mayer Rothschild is born.

1781: On July 2nd, Isabella Rothschild is born.

1784: On August 29th, Babette Rothschild is born.

Adam Weishaupt issues his order in the form of a book for the French Revolution to be started by Maximilien Robespierre. This book is written by one of Weishaupt's associates, Xavier Zwack, and sent by courier from Frankfurt to Paris. However, en-route there the courier is struck by lightning. The book detailing this plan is discovered by the police and handed over to the Bavarian authorities.

As a consequence, the Bavarian government orders the

police to raid Weishaupt's Masonic Lodges of the Grand Orient, and the homes of his most influential associates. Clearly, the Bavarian authorities were convinced that the book that was discovered was a very real threat by a private group of influential people, who planned the use of wars and revolutions to achieve their political ends.

1785: The Bavarian government outlaw the "Illuminati," and close all the Bavarian lodges of the Grand Orient.

Mayer Amschel Rothschild moves his family home to a five storey house in Frankfurt which he shares with the Schiff family.

1786: The Bavarian government publishes the details of the "Illuminati" plot in a document entitled, "The Original Writings of The Order and Sect of The Illuminati." They then send this document to all the heads of church and state throughout Europe, who sadly ignore their warning.

1788: On April 24th, Kalmann (Carl) Mayer Rothschild is born.

1789: Due to the European ignorance of the Bavarian government's warning, the "Illuminati's" plan for a French Revolution succeeds from this year to its' completion in 1793. This revolution is a central bankers' dream, as it establishes a new constitution and passes laws that both forbids the Roman Church from levying tithes (taxes) and also removes the Church's exemption from taxation.

1790: Mayer Amschel Rothschild states,

> "Let me issue and control a nation's money and I care not who writes the laws."

On May 1st, Julie Rothschild is born.

1791: The Rothschilds get "control of a nation's money" through Alexander Hamilton (their agent in George Washington's cabinet) when they set up a central bank in the United States called the First Bank of the United States. This is established with a 20 year charter.

Within the first five years of the life of this central bank, the American Government will borrow $8,200,000 from it, and prices in the country will increase by 72%. In relation to this excessive borrowing and inflation, Thomas Jefferson, then Secretary of State goes on to state,

> "I wish it were possible to obtain a single amendment to our constitution taking from the Federal Government their power of borrowing."

Henriette ("Jette") Rothschild is born, who goes on to

marry Moses Montefiore. Montefiore will become the President of the Board of Deputies of British Jews from 1835-1874.

1792: On May 15th, the last of Mayer Amschel Rothschild's children, Jacob (James) Mayer Rothschild is born.

1796: Amschel Mayer Rothschild marries Eva Hanau.

1798: John Robison publishes a book entitled, "Proofs of a Conspiracy Against All the Religions and Governments of Europe Carried on in the Secret Meetings of Freemasons, Illuminati and Reading Societies." In this book, Professor Robison of the University of Edinburgh, one of the leading intellects of his time, who in 1783 was elected general secretary of the Royal Society of Edinburgh, gives details of the whole Rothschild "Illuminati" plot.

He advises how he had been a high degree mason in the Scottish Rite of Freemasonry and had been invited by Adam Weishaupt to Europe, where he was given a revised copy of Weishaupt's conspiracy. However, although he pretended to go along with it, Professor Robison did not agree with it and therefore published his aforementioned book to expose it. The book included details of the Bavarian government's investigation into the "Illuminati" and the French Revolution.

That same year on July 19th, David Pappen, President of

Harvard University, lectures the graduating class on the influence "Illuminism" is having on American politics and religion.

At the age of twenty-one, Nathan Mayer Rothschild leaves Frankfurt for England where, with a large sum of money given to him by his father, he sets up a banking house in London.

1800: In France, the Bank of France is set up. Napoleon would soon see that a free France would mean a country free of debt, and he subsequently states,

> "The hand that gives is among the hand that takes. Money has no motherland, financiers are without patriotism and without decency. Their sole object is gain."

Salomon Mayer Rothschild marries Caroline Stern.

1806: Napolean states that it is his

> "object to remove the house of Hesse-Cassel from rulership and to strike it out of the list of powers."

On hearing this, Prince William IX of Hesse-Hanau, flees Germany, goes to Denmark and entrusts his fortune, valued at $3,000,000 at that time, to Mayer Amschel Rothschild for safekeeping.

Nathan Mayer Rothschild marries Hannah Barent Cohen, the daughter of a wealthy London merchant.

1807: President Thomas Jefferson (the third President of the United States from 1801-1809), provides one of the first honest insights into the dishonesty and corruptibility of the media when he states,

> "Nothing can now be believed which is seen in a newspaper. Truth itself becomes suspicious by being put into that polluted vehicle. The real extent of this state of misinformation is known only to those who are in situations to confront facts within their knowledge with the lies of the day."

1808: Nathan Mayer Rothschild has his first son, born Lionel Nathan de Rothschild.

1810: Sir Francis Baring and Abraham Goldsmid die. This leaves Nathan Mayer Rothschild as the remaining major banker in England.

Salomon Mayer Rothschild goes to Vienna, Austria and sets up the bank, M. von Rothschild und Söhne.

1811: The charter for the Rothschilds' Bank of the United States runs out and Congress votes against its renewal. Nathan Mayer Rothschild is not amused and he states,

> "Either the application for renewal of the charter is granted, or the United States will find itself involved in a most disastrous war."

However the United States stands firm and the charter is not renewed, which causes Nathan Mayer Rothschild to issue another threat, in which he states,

> "Teach those impudent Americans a lesson. Bring them back to colonial status."

1812: Backed by Rothschild money, and Nathan Mayer Rothschild's orders, the British declare war on the United States. The Rothschilds' plan is to cause the United States to build up such a debt in fighting this war that they have no option but to surrender to the British and allow the charter for the Rothschild owned First Bank of the United States to be renewed. However, as the British are still busy fighting Napoleon, they are unable to mount much of an assault and the war ends in 1814 with America undefeated.

On September 19th, Mayer Amschel Rothschild dies. In his will he lays out specific laws that the House of Rothschild are to follow:

> 1) All key positions in the family business are only to be held by family members.
>
> 2) Only male members of the family are allowed to participate in the family business. This included a reported sixth secret bastard son (It is

important to note here that Mayer Amschel Rothschild also had five daughters, so today the spread of the Rothschild dynasty *without* the Rothschild name is far and wide, and Jews believe the mixed offspring of a Jewish mother is solely Jewish).

3) The family is to intermarry with its' first and second cousins to preserve the family fortune (interestingly, according to the Jewish Encyclopaedia of 1905, of the fifty-eight Rothschild marriages to that date, exactly half, or twenty-nine, had been to first cousins—a practice known today as inbreeding).

4) No public inventory of his estate is to be published.

5) No legal action is to be taken with regard to the value of the inheritance.

6) The eldest son of the eldest son is to become the head of the family (this condition could only be overturned when the majority of the family agreed otherwise).

Law number six is straightaway put into effect when Nathan Mayer Rothschild is elected his father's successor as head of the family.

Jacob (James) Mayer Rothschild goes to Paris, France to set up the bank, de Rothschild Frères.

Nathaniel de Rothschild, the son of Nathan Mayer Rothschild, is born.

1814: With regard to the $3,000,000 Prince William IX of Hesse-Hanau had entrusted to Mayer Amschel Rothschild for safekeeping, the Jewish Encyclopaedia, 1905 edition, Volume 10, page 494, gives the following account of where it ended up,

> "According to legend this money was hidden away in wine casks, and, escaping the search of Napoleon's soldiers when they entered Frankfurt, was restored intact in the same casks in 1814, when the elector (Prince William IX of Hesse-Hanau) returned to the electorate (Germany). The facts are somewhat less romantic, and more businesslike."

This last line indicates the money was never returned by Rothschild to Prince William IX of Hesse-Hanau. The encyclopaedia goes on to state,

> "Nathan Mayer Rothschild invested this $3,000,000 in, gold from the East India company knowing that it would be needed for Wellington's peninsula campaign."

Furthermore, on the stolen money Nathan made,

> "no less than four profits:
>
> 1) On the sale of Wellington's paper which he bought at 50 cents on the dollar and collected at par.

2) On the sale of gold to Wellington.

3) On its' repurchase.

4) On forwarding it to Portugal."

1815: The five Rothschild brothers work to supply gold to both Wellington's army (through Nathan in England), and Napoleon's army (through Jacob in France), and begin their policy of funding both sides in wars. The Rothschilds love wars because they are massive generators of risk free debt.

Risk free, because the debts are guaranteed by the government of a country, and therefore the efforts of the population of that country, and furthermore it doesn't matter which country loses the war because the loans are given on the guarantee that the victor will honour the debts of the vanquished.

Whilst the Rothschilds are funding both sides in this war, they use the banks they have spread out across Europe to give them the opportunity to set up an unrivalled postal service network of secret routes and fast couriers. Mail that these couriers carry is opened up by the couriers and the details of their contents given to the Rothschilds so they are always one step ahead of current events.

These Rothschild couriers are the only merchants allowed to pass through the English and French blockades, and they use this advantage to keep Nathan Mayer Rothschild up to date with how the war is going so he is able to use that intelligence to buy and sell from his position on the stock exchange in accordance with that intelligence.

One of Rothschild's couriers, a man named Rothworth, upon learning the British won the Battle of Waterloo, takes off for the Channel and delivers this news to Nathan Mayer Rothschild a full 24 hours before Wellington's own courier.

Nathan Mayer Rothschild subsequently enters the stock exchange and instructs all his workers to start selling consuls (known as bonds today). Due to Rothschild's reputation for being one step ahead with regard to information, the other traders panic, think the British have lost the war, and start selling frantically.

As a result the consuls plummet in value, at which point Nathan Mayer Rothschild discreetly instructs his workers to purchase all the consuls they can lay their hands on.

When the news comes through that the British had actually won the war, the consuls rocket up to a level even higher than before the war started, leaving Nathan Mayer Rothschild with a return of approximately twenty to one on his investment. In fact, Nathan Rothschild openly brags that in his seventeen years in England he has increased his initial £20,000 stake given to him by his father, 2500 times to £50,000,000.

The ownership of these bonds, or consuls, gives the Rothschild family complete control of the British economy, now the undisputed financial centre of the world (following Napoleon's defeat) and forces the British to set up a new Bank of England under the control of Nathan Mayer Rothschild.

Interestingly, one hundred years later The New York Times would run a story stating that Nathan Mayer Rothschild's grandson had attempted to secure a court order to suppress publication of a book which had this insider trading story in it. The Rothschild family claimed the story was untrue and libellous, but the court denied the Rothschilds' request and ordered the family to pay all court costs.

Back to 1815, this is the year Nathan Mayer Rothschild makes his famous statement,

> "I care not what puppet is placed upon the throne of England to rule the Empire on which the sun never sets. The man who controls Britain's money supply controls the British Empire, and I control the British money supply."

The Rothschilds also use their control of the Bank of England to replace the method of shipping gold from country to country and instead use their five banks spread across Europe to set up a system of paper debits and credits, the banking system of today.

By the end of this century, a period of time that becomes known as the "Age of the Rothschilds," it is estimated that the Rothschild family controls over half the wealth of the world.

Indeed, a letter to Nathan Rothschild from Soloman Rothschild dated February 28th of this year states,

> "We are like the mechanism of a watch, each part is essential."

However something that did not go as well as the Rothschilds would have liked this year is the Congress of Vienna, which started in September, 1814 and concluded in June of this year. The reason for this Congress of Vienna was for the Rothschilds to create a form of world government, using the debt that many European governments owed them as leverage to give them complete political control over much of the civilized world.

The Congress started well, when the Rothschilds managed to get Switzerland declared forever neutral in wars, in order to provide them with a sovereign territory from which to finance both sides in their manufactured debt creating wars. They also had Switzerland's borders extended to include within its' territory Valais; Neuchatel; and Geneva. However their ultimate plan for world government fails when Tsar Alexander I of Russia, one of the few great powers who had not succumbed to a Rothschild central bank, refuses to accept world government.

Enraged by this, Nathan Mayer Rothschild swears that some day he or his descendants will destroy the Tsar Alexander Ist's entire family and descendants. Unfortunately he would prove to be true to his word when one hundred and two years later Rothschild funded Jewish Bolsheviks would act upon that promise.

Interestingly, world government fanatic and Ashkenazi Jew, Henry Kissinger, did his doctoral dissertation on the Congress of Vienna.

On June 19th, Julie Rothschild dies.

1816: The American Congress pass a bill permitting yet another Rothschild dominated central bank, which gives the Rothschilds control of the American money supply again. This is called the Second Bank of the United States and is given a twenty year charter. This of course means the end of the British war against America with the deaths of thousands of British and American soldiers, and the formation of another Rothschild owned central bank.

1818: Following the French securing massive loans in 1817 in order to help rebuild after their disastrous defeat at Waterloo, Rothschild agents purchase vast amounts of French government bonds causing their value to increase.

On November 5th they dump the lot on the open market causing their value to plummet and France as a whole to go into a financial panic. The Rothschilds then step in to take control of the French money supply in a similar way to their manipulation of the British stock market 6 years earlier.

1821: Kalmann (Carl) Mayer Rothschild is sent to Naples, Italy. He goes on to do a great deal of business with the Vatican, and Pope Gregory XVI subsequently confers upon him the Order of St. George.

Also, whenever the Pope receives Kalmann, he gives him his hand rather than the customary toe to kiss, which causes concern with regard to the extent of Kalmann Rothschild's power over the Vatican.

1822: The emperor of Austria makes the five Rothschild brothers, "Barons." Nathan Mayer Rothschild chooses not to take up the title.

1823: The Rothschilds take over the financial operations of the Catholic Church, worldwide.

1827: Sir Walter Scott publishes his nine volume set, "The Life of Napoleon," and in volume two he states that the French Revolution was planned by the "Illuminati" (Adam Weishaupt) and financed by the money changers of Europe (The Rothschilds).

1828: After 12 years during which the Second Bank of the United States ruthlessly manipulated the American economy to the detriment of the people but to the benefit of their own money grabbing ends, the American people had enough, and opponents of this bank nominated Senator Andrew Jackson of Tennessee to run for President.

To the dismay of the Rothschilds, Jackson wins the Presidency and makes it quite clear he is going to use his mandate to kill this bank at his first opportunity. He starts out during his first term in office rooting out the bank's many minions from government service. To illustrate how deep this cancer was rooted in government, in order to achieve this end he had to fire 2,000 of the 11,000 employees of the Federal Government.

1830: David Sassoon, a Jew and Jewish banker of David Sassoon & Co., with branches in China, Japan and Hong Kong, uses his monopoly of the opium-trade in this area on behalf of the Rothschild controlled British government to traffic 18,956 chests of opium. This earned millions of dollars for the Rothschilds and the British Royal family.

1832: The Second Bank of the United States asks Congress to pass a renewal of the bank's charter, four years early. Congress complies and sends the bill to President Jackson (the 7th President of the United States, serving from 1829 to 1837), for signing. President Jackson vetoes this bill and in his veto message he states the following,

> "It is not our own citizens only who are to receive the bounty of our Government. More than eight millions of the stock of the Bank are held by foreigners…Is there no danger to our liberty and independence in a bank that in its nature has so little to bind it to our country?

> Controlling our currency, receiving our public moneys, and holding thousands of our citizens in dependence...would be more formidable and dangerous than a military power of the enemy. If government would confine itself to equal protection, and, as Heaven does its rains, shower the favor alike on the high and the low, the rich and the poor, it would be an unqualified blessing.
>
> In the act before me there seems to be wide and unnecessary departure from these just principles."

In July, Congress is unable to override President Jackson's veto. President Jackson then stands for re-election and for the first time in American history he takes his argument directly to the people by taking his re-election campaign on the road. His campaign slogan is, "Jackson And No Bank!"

Even though the Rothschilds pour over $3,000,000 into the campaign of President Jackson's opponent, the Republican, Senator Henry Clay, President Jackson is re-elected by a landslide in November. However, President Jackson knows the battle is only beginning, and following his victory he states,

> "The hydra of corruption is only scorched, not dead!"

1833: President Jackson starts removing the government's deposits from the Rothschild controlled,

Second Bank of the United States and instead deposits them into banks directed by independant bankers.

This causes the Rothschilds to panic and so they do what they do best, by contracting the money supply and causing a depression. President Jackson knows what they are up to and later states,

> "You are a den of thieves vipers, and I intend to rout you out, and by the Eternal God, I will rout you out."

1834: The Italian revolutionary leader, Guiseppe Mazzini, is selected by the "Illuminati" to direct their revolutionary program throughout the world and goes on to serve in that capacity until his death in 1872.

1835: On January 30th, an assassin tries to shoot President Jackson, but miraculously both of the assassin's pistols misfire. President Jackson later claims that he knew the Rothschilds were responsible for that attempted assassination. He is not the only one. Indeed, even the assassin, Richard Lawrence, who was found not guilty by reason of insanity, later brags that powerful people in Europe had hired him and promised to protect him if he were caught.

The Rothschilds acquire the rights to the Almadén quicksilver mines in Spain. At the time this is the biggest concession in the world and as quicksilver is a vital component in the refining of gold or silver this gives the

Rothschilds a virtual world monopoly. As a result of this acquisition, N. M. Rothschild & Sons would subsequently begin refining gold and silver for the Royal Mint, the Bank of England, and many other international customers.

1836: Following his years of fighting against the Rothschilds and their central bank in America, President Andrew Jackson finally succeeds in throwing the Rothschilds central bank out of America, when the bank's charter is not renewed. It would not be until 1913 that the Rothschilds would be able to set up their third central bank in America, the Federal Reserve.

On July 28th, Nathan Mayer Rothschild dies and the control of his bank, N. M. Rothschild & Sons, is passed on to his younger brother, James Mayer Rothschild.

David Sassoon, the Rothschilds' drug dealer over in China, increases his trade to over 30,000 chests of opium annually and drug addiction in coastal cities becomes endemic.

1837: The Rothschilds send one of their own, August Belmont, an Ashkenazi Crypto-Jew (real name Schönberg), to America to immediately start work on salvaging their banking interests, which were destroyed by President Jackson.

1838: On January 8th President Jackson pays off the final instalment of the national debt, which had been created by allowing the banks to issue currency for government bonds, rather than simply issuing treasury notes without such debt. He becomes the only President to ever pay off the debt.

1839: Due to the rampant opium addiction in China, profiting David Sassoon, the British Royal family, and the Rothschilds, the Manchu Emperor orders the trade be stopped. He names the Commissioner of Canton, Lin Tse-Hsu, as leader of a campaign against opium. Lin Tse-Hsu organises the seizing of 2,000 chests of Sassoon opium and orders it to be thrown into the river. David Sassoon informs the Rothschilds of this and they demand that the armed forces of Great Britain retaliate in order to protect their drug running interests.

Thus, the Opium Wars begin with the British Army once again fighting as mercenaries for Rothschild interests. They attack cities and blockade ports. The Chinese Army, by now decimated by 10 years of rampant opium addiction, prove no match for the British Army. The war ends in 1842 with the signing of the Treaty of Nanking. This includes the following provisions designed to guarantee the Rothschilds, through their puppet, David Sassoon, the right to provide an entire population with opium:

1) Full legalisation of the opium trade in China.

2) Compensation to David Sassoon of two million pounds for the opium dumped into the river by Lin Tse-Hsu.

> 3) Territorial sovereignty for the British Crown over several designated offshore islands.

1840: The Rothschilds name themselves the Bank of England's bullion brokers. They set up agencies in California and Australia.

1841: President John Tyler (the 10th President of the United States From 1841 to 1845) vetoes the act to renew the charter for the Bank of the United States, which Rothschild agents had been touting around Congress. He goes on to receive hundreds of letters threatening him with assassination.

1844: Salomon Mayer Rothschild purchases the United Coal Mines of Vítkovice and Austro-Hungarian Blast Furnace Company that go on to be one of the top ten global industrial concerns.

Benjamin Disraeli, a Sephardic Jew (who would go on to become British Prime Minister) publishes Coningsby, in which he characterises Nathan Mayer Rothschild as,

> "…the Lord and Master of the money markets of the world, and of course virtually Lord and Master of everything else. He literally held the revenues of Southern Italy in pawn, and Monarchs and Ministers of all countries courted his advice and were guided by his suggestions."

Disraeli would also make the following interesting statement,

> "The racial question is the key to world history…All is race, there is no other truth."

1843: The B'nai B'rith is established by Jews in New York City as a Masonic Lodge. 70 years later this group will establish the notorious Anti-Defamation League, designed to smear and defame any critics of Jewish supremacism or criminality as "anti-Semitic."

1845: Andrew Jackson (7th President of the United States) dies. He leaves instructions for the following inscription to be placed upon his tombstone, in accordance with what he regarded as his greatest service to humanity. The inscription is,

> "I Killed The Bank."

This is done and is, of course, in reference to the fact he destroyed the Rothschilds' Second Bank of the United States in 1836.

Jacob (James) Mayer Rothschild (who by now had married his niece, Betty, Salomon Mayer Rothschild's daughter), now known as Baron James de Rothschild, wins the contract to build the first major railway line across the country. This was called the, "Chemin De Fer Du Nord," and ran initially from Paris to Valenciennes and then joined with the Austrian rail network built by his brother (who is of course also his wife's father), Salomon Mayer Rothschild.

Edmond de Rothschild is born to James Mayer Rothschild and Betty von Rothschild. He is their youngest child.

1847: Lionel de Rothschild, who is now married to the daughter of his uncle, Kalmann (Carl) Mayer Rothschild, is elected to the parliamentary seat for the City of London.

A requirement for entering parliament is to take an oath in the true faith of a Christian. Lionel de Rothschild refuses to do this due to his Judaic faith, which renounces Christ, and as a result his seat in parliament remains empty for eleven years until new oaths are allowed. Interestingly he managed to keep his parliamentary seat for eleven years, whilst he remained unable to represent his constituency at any votes in parliament during that time.

1848: Ashkenazi Jew, Karl Marx (a Crypto-Jew, real name Moses Mordechai Levy), publishes "The Communist Manifesto." Interestingly, at the same time as he is working on this, Karl Ritter of Frankfurt University is writing the antithesis which goes on to form the basis for Freidrich Wilhelm Nietzsche's "Nietzscheanism." This "Nietzecheanism" is later developed into Fascism and Nazism and will be used to foment the first and second world wars.

Marx, Ritter, and Nietzsche are all funded and under the instruction of the Rothschilds. The idea behind this scheme is that those who direct the overall conspiracy could use the differences in so-called ideologies to enable them to divide larger and larger factions of the human race into opposing camps so that they could be armed and then brainwashed into fighting and destroying each other, and particularly, in destroying all political and religious institutions. This is essentially the same plan put forward by Weishaupt in 1776.

Interestingly, Marxism, Communism and its derivative, Socialism, when seen years later in practice, are nothing but state-capitalism and rule by a privileged minority, exercising despotic and total control over a majority which is left with virtually no property or legal rights. This explains why the Rothschilds were so interested in funding these ideologies, which would subsequently develop into "democracy," a system of the two party state in which both parties are controlled by the same force, and whilst they may squabble over insignificant issues, to give the impression of opposing one another, they actually follow the same basic ideology. This is why the inhabitants of democracies soon discover that it doesn't matter who they vote for, nothing ever changes.

Eva Hanau, Amschel Mayer Rothschild's wife, dies.

1849: Gutle Schnaper, Mayer Amschel Rothschild's wife, dies. Before her death she would nonchalantly state,

> "If my sons did not want wars, there would be none."

1850: Construction begins this decade on the manor houses of Mentmore in England and Ferrières in France. More Rothschilds' Manors will follow throughout the world, all of them filled with priceless works of art.

Jacob (James) Rothschild in France is said to be worth 600 million francs, which is 150 million francs more than all the other bankers in France put together.

1852: Future British Prime Minister William Gladstone states the following about the Bank of England and the City of London, when he becomes Chancellor of the Exchequer this year,

> "From the time I took office as Chancellor of the Exchequer, I began to learn that the State held, in the face of the Bank and the City, an essentially false position as to finance. The Government itself was not to be a substantive power, but was to leave the Money Power supreme and unquestioned."

1853: David Sassoon, the Rothschild drug dealer in China, becomes a naturalised British citizen. He keeps the dress and manners of the Baghdadi Jews, but allows his sons to adopt English manners. His son, Abdullah, changes his name to Albert, moves to England with his father, and goes on to have a son, Edward Albert, who will marry into the Rothschild family.

David Sassoon in honour of his Jewish heritage, builds synagogues in India. One in the area of Fort and another in Byculla.

Nathaniel de Rothschild, the son of Nathan Mayer Rothschild and son in law of Jacob (James) Mayer Rothschild, purchases Château Brane Mouton, the Bordeaux vineyard of Mouton, and renames it Château Mouton Rothschild.

1854: Caroline Stern, Salomon Mayer Rothschild's wife, dies.

1855: On March 10th, Kalmann (Carl) Mayer Rothschild dies.

On July 28th, Salomon Mayer Rothschild dies.

On December 6th, Amschel Mayer Rothschild dies.

1856: On May 6th, Ashkenazi Jew, psychoanalyst Sigmund Freud is born. Freud would go on to attack Western morality, criticizing what he considered Western Man's neurotic emphasis on sex, which he insisted should be replaced with Jewish values of promiscuity. Interestingly he promoted the ideas of incest and paedophilia as normal, something also permitted by the Jews most holy book, the Talmud.

1858: Lionel de Rothschild finally takes his seat in parliament when the requirement to take an oath in the true faith of a Christian is broadened to include other oaths. He becomes the first openly Jewish member of the British parliament.

On July 12th, Lord Harrington gives a speech in the House of Lords opposing the admission of Jewish immigrants to England, in which he states the following,

> "They are the great moneylenders and loan contractors of the world.... The consequence is that the nations of the world are groaning under heavy systems of taxation and national debt. They have ever been the greatest enemies of freedom."

1859: Schönche Jeannette Rothschild dies.

1860: In the American South, since American independence, a close business relationship had developed between the cotton growing aristocracy and the cotton manufacturers in England. The cotton was even delivered from America to France and Britain on Rothschild owned ships. The Rothschilds decided that this was America's achilles heel that they could exploit to re-establish themselves in America, following the destruction of their central bank by President Andrew Jackson in 1836.

The Rothschilds had prepared long for this, and this year the Southern States of America contained a vast number of Rothschild agents. They carefully manipulated the population by conspiring with local politicians they had in their pocket, and spreading propaganda amongst the people. This resulted in the secession of South Carolina on December 29th, 1860. Only a few weeks later, another six states would join the conspiracy against the Union and form a breakaway nation called the "Confederate States of America," with Jefferson Davis as its President.

In order to provoke the North, these Rothschild agents and their brainwashed followers raid armies, seize forts, arsenals, mints and other Union property. Even members of President Buchanan's cabinet conspire to destroy the Union by damaging the public credit and working to bankrupt the nation. Buchanan claims to deplore secession but takes no steps to check it, even when a United States ship is fired upon by South Carolina shore batteries.

1861: One month after the inauguration of President Abraham Lincoln (16th President of the United States from 1860 till his assassination in 1865), the American Civil War gets underway at Fort Sumter, South Carolina, after South Carolina leaves the Union. Slavery has always been cited as the cause of the war but this was simply not the case, as President Lincoln himself stated,

> "I have no purpose directly or indirectly to interfere with the institution of slavery in the states where it now exists. I believe I have no lawful right to do so, and I have no inclination to do so.... My paramount objective is to save the Union and it is not either to save or destroy slavery. If I could save the Union without freeing any slave, I would do it."

The real reason for the war is that the Southern States were in a dire economic situation due to the actions of the Northern States. Northern industrialists had used trade tariffs to prevent the Southern States from buying cheaper European goods. Europe subsequently retaliated by stopping cotton imports from the South. Thus the South had been forced to pay more for goods whilst having their income slashed.

This is when the money changers saw the opportunity to divide and conquer America by plunging it into Civil War. This is confirmed by Otto Von Bismark when he was Chancellor of Germany (1871-1890), who stated the following in 1876,

> "The division of the United States into federations of equal force was decided long before the Civil War by the high financial powers of Europe, these bankers were afraid that the United States if they remained as one block and as one nation, would attain economic and financial independence which would upset their financial domination over the world.

> The voice of the Rothschilds predominated. They foresaw the tremendous booty if they could substitute two feeble democracies, indebted to the financiers, for the vigorous Republic, confident and self-providing. Therefore they started their emissaries in order to exploit the question of slavery and thus dig an abyss between the two parts of the Republic."

Indeed, only months after these first shots in South Carolina, the Rothschilds loaned Napoleon III of France (the Napoleon of the battle of Waterloo's nephew), 210 million francs to seize Mexico and then station troops along the Southern border of the United States, taking advantage of the American Civil War to return Mexico to colonial rule.

This was in violation of the "Monroe Doctrine," which was issued by President James Monroe during his seventh annual State of the Union address to Congress, in 1823. This doctrine proclaimed the United States' opinion that European powers should no longer colonize the Americas or interfere with the affairs of sovereign nations located in the Americas, such as the United States, Mexico, and others.

In return, the United States planned to stay neutral in wars between European powers and in wars between a European power and its colonies. However, if these latter type of wars were to occur in the Americas, the United States would view such action as hostile toward itself.

Whilst the French were breaching the Monroe Doctrine in Mexico, the British followed suit by moving 11,000 troops into Canada and positioning them along America's Northern border. President Lincoln knew he was in trouble, so he went with his Secretary to the Treasury, Salomon P. Chase, to New York to apply for the loans necessary to fund America's defence.

The Rothschilds had engineered the war to make the Union fail, and were not about to save it now, so they instructed their American banks to offer loans at 24% to 36% interest. President Lincoln declined this as they knew he would and returned to Washington, where he sent for Colonel Dick Taylor of Chicago, who he put in charge of the problem of how he should finance the war.

During one meeting President Lincoln asked Colonel Taylor what proposals he had come up with to finance the war. Colonel Taylor stated,

> "Why Lincoln, that is easy, just get Congress to pass a bill authorizing the printing of full legal tender treasury notes...and pay your soldiers with them and go ahead and win your war with them also."

President Lincoln asked Colonel Taylor if the people of the United States would accept the notes, to which Colonel Taylor replied,

> "The people or anyone else will not have any choice in the matter, if you make them full legal tender. They will have the full sanction of the government and be just as good as any money, as

> Congress is given that express right by the Constitution."

Isabella Rothschild dies.

1862: President Lincoln begins the printing of $450,000,000 worth of American currency. These bills are printed in green ink on the reverse side, in order to distinguish them from other bills in circulation, and are called "Greenbacks." These are printed at no interest to the Federal Government and are used to pay the troops and purchase their supplies. President Lincoln would be the last President to issue debt free United States notes, and on this subject he states,

> "The Government should create, issue and circulate all the currency and credit needed to satisfy the spending power of the Government and the buying power of consumers. The privilege of creating and issuing money is not only the supreme prerogative of Government, but it is in the Government's greatest creative opportunity. By the adoption of these principles…the taxpayers will be saved immense sums of interest. Money will cease to be master and become the servant of humanity."

He also states,

> "We gave the people of this republic the greatest blessing they ever had, their own paper money to pay their own debts."

That same year The Times of London illustrates who's pulling its strings, when it publishes a story containing the following statement,

> "If that mischievous financial policy, which had its origin in the North American Republic, should become indurated down to a fixture, then that government will furnish its own money without cost. It will pay off debts and be without a debt. It will have all the money necessary to carry on its commerce.
>
> It will become prosperous beyond precedent in the history of civilized governments of the world. The brains and the wealth of all countries will go to North America. That government must be destroyed or it will destroy every monarchy on the globe."

A Hazard circular from the Rothschild controlled Bank of England comes to light some years later that provides further information as to why Lincoln's debt-free money, the greenback, had to be stopped,

> "Slavery is likely to be abolished by the war power and chattel slavery destroyed. This, I and my (Jewish) European friends are glad of, for slavery is but the owning of labour and carries with it the care of the labourers, while the European plan, led by England, is that capital shall control labour by controlling wages.
>
> This can be done by controlling the money. The great debt that capitalists will see to it is made

> out of the war, must be used as a means to control the volume of money. To accomplish this, the bonds must be used as a banking basis. We are now awaiting for the Secretary of the Treasury to make his recommendation to Congress. It will not do to allow the greenback, as it is called, to circulate as money any length of time, as we cannot control that."

1863: President Abraham Lincoln discovers the Tsar of Russia, Alexander II (1855-1881), has been having problems with the Rothschilds as well, as he had been refusing their continual attempts to set up a central bank in Russia. The Tsar then gives President Lincoln some unexpected help.

The Tsar issues orders that if either England or France actively intervene in the American Civil War, and help the South, Russia would consider such action a declaration of war, and take the side of President Lincoln. To show that he wasn't messing about, he sends part of his Pacific Fleet to port in San Francisco and another part to port in New York.

The Rothschild banking house in Naples, Italy, C. M. de Rothschild e figli, closes following the unification of Italy.

The Rothschilds use one of their own in America, John D. Rockefeller, to form an oil business called Standard Oil which eventually takes over all of its competition.

1864: President Lincoln is re-elected on November 8th and on November 21st he writes a friend the following,

> "The money power preys upon the nations in times of peace and conspires against it in times of adversity. It is more despotic than monarchy, more insolent than autocracy, more selfish than bureaucracy."

Rothschild agent, August Belmont, who by now is the Democratic Party's National Chairman (1860-1872), supports General George McClellan as the Democratic nominee to run against President Abraham Lincoln in this year's election. Much to the anger of Belmont, President Lincoln wins the election.

1865: In a statement to Congress, President Abraham Lincoln states,

> "I have two great enemies, the Southern Army in front of me, and the financial institutions in the rear. Of the two, the one in my rear is my greatest foe."

On April 14th, forty-one days after his second inauguration, and just five days after General Lee surrendered to General Grant at Appomattox, President Lincoln is shot by John Wilkes Booth, at Ford's Theater. He would later die of his injuries, less than two months before the end of the American Civil War.

More than seventy years later, Booth's granddaughter

Izola Forrester, reveals in her book on Booth, "This One Mad Act," that he had been put up to this assassination by powerful interests in Europe, and contrary to reports that Booth was later killed by the American authorities, he actually escaped to Europe and died in Calais at the age of thirty-nine.

Subsequent allegations that international bankers were responsible for President Lincoln's assassination would be made in the Canadian House of Commons nearly seventy years later, in 1934. The person who revealed this was a Canadian Attorney, Gerald G. McGeer.

He had obtained evidence deleted from the public record provided to him by Secret Service agents at the trial of John Wilkes Booth, after Booth's alleged death. McGeer stated that it showed that John Wilkes Booth was a mercenary working for the international bankers. His speech would be reported in an article in the Vancouver Sun, dated, 2nd May 1934, which stated,

> "Abraham Lincoln, the murdered emancipator of the slaves, was assassinated through the machinations of a group representative of the International Bankers, who feared the United States President's National Credit ambitions.
>
> There was only one group in the world at that time who had any reason to desire the death of Lincoln.
>
> They were the men opposed to his national currency program and who had fought him throughout the whole Civil War on his policy of Greenback currency."

Gerald G. McGeer also stated that Lincoln's assassination was not purely because the International Bankers wanted to re-establish a central bank in America, but also because they wanted to base America's currency on gold, which they of course controlled. They wanted to put America on a Gold Standard. This was in direct opposition to President Lincoln's policy of issuing Greenbacks, based solely on the good faith and credit of the United States.

The Vancouver Sun article also quoted Gerald G. McGeer with the following statement,

> "They were the men interested in the establishment of the Gold Standard and the right of the bankers to manage the currency and credit of every nation in the world. With Lincoln out of the way they were able to proceed with that plan and did proceed with it in the United States. Within eight years after Lincoln's assassination, silver was de-monetized and the Gold Standard system set up in the United States."

Interestingly, there has been much speculation that Abraham Lincoln was actually the illegitimate son of A. A. Springs (pre Crypto-Jew name—Springstein), a Rothschild.

Following a brief training period in the Rothschilds' London Bank, Jacob Schiff, a Rothschild, born in their house in Frankfurt, arrives in America at the age of eighteen, with instructions and the finance necessary to buy into a banking house there. The purpose of this is to carry out the following tasks:

1) Gain control of America's money system through the establishment of a central bank.

2) Find desirable men who, for a price, are willing to serve as stooges for the "Illuminati" and promote them into high places in the Federal Government, the Congress, the Supreme Court, and all the federal agencies.

3) Create minority group strife throughout the nations, particularly targeting the whites and blacks.

4) Create a movement to destroy religion in the United States, with Christianity as the main target.

Nathaniel de Rothschild becomes Member of Parliament for Aylesbury in Buckinghamshire.

1866: Henriette ("Jette") Rothschild dies.

1868: On November 15th, Jacob (James) Mayer Rothschild dies, shortly after purchasing Château Lafite, one of the four great premier grand cru estates of France. He is the last of Mayer Amschel Rothschild's sons to die.

1869: At the funeral of Grand Rabbi Simeon Ben-Iudah, Rabbi Reichorn makes the following revealing statement,

> "Thanks to the terrible power of our International Banks, we have forced the Christians into wars without number. Wars have a special value for Jews, since Christians massacre each other and make more room for us Jews. Wars are the Jews' Harvest, the Jew banks grow fat on Christian wars. Over one hundred million Christians have been swept off the face of the earth by wars, and the end is not yet."

On March 16th, Babette Rothschild dies.

1870: Nathaniel de Rothschild dies.

1871: An American General named Albert Pike, who had been enticed into the "Illuminati" by Guisseppe Mazzini, completes his military blueprint for three world wars and various revolutions throughout the world, culminating into moving this great conspiracy into its final stage. These details are as follows:

The First World War is to be fought for the purpose of destroying the Tsar in Russia, as promised by Nathan Mayer Rothschild in 1815. The Tsar is to be replaced with communism which is to be used to attack religions, predominantly Christianity. The differences between the British and German empires are to be used to foment this war.

The Second World War is to be used to foment the controversy between fascism and political Zionism with the oppression of Jews in Germany a lynchpin in bringing hatred against the German people. This is designed to destroy fascism (which the Rothschilds created) and increase the power of political Zionism. This war is also designed to increase the power of communism to the level that it equals that of united Christendom.

The Third World War is to be played out by stirring up hatred of the Muslim world for the purposes of playing the Islamic world and the political Zionists off against one another. Whilst this is going on, the remaining nations would be forced to fight themselves into a state of mental, physical, spiritual and economic exhaustion.

On August 15th of this year, Albert Pike writes a letter (now catalogued in the British Museum) to Guiseppe Mazzini in which he states the following,

> "We shall unleash the nihilists and the atheists and we shall provoke a great social cataclysm which in all its horror will show clearly to all nations the effect of absolute atheism; the origins of savagery and of most bloody turmoil.
>
> Then everywhere, the people will be forced to defend themselves against the world minority of the world revolutionaries and will exterminate those destroyers of civilization and the multitudes disillusioned with Christianity whose spirits will be from that moment without direction and leadership and anxious for an

> ideal, but without knowledge where to send its adoration, will receive the true light through the universal manifestation of the pure doctrine of Lucifer brought finally out into public view.
>
> A manifestation which will result from a general reactionary movement which will follow the destruction of Christianity and Atheism; both conquered and exterminated at the same time."

Pike, who had been elected as Sovereign Grand Commander of the Scottish Rite of Freemasonry's Southern Jurisdiction in 1859, was the most powerful Freemason in America. He would retain that post for thirty-two years until his death in 1891. He also published a book on the subject in 1872 entitled, "Morals and Dogma of the Ancient and Accepted Scottish Rite of Freemasonry," in which he candidly states the following,

> "The true name of Satan, the Kabbalists say, is that of Yahweh reversed; for Satan is not a black god, but the negation of God.... For the Initiates, this is not a Person, but a Force, created for good, but which may serve for evil. It is the instrument of Liberty and Free Will...
>
> LUCIFER, the Light-bearer! Strange and mysterious name to give to the Spirit of Darkness! Lucifer, the Son of the Morning! Is it he who bears the Light, and with its splendors intolerable blinds feeble, sensual or selfish Souls? Doubt it not!"

Interestingly, in the same book, Pike emphasizes that Freemasonry is a religion based on the occult Jewish philosophy found in the Kabbalah.

1872: Prior to Guiseppe Mazzini's death this year, he makes another revolutionary leader named Adrian Lemmy his successor. Lemmy will be subsequently succeeded by Lenin and Trotsky, then by Stalin. The revolutionary activities of all these men are financed by the Rothschilds.

1873: The Rio Tinto copper mines in Spain are purchased by a group of foreign financiers including the Rothschilds. These mines are Europe's largest source of copper.

1875: On January 1st, Jacob Schiff, now Solomon Loeb's son-in-law after marrying his daughter, Teresa, takes control of the banking house, Kuhn, Loeb & Co. Schiff goes on to finance the Standard Oil Company of Crypto-Jew, John D. Rockefeller. He also finances Edward R. Harriman's Railroad Empire, and Andrew Carnegie's Steel Empire. This is all with Rothschild money.

He then identifies the other largest bankers in America at that time. They are, J. P. Morgan who controls Wall Street, and the Drexels and the Biddles of Philadelphia. All the other financiers, large and small, would dance to the tune of those three houses. Schiff then gets the European Rothschilds to set up European branches of these three large banks on the understanding that Schiff, and therefore Rothschild, is to be the boss of banking in New York and therefore America.

N. M. Rothschild & Sons undertake a share issue to raise capital for the first channel tunnel project to link France to England, with half of its capital coming from the Rothschild owned, "Compagnie du Chemin de Fer du Nord."

The Rothschilds needed to control the Suez Canal to protect their huge business interests in the region, so Lionel de Rothschild instructs Jewish Prime Minister, Benjamin Disraeli, to purchase the shares in the Suez Canal from Khedive Said of Egypt. The Rothschilds loaned the money to the British government to facilitate this purchase, they did not want to own it themselves, as they needed a government they controlled to own it, so that they could use the military of that government to protect it.

1878: Archibald Philip Primrose, the 5th Earl of Rosebery, who would go on to be British Prime Minister in 1894, marries Hannah de Rothschild, the daughter of Baron Mayer de Rothschild. The marriage produces four children: Harry Primrose, Lord Dalmeny (later 6th Earl of Rosebery); the honourable Neil Primrose; Lady Sybil Primrose; and Lady Margaret Primrose.

1879: Lionel de Rothschild dies.

1880: Rothschild agents begin fomenting a series of pogroms predominantly in Russia, but also in Poland, Bulgaria and Romania. These pogroms result in the slaughter of thousands of Jews, causing approximately two million to flee, mainly to New York, but also to Chicago, Philadelphia, Boston and Los Angeles. However some are assisted with Rothschild money to begin settling in Palestine.

The reason these pogroms were initiated was to create a large Jewish base in America, who when they arrived, would be educated to register as Democrat voters. Some twenty years later, this would result in a massive Democratic power base in the United States and be used to elect Rothschild front men such as Woodrow Wilson to the Presidency to carry out the bidding of the Rothschilds.

In America, John Swinton, then the pre-eminent New York journalist, was the guest of honour at a banquet given him by the leaders of his craft. Someone who knew neither the press nor Swinton offered a toast to the independent press. Swinton outraged his colleagues by replying,

> "There is no such thing, at this date of the world's history, in America, as an independent press. You know it and I know it.
>
> There is not one of you who dares to write your honest opinions, and if you did, you know beforehand that it would never appear in print. I am paid weekly for keeping my honest opinion out of the paper I am connected with.

> Others of you are paid similar salaries for similar things, and any of you who would be so foolish as to write honest opinions would be out on the streets looking for another job. If I allowed my honest opinions to appear in one issue of my paper, before twenty-four hours my occupation would be gone.
>
> The business of the journalists is to destroy the truth, to lie outright, to pervert, to vilify, to fawn at the feet of mammon, and to sell his country and his race for his daily bread. You know it and I know it, and what folly is this toasting an independent press?
>
> We are the tools and vassals of rich men behind the scenes. We are the jumping jacks, they pull the strings and we dance. Our talents, our possibilities and our lives are all the property of other men. We are intellectual prostitutes."

1881: President James A. Garfield (The 20th President of the United States who lasted only one hundred days) states two weeks before he is assassinated,

> "Whoever controls the volume of money in our country is absolute master of all industry and commerce…and when you realize that the entire system is very easily controlled, one way or another, by a few powerful men at the top, you will not have to be told how periods of inflation and depression originate."

On March 13th, The Tsar of Russia, Alexander II is assassinated in St. Petersburg, following several assassination attempts that began in 1866, less than a year after President Lincoln's victory in the American Civil War.

Edmond James de Rothschild has a son, Maurice de Rothschild.

1883: After 6,000 feet of tunnel in the channel tunnel project has been excavated, the British government halt the project citing the fact that it would be a threat to Britain's security.

1885: Nathaniel Rothschild, son of Lionel de Rothschild, becomes the first Jewish peer and takes the title of Lord Rothschild.

1886: The French Rothschild bank, de Rothschild Frères obtains substantial amounts of Russia's oil fields and forms the Caspian and Black Sea Petroleum Company, which quickly becomes the world's second largest oil producer.

1887: Edward Albert Sassoon, grandson of Rothschild opium monopolist David Sassoon, marries Aline Caroline de Rothschild, the grand-daughter of Jacob (James) Mayer Rothschild. Aline Caroline's father, Gustave, together with his brother, Alphonse, took over the Rothschilds' french arm following their father Jacob's death.

The Rothschilds finance the amalgamation of the Kimberley diamond mines in South Africa. They subsequently become the biggest shareholders of this company, De Beers, and mine precious stones in Africa and India.

1888: Noémie Halphen, future wife of Maurice de Rothschild, is born.

1891: The British Labour Party Leader makes the following statement on the subject of the Rothschilds,

> "This blood-sucking crew has been the cause of untold mischief and misery in Europe during the present century, and has piled up its prodigious wealth chiefly through fomenting wars between States which ought never to have quarrelled.
>
> Whenever there is trouble in Europe, wherever rumours of war circulate and men's minds are distraught with fear of change and calamity you may be sure that a hook-nosed Rothschild is at his games somewhere near the region of the disturbance."

Comments like this worry the Rothschilds and towards the end of the 1800's they purchase Reuters news agency so they can exercise some control over the media.

1895: Edmond James de Rothschild, the youngest son of Jacob (James) Mayer Rothschild, visits Palestine to see the Jewish colonies he funded as a result of the Rothschild engineered pogroms in Russia, Poland, Bulgaria and Romania. He is impressed and vows to continue to supply funds to these colonies in furtherance of the long term Rothschild objective of creating a Rothschild owned Jewish state.

1897: The Rothschilds found the World Zionist Congress to promote Zionism. Zionism is portrayed as a political movement seeking to secure a homeland for the Jews, but is in reality a conspiracy to bring the entire world under a World Government administered and controlled by Jews, and in particular, the Rothschilds.

The first meeting of the World Zionist Congress is arranged to take place in Munich; however, due to opposition from local Jews, this meeting has to be moved to Basle, Switzerland and takes place on 29th August. The meeting is chaired by Ashkenazi Jew, Theodor Herzl, who would go on to state in his diaries,

> "It is essential that the sufferings of Jews... become worse...this will assist in realization of our plans.... I have an excellent idea.... I shall induce anti-Semites to liquidate Jewish wealth.... The anti-Semites will assist us thereby in that they will strengthen the persecution and oppression of Jews. The anti-Semites shall be our best friends."

Herzl is subsequently elected President of the World

Zionist Organisation which adopts the "Rothschild Red Hexagram," as the Zionist flag which fifty-one years later will end up on the flag of Israel.

At this conference, Chaim Weizmann, who would go on to become its head, declares,

> "There are no English, French, German or American Jews, but only Jews living in England, France, Germany or America."

Edward Henry Harriman becomes a director of the Union Pacific Railroad and goes on to take control of the Southern Pacific Railroad. This is all financed by the Rothschilds.

1898: At the World Zionist Congress in July, Max Mandelstam, makes the following statement,

> "The Jews energetically reject the idea of fusion with the other nationalities and cling firmly to their historical hope of World Empire."

1898: Pope Leo XIII states the following on the subject of usury (the charging of interest on money),

> "On the one hand there is the party which holds the power because it holds the wealth, which has in its grasp all labour and all trade, which manipulates for its own benefit and its own purposes all the sources of supply, and which is

> powerfully represented in the councils of State itself. On the other side there is the needy and powerless multitude, sore and suffering.
>
> Rapacious usury, which, although more than once condemned by the Church, is nevertheless under a different form but with the same guilt, still practiced by avaricious and grasping men… so that a small number of very rich men have been able to lay upon the masses of the poor a yoke little better than slavery itself."

Ferdinand de Rothschild dies.

1899: Due to the discovery of a vastly increasing amount of wealth in gold and diamonds within South Africa, the Rothschilds, through their agents Lord Alfred Milner and Cecil Rhodes, send 400,000 British soldiers over there to fight against the, "enemy," which consist of 30,000 Boer farmers with rifles who would rather not leave their own land.

It is during this so-called war that the concentration camp is invented, when the British rounded up anyone sympathetic to the Boers, which included women and children, and placed them in unsanitary, fever ridden camps. The Rothschild British Army goes on to win this war, and thus the vast wealth in gold and diamonds, for the Rothschilds.

Indeed, in a speech he gave on October 30th, 1937, Rear Admiral Henry Hamilton Beamish had the following to say on the subject of the Boer War,

> "The Boer War occurred 37 years ago. Boer means farmer. Many criticized a great power like Britain for trying to wipe out the Boers. Upon making inquiry, I found all the gold and diamond mines of South Africa were owned by Jews; that Rothschild controlled gold; Samuels controlled silver, Baum controlled other mining, and Moses controlled base metals. Anything these people touch they inevitably pollute."

The current President of the Transvaal Republic in South Africa, Stephanus Johannes Paul Kruger, would state the following this year, regarding the only way he could envision peace in South Africa,

> "If it were conceivable, to eject the Jew monopolist from this country neck and crop without incurring war with Great Britain, then the problem of everlasting peace would be solved."

1901: The Jews from the colonies set up in Palestine by Edmond James de Rothschild send a delegation to him which states the following,

> "If you wish to save the Yishuv (the Jewish settlement) first take your hands from it, and…for once permit the colonists to have the possibility of correcting for themselves what needs correcting."

Edmond James de Rothschild is not at all pleased to receive this delegation and he says to them,

> "I created the Yishuv, I alone. Therefore no men, neither colonists nor organisations, have the right to interfere in my plans."

The Rothschild banking house in Frankfurt, Germany, M. A. von Rothschild und Söhne, closes as there is no male Rothschild heir to take it on.

1902: Philippe de Rothschild is born.

1903: In August at the sixth World Zionist Congress in Basle, Switzerland, a discussion takes place regarding an offer from Britain to provide Uganda as a base for a future Jewish Zionist state.

The Jews present complain they want Palestine, and then suddenly Max Nordau makes the following shocking statement regarding how the Jews will get Palestine through a stepping stone process, which would play out to the letter more than 15 years later. This is what he said,

> "Let me tell you the following words as if I were showing you the rungs of a ladder leading upward and upward: Herzl; the World Zionist Congress; the English Uganda proposition; the future world war; the peace conference where with the help of England a free and Jewish Palestine will be created."

1905: A group of Rothschild backed Zionist Jews led by Georgi Apollonovich Gapon attempt to overthrow the Tsar of Russia in a Communist Coup. They fail and are forced to flee Russia only to be given refuge in Germany.

This year's Jewish Encyclopaedia (Vol. 2, p.497), on the subject of control of the Catholic Church, states,

> "It is a somewhat curious sequel to the attempt to set up a Catholic competitor to the Rothschilds that at the present time the latter are the guardians of the papal treasure."

1906: The Rothschilds claim that due to growing instability in the region and increasing competition from Rockefeller (the Rockefeller family are Rothschild descendants through a female bloodline) owned Standard Oil, they decide to sell their Caspian and Black Sea Petroleum Company to Royal Dutch and Shell. This is another example of the Rothschilds trying to hide their true wealth which they are actually consolidating.

1907: Rothschild, Jacob Schiff, the head of Kuhn, Loeb and Co., in a speech to the New York Chamber of Commerce, warns that,

> "Unless we have a Central Bank with adequate control of credit resources, this country is going to undergo the most severe and far reaching money panic in its' history."

Suddenly America finds itself in the middle of another financial crisis, known as the, "Panic of 1907," which goes on to decimate the lives of millions of Americans.

1909: Jacob Schiff founds the National Advancement for the Association of the Coloured People (NAACP). This is done to incite black people into rioting, looting and other forms of disorder, in order to cause a rift between the black and white communities.

Jewish historian Howard Sachar states the following in his book, "A History of the Jews in America,"

> "In 1914, Professor Emeritus Joel Spingarn of Columbia University became chairman of the NAACP and recruited for its board such Jewish leaders as Jacob Schiff, Jacob Billikopf, and Rabbi Stephen Wise."

Other Ashkenazi Jew co-founders included Julius Rosenthal, Lillian Wald and Rabbi Emil G. Hirsch. It would not be until over 60 years later, in the 1970's, that the NAACP would appoint its first black president, Benjamin Hooks.

Interestingly, the Jewish Talmud is the proponent of the racist Hamitic Myth, a subject on which former employee of The Simon Wiesenthal Center, Harold Brackman, wrote the following in his doctoral dissertation entitled, "The Ebb and Flow of Conflict: The History of Black-Jewish Relations Through 1900,"

> "There is no denying that the Babylonian

> Talmud was the first source to read a Negrophobic content into the episode by stressing Canaan's fraternal connection with Cush…The more important version of the myth, however, ingeniously ties in the origins of blackness—and of other, real and imagined Negroid traits—with Noah's Curse itself.
>
> According to it, Ham is told by his outraged father that, because you have abused me in the darkness of the night, your children shall be born black and ugly; because you have twisted your head to cause me embarrassment, they shall have kinky hair and red eyes; because your lips jested at my exposure, theirs shall swell; and because you neglected my nakedness, they shall go naked with their shamefully elongated male members exposed for all to see…"

Maurice de Rothschild marries Ashkenazi Jew, Noémie Halphen.

1911: Werner Sombart, in his book, "The Jews and Modern Capitalism," states that from 1820 on, it was the "Age of the Rothschild" and concluded that there was, "Only one power in Europe, and that is Rothschild." He also stated,

> "Jewish influence made the United States just what they are—that is, American. For what we call Americanism is nothing else, if we may say so, than the Jewish spirit distilled…modern

> capitalism is nothing more nor less than an expression of the Jewish spirit…
>
> Capitalism was born from the money loan. Money lending contains the root idea of capitalism. Turn to the pages of the Talmud and you will find that the Jews made an art of lending money. They were taught early to look for their chief happiness in the possession of money. They fathomed all the secrets that lay hidden in money. They became Lords of Money and Lords of the World…"

1912: In the December issue of "Truth" magazine, George R. Conroy states of banker Jacob Schiff,

> "Mr Schiff is head of the great private banking house of Kuhn, Loeb, and Co., which represents the Rothschilds' interests on this side of the Atlantic.
>
> He has been described as financial strategist and has been for years the financial minister of the great impersonal power known as Standard Oil.
>
> He was hand in glove with the Harrimans, the Goulds, and the Rockefellers in all their railroad enterprises and has become the dominant power in the railroad and financial power of America."

1913: On March 4th, Woodrow Wilson is elected the

28th President of the United States. Shortly after he is inaugurated, he is visited in the White House by Ashkenazi Jew, Samuel Untermyer, of law firm Guggenheim, Untermyer, and Marshall, who tries to blackmail him for the sum of $40,000 in relation to an affair Wilson had whilst he was a professor at Princeton University, with a fellow professor's wife.

President Wilson does not have the money, so Untermyer volunteers to pay the $40,000 out of his own pocket to the woman Wilson had had the affair with, on the condition that Wilson promise to appoint to the first vacancy on the United States Supreme Court a nominee to be recommended to President Wilson by Untermyer. Wilson agrees to this.

On March 31st, J. P. Morgan, alleged owner of the J. P. Morgan banking empire, dies. He is thought to be the richest man in America, but his will revealed he owned only 19% of J. P. Morgan companies. The other 81%? Owned by the Rothschilds.

Jacob Schiff sets up the Anti-Defamation League (ADL) as a branch of the B'nai B'rith in the United States. This organisation is created for the purpose of identifying anyone who questions or challenges the unlawful actions of elitist Jews or the Rothschild global conspiracy as "anti-Semitic" and against the Jewish race as a whole.

Strangely enough, the same year that they do this Jews also set up their last and current central bank in America, the Federal Reserve. In order to get support for this from the public, they brazenly state that only a Central Bank could curb inflations and depressions when, in fact, the very idea of a central bank is to manipulate the money supply to cause this.

Following the passing of the Federal Reserve Act on December 23rd, Congressman Charles Lindbergh states,

> "The Act establishes the most gigantic trust on earth. When the President signs this Bill, the invisible government of the monetary power will be legalized...The greatest crime of the ages is perpetrated by this banking and currency bill."

It is important to note that the Federal Reserve is a private company, it is neither Federal nor does it have any Reserve. It is conservatively estimated that profits exceed $150 billion per year, yet the Federal Reserve has never once in its history published accounts. Some recent evidence has come forward as to who really owns the Federal Reserve, and they are the following banks:

Rothschild Bank of London
Warburg Bank of Hamburg
Rothschild Bank of Berlin
Lehman Brothers of New York
Lazard Brothers of Paris
Kuhn Loeb Bank of New York
Israel Moses Seif Banks of Italy
Goldman, Sachs of New York
Warburg Bank of Amsterdam
Chase Manhattan Bank of New York

These are all Rothschild banks.

1914: The start of World War 1. In this war, the German Rothschilds loan money to the Germans, the British Rothschilds loan money to the British, and the French Rothschilds loan money to the French.

Futhermore, the Rothschilds have control of the three European news agencies, Wolff (est. 1849) in Germany, Reuters (est. 1851) in England, and Havas (est. 1835) in France.

The Rothschilds use Wolff to manipulate the German people into a fervour for war. It is around this time that the Rothschilds are rarely reported on in the media, because they own the media.

1915: The Islamic Ottoman Government of Turkey is overthrown by Masonic Jewish socialists, who deceptively called themselves the "Young Turks." The upshot of this is a Jewish led genocide of two million Christian Armenians, many of whom are tortured and have their hands cut off. Indeed, according to the British Consul, there were so many severed hands that if they were laid side by side, a highway could have been made out of them.

As a result of this revolution, the man who would become known as Mustafa Kemal Ataturk, an alcoholic Crypto-Jew, would rise to dictatorial power in Turkey.

1916: On June 4th, Ashkenazi Jew, Louis Dembitz Brandeis is appointed to the Supreme Court of the United States by President Wilson, as per his agreed blackmail payment to Samuel Untermyer some three years earlier. Justice Brandeis is also the elected leader of the Executive Committee for Zionist Affairs, a position he has held since 1914.

The middle of World War 1. Germany is winning the war as it is being financed by the Rothschilds to a greater extent than France, Italy and England, simply because the Rothschilds do not want to support the Tsar in Russia and, of course, Russia was on the same side as France, Italy and England.

Then a significant event occurs. On December 12th, Germany, although it was winning the war and not one foreign soldier had set foot on its soil, offers armistice to Britain with no requirement of reparations. The Rothschilds are anxious to make sure this is not accepted by the British as they have a few cards left up their sleeve in relation to what they initiated this war for.

So, whilst the British are considering Germany's offer, Rothschild agent Louis Brandeis sends a Zionist delegation from America to Britain to promise to bring America into the war on the side of the British, provided the British agree to give the land of Palestine to the Rothschilds.

The Rothschilds wanted Palestine so they could protect the great business interests they had in the East. They also desired their own State in that area along with their own military which they could use as an aggressor to any State that threatened those interests.

The British subsequently agree to the deal for Palestine and the Zionists in London contact their counterparts in America and inform them of this fact. Suddenly all the major newspapers in America that up to that point had been pro-German turn on Germany, running propaganda pieces to manipulate the American public against the Germans, such as: German soldiers are killing Red Cross Nurses; and, German soldiers are cutting off babies' hands.

Interestingly, Woodrow Wilson is re-elected President this year, the slogan of his campaign being, "Re-elect the man who will keep your sons out of the war."

1917: As a result of Germany's offer of peace, the Rothschild war machine goes into total overdrive in America, spreading anti-German propaganda throughout the American media which leads to President Wilson, under the instructions of the Jewish American Supreme Court Justice, Louis Dembitz Brandeis, reneging on his promise to the electorate and taking America into World War 1 on April 6th.

As per the Rothschild promise to the British to take America into the war, they decide they want something in writing from the British to prove that they will uphold their side of the bargain. The British Foreign Secretary, Arthur James Balfour, a Jew, therefore drafts a letter which is commonly known as the "Balfour Declaration," which is reprinted following:

Foreign Office

November 2nd, 1917

Dear Lord Rothschild,

I have much pleasure in conveying to you, on behalf of His Majesty's Government, the following declaration of sympathy with Jewish Zionist aspirations which has been submitted to, and approved by, the Cabinet.

His Majesty's Government view with favour the establishment in Palestine of a national home for the Jewish people, and will use their best endeavours to facilitate the achievement of this object, it being clearly understood that nothing shall be done which may prejudice the civil and religious rights of existing non-Jewish communities in Palestine, or the rights and political status enjoyed by Jews in any other country.

I should be grateful if you would bring this declaration to the knowledge of the Zionist Federation.

Yours sincerely,

Arthur James Balfour

The Rothschilds order the execution by the Jewish Bolsheviks they control, of Tsar Nicholas II and his entire family in Russia, even though the Tsar had already abdicated on March 2nd. This is to get control of the country and an act of revenge for Tsar Alexander I blocking their world government plan in 1815 at the

Congress of Vienna, and Tsar Alexander II siding with President Abraham Lincoln in 1864.

It is extremely important for them to slaughter the entire family including women and children in order to make good on the promise to do so made by Nathan Mayer Rothschild in 1815. This act is a show of power-play and defiance by the Jews to the rest of the world.

United States Congressman Oscar Callaway informs Congress that J. P. Morgan is a Rothschild front and has taken control of the American media industry. He states,

> "In March, 1915, the J. P. Morgan interests, the steel, shipbuilding, and powder interest, and their subsidiary organizations, got together twelve men high up in the newspaper world and employed them to select the most influential newspapers in the United States and sufficient number of them to control generally the policy of the daily press...
>
> They found it was only necessary to purchase the control of 25 of the greatest papers.... An agreement was reached. The policy of the papers was bought, to be paid for by the month, an editor was furnished for each paper to properly supervise and edit information regarding the questions of preparedness, militarism, financial policies, and other things of national and international nature considered vital to the interests of the purchasers."

1918: The real purpose of Communism becomes apparent less than a year after the Bolshevik revolution in Russia, the stealing of the wealth of the people (especially the Rothschilds' favourite—Gold!) for the benefit of the State, the State which is of course now owned by the Rothschild family and administered by Jews. This is highlighted by the following despatch from Petrograd reported in The New York Times on January 30th,

> "The people's commissaries have decreed a State Monopoly of gold. Churches, museums and other public institutions are required to place their gold articles at the disposal of the State. Gold articles belonging to private persons must be handed over to the State. Informants will receive one-third of the value of the articles."

In March of this year, Lenin makes a statement against anti-Semitism which is put onto phonograph record and circulated around the country, as part of a massive campaign to stifle the burgeoning counter-revolutionary movement against the Jews.

In April, the London Times correspondent to Russia, Robert Wilton, produces a table showing the ethnic structure of the 384 Commissars in the new Communist Russian government. These Commissars include: 2 Negroes; 13 Russians; 15 Chinamen; 22 Armenians; and more than 300 Jews. Of those Jews, 264 had come to Russia from the United States since the downfall of the Imperial Government.

The President of the University of Wisconsin, Charles R. Van Hise, delivers an address entitled, "The Foundation of a New World Order," to the "Wisconsin State Convention of the League to Enforce Peace." During this address he states,

> "The world has become one body, and no great member of it can proceed independently of the other members. They must act together, and this is possible only through formal treaty covenants."

1919: In January, Jew, Karl Liebknecht and Sephardic Jew, Rosa Luxemburg, are killed as they attempt to lead another Rothschild funded Communist coup, this time in Berlin, Germany.

On January 18th, the Versailles peace conference commences, to decide reparations that the Germans are required to pay to the victors following the end of World War 1. A delegation of 117 Jews headed up by Ashkenazi Jew, Bernard Baruch (who would go on to state to a select committee of the United States Congress, "I probably had more power than perhaps any other man did in the war, doubtless that is true,") bring up the subject of the promise of Palestine for them. At this point the Germans realised why America had turned on them and under whose influence, the Rothschilds.

The Germans, naturally, felt they had been betrayed by their Jewish population. This is because, at the time the Rothschilds made their deal with Britain for Palestine in exchange for bringing America into the war, Germany was the most friendly country in the world towards the Jews. Indeed, the German Emancipation Edict of 1822 guaranteed Jews in Germany all civil rights enjoyed by Germans.

Also, Germany was the only country in Europe which did not place restrictions on Jews, even giving them refuge when they had to flee from Russia after their first attempted Communist coup failed there in 1905.

Nevertheless, Palestine is confirmed as a Jewish homeland, and whilst its handover to the Rothschilds takes place, it is to remain under the control of Britain as the Rothschilds control Britain. At the time, less than one percent of the population of Palestine is Jewish. Interestingly, the host of the Versailles Peace Conference is its Jewish boss, Baron Edmond de Rothschild.

Indeed in his book, "The Inside Story of the Peace Conference," Emile Joseph Dillon states the following of the Versailles Peace Conference,

> "It may seem amazing to some readers, but it is not the less a fact that a considerable number of delegates (to the Peace Conference at Versailles) believed that the real influences behind the Anglo-Saxon people were Jews…
>
> The formula into which this policy was thrown by the members of the conference, whose countries it affected, and who regarded it as fatal to the peace of Eastern Europe ends thus: Henceforth the world will be governed by the

> Anglo-Saxon peoples, who, in turn, are swayed by their Jewish elements."

Furthermore, the Rothschilds use this conference to obtain the German owned railway rights in Palestine and give them control over the nation's infrastructure.

On May 30th, a spin-off meeting from this so-called peace conference is held, also chaired by Baron Edmond de Rothschild, at the Hotel Majestic in Paris, where it is decided that an organization be set up to advise (control) what governments do.

This body is called the "Institute Of International Affairs," which would subsequently metamorphosize into two arms, the British "Royal Institute Of International Affairs (RIIA)," in 1920, and its American counterpart, the "Council On Foreign Relations (CFR)," in 1921. Both of these bodies are to be controlled by the Rothschilds.

Finally, the Rothschilds also use the Versailles Peace Conference to set up their second overt attempt at world government, which they promote under the pretext of ending all wars (which they of course create). They call this the "League of Nations."

Fortunately, this would not be accepted by enough countries, and would therefore fade away, but before it did, the future President of the World Zionist Congress, Nahum Sokolow, would state the following of it,

> "The League of Nations is a Jewish idea. We created it after a fight of twenty-five years."

On March 29th The Times of London reports the following on the Bolsheviks in Russia,

> "One of the curious features of the Bolshevist movement is the high percentage of non-Russian elements among its leaders. Of the twenty or thirty commissaries, or leaders, who provide the central machinery of the Bolshevist movement, not less than 75% were Jews."

It is reported that the Rothschilds are angry with the Russians because they were not prepared to allow them to form a central bank within their nation. They therefore gathered groups of Jewish spies and sent them into Russia to drum up a revolution for the benefit of the common man, which was actually a takeover of Russia by a Rothschild controlled Jewish elite. Indeed, one of these leading Jewish spies, Leon Trotsky, even used to play chess with Baron Rothschild whilst he was in Vienna.

These Jewish spies were, in age-old deceptive Ashkenazi Crypto-Jew tradition, given Russian names. For example, Trotsky was a leading member of the first group and his original name was Bronstein. These groups were sent to areas throughout Russia to incite riots and rebellion.

The Jewish Post International Edition, week ending January 24th 1991, confirms Vladimir Lenin was Jewish. He was a Crypto-Jew, and was born Vladimir Ilyich Ulyanov. Lenin is on record as having stated,

> "The establishment of a central bank is 90% of communizing a nation."

These Jewish, Rothschild funded Bolsheviks would go on in the course of history to slaughter 60 million Christians and non-Jews in Soviet controlled territory. Indeed the author Aleksandr Solzhenitsyn in his work, "Gulag Archipelago, Vol. 2," affirms that Jews created and administered the organized Soviet concentration camp system in which these tens of millions of Christians and non-Jews died. On page 79 of this book he even names the administrators of this, the greatest killing machine in the history of the world. They are: Aron Solts; Yakov Rappoport; Lazar Kogan; Matvei Berman; Genrikh Yagoda; and Naftaly Frenkel. All six are Jews. In 1970 Solzhenitsyn would be awarded the Nobel Peace Prize for literature.

Indeed, in April, George Pitter-Wilson, of the London Globe, wrote an article which contained the following definition of Bolshevism,

> "Bolshevism is the dispossession of the Christian nations of the world to such an extent that no capital will remain in the hands of the Christians, that all Jews may jointly hold the world in their hands and reign wherever they choose."

On July 23rd, Scotland Yard report the following to the American Secretary of State,

> "There is now definite evidence that Bolshevism is an international movement controlled by Jews; communications are passing between the leaders in America, France, Russia and England, with a view toward concerted action."

On June 19th, Australian Prime Minister Billy Hughes is quoted with the following statement in the Saturday Evening Post,

> "The Montefiores have taken Australia for their own, and there is not a gold field or a sheep run from Tasmania to New South Wales that does not pay them a heavy tribute. They are the real owners of the antipodean continent. What is the good of our being a wealthy nation, if the wealth is all in the hands of German Jews?"

N. M. Rothschild & Sons are given a permanent role to fix the world's daily gold price. This takes place in the City of London offices, daily at 1100 hours, in the same room, until 2004.

1920: Winston Churchill (whose mother, Jenny (Jacobson) Jerome, was Jewish—meaning he is Jewish under Israeli immigration law as he was born of a Jewish mother)—writes the following in an article on page 5 of the Illustrated Sunday Herald, dated February 8th,

> "Some people like Jews and some do not; but no thoughtful man can doubt the fact that they are beyond all question the most formidable and the most remarkable race which has ever appeared in the world.
>
> And it may well be that this same astounding race may at the present time be in the actual process of producing another system of morals

and philosophy, as malevolent as Christianity was benevolent, which, if not arrested would shatter irretrievably all that Christianity has rendered possible….

From the days of Spartacus-Weishaupt to those of Karl Marx, and down to Trotsky (Russia), Bela Kun (Hungary—pre Crypto-Jew name, Cohen), Rosa Luxemburg (Germany), and Emma Goldman (United States), this world-wide conspiracy for the overthrow of civilisation and for the reconstitution of society on the basis of arrested development, of envious male-volence, and impossible equality, has been steadily growing.

It played…a definitely recognisable part in the tragedy of the French Revolution. It has been the mainspring of every subversive movement during the Nineteenth Century; and now at last this band of extraordinary personalities from the underworld of the great cities of Europe and America have gripped the Russian people by the hair of their heads and have become practically the undisputed masters of that enormous empire.

There is no need to exaggerate the part played in the creation of Bolshevism and in the actual bringing about of the Russian revolution by these international, and for the most part atheistic Jews. It is certainly a very great one; it probably outweighs all others. With the notable exception of Lenin (subsequently revealed as a Jew), the majority of the leading figures are Jews."

In the September 10th edition of, The American Hebrew," it is stated,

> "The Bolshevist revolution in Russia was the work of Jewish brains, of Jewish dissatisfaction, of Jewish planning, whose goal is to create a new order in the world. What was performed in so excellent a way in Russia, thanks to Jewish brains, and because of Jewish dissatisfaction, and by Jewish planning, shall also, through the same Jewish mental and physical forces, become a reality all over the world."

In, "The Cause Of World Unrest," published this year, H. A. Gwynne, contributes an introduction in which he states the following,

> "In earlier history...kings, princes, governors stood between the masses and their exploiters... roughly speaking, the people were prevented by established authority from being victimized. Today all that is changed, and we now live in an age which will we be known, perhaps, in history as the age of the exploitation of the people....
>
> The pages of this book will trace the threads of a conspiracy engineered by people whose main object has been to destroy utterly anything—kings, governments, or institutions—which might stand between them and the people they would exploit...
>
> The main outline of the contents of this book is,

> in brief, that there has been for centuries a hidden conspiracy, chiefly Jewish, whose objects have been and are to produce revolution, communism and anarchy, by means of which they hope to arrive at the hegemony of the world by establishing some sort of despotic rule."

Also this year, the "Protocols Of The Learned Elders Of Zion" is published in England, having first been deposited in the British Museum in 1905. This document is the blueprint for the domination of the world by Jews, and is said to have formed the minutes of the first World Zionist Congress held in Basle, Switzerland, in 1897.

It is immediately slammed as anti-Semitic by the Jews, who claim it is a forgery, but interestingly will not go as far as to call it a fake. The only way to determine if this plan for Jewish domination of the world is real is to look at the evidence and establish whether the Jews have dominated the world, or have made clear efforts to do so. There is more than enough evidence for the former to be the case and in fact this is what Henry Ford said about the Protocols, 85 years ago, in 1921,

> "The only statement I care to make about the Protocols is that they fit in with what is going on. They are sixteen years old, and they have fitted the world situation up to this time. They fit it now."

1921: In her book, published this year, "World Revolution or the Plot Against Civilization," noted historian, Nesta Webster, states the following of the Jews,

> "Since the earliest times it is as the exploiter that the Jew has been known amongst his fellow men of all races and creeds. Moreover, he has persistently shown himself ungrateful.... The Jews have always formed a rebellious element in every state."

Under the orders of Jacob Schiff, the Council on Foreign Relations (CFR) is founded by Ashkenazi Jews, Bernard Baruch and Colonel Edward Mandell House. Schiff gave his orders prior to his death in 1920, as he knew an organisation in America needed to be set up to select politicians to carry on the Rothschild conspiracy. Indeed, the formation of the CFR was actually agreed in a meeting on May 30th, 1919 at the Hotel Majestic in Paris, France.

The CFR membership at the start is approximately 1,000 people in the United States. This membership includes the heads of virtually every industrial empire in America, all the American based international bankers, and the heads of all their tax free foundations. In essence all those people who would provide the capital required for anyone who wished to run for Congress, the Senate or the Presidency.

The first job of the CFR is to gain control of the press. This task is given to John D. Rockefeller who sets up a number of national news magazines such as Life and Time. He finances the Jew, Samuel Newhouse, to buy up and establish a chain of newspapers all across the country, and another Jew, Eugene Meyer, who would go on to buy up many publications such as the Washington Post, Newsweek, and The Weekly Magazine.

The idea of controlling the press is not simply to censor news the Rothschilds don't want you to hear. It is primarily to be used as an education tool to condition the public by emphasising what news is important and what news isn't. A perfect example of this is a newspaper which runs lead stories about the shenanigans of whatever flavour of the month celebrity they choose, yet bury within the inside pages some brief account of an ongoing war that will overtly or covertly have an effect on each and every one of us. Another example of this is putting more and more emphasis on sports as opposed to news.

The CFR also needed to get control of radio, television and the motion picture industry. This task is split amongst the international bankers from Kuhn Loeb, Goldman Sachs, the Warburgs, and the Lehmanns. Interestingly the Jewish Encyclopaedica Judaica would have the following to say on this subject,

> "All the large Hollywood companies, with the exception of United Artists, were founded and controlled by Jews."

Finally the CFR needed to control what was being taught in the schools, and that task was given to the Carnegies.

In Germany, Jacob Klatzkin, a Jewish political Zionist

ideologist in Germany at the time, where incidentally the Jews of Germany were enjoying full political and civil rights, makes the following provocative statement hoping it will undermine the Jewish community in Germany and make them flee to Palestine,

> "We Jews are aliens…a foreign people in your midst and we…wish to stay that way. A Jew can never be a loyal German. Whoever calls the foreign land his Fatherland is a traitor to the Jewish people."

1922: President Theodore Roosevelt, who died in 1919, is quoted in the March 27th edition of the New York Times with the following statement,

> "These International bankers and Rockefeller-Standard Oil interests control the majority of newspapers and the columns of these newspapers to club into submission or drive out of public office officials who refuse to do the bidding of the powerful corrupt cliques which compose the invisible government."

The reason the New York Times ran this article, was due to the Mayor of New York, John Hylan, who had been reported in the same paper the previous day, March 26th, with the following statement,

> "The warning of Theodore Roosevelt has much timeliness today, for the real menace of our republic is this invisible government which like a giant octopus sprawls its slimy length over

> city, state, and nation.... It seizes in its long and powerful tentacles our executive officers, our legislative bodies, our schools, our courts, our newspapers, and every agency created for the public protection...
>
> To depart from mere generalizations, let me say that at the head of this octopus are the Rockefeller-Standard Oil interest and a small group of powerful banking houses generally referred to as international bankers. This little coterie of powerful international bankers virtually run the United States Government for their own selfish purposes.
>
> They practically control both parties, write political platforms, make cats-paws of party leaders, use the leading men of private organizations, and resort to every device to place in nomination for high public office only such candidates as will be amenable to the dictates of corrupt big business...these International Bankers and Rockefeller-Standard Oil interests control the majority of newspapers and magazines in this country."

In his book, "The Jews," published this year, noted historian, Hilaire Belloc, states the following in relation to the increasing phenomenon of the, "Crypto-Jew,"

> "Take the particular trick of false names. It seems to us particularly odious. We think when we show our contempt for those who use this

> subterfuge that we are giving them no more than they deserve. It is a meanness which we associate with criminals and vagabonds; a piece of crawling and sneaking....Men whose race is universally known, will unblushingly adopt a false name as a mask, and after a year or two pretend to treat it as an insult if their original and true name be used in its place."

He goes onto reveal how some Jews did not need to change their name as they simply intermarried with the aristocracy of England when he states,

> "The Jew might almost be called a British agent upon the Continent of Europe and still more in the Near and Far East...He was admitted to every institution in the State. A prominent member of his nation became chief officer of the English executive, and, an influence more subtle and penetrating, marriages began to take place, wholesale, between what had once been the aristocratic territorial families of this country and the Jewish commercial fortunes.
>
> After two generations of this, with the opening of the twentieth century those of the great territorial English families in which there was no Jewish blood were the exception. In nearly all of them was the stain more or less marked, in some of them so strong that though the name was still an English name and the tradition those of a purely English lineage of the long past, the physique and character had become wholly Jewish and the members of the family were

> taken for Jews whenever they travelled in countries where the gentry had not yet suffered or enjoyed the admixture."

1924: Josef Stalin, a Georgian, becomes Premier of the Soviet Union. Joseph Stalin's real name is Djugashvili, which translates from Georgian as, "son of a Jew." In the Georgian language, "shvili," means son of, and, "Djuga," means Jew. Stalin also has three wives in his lifetime. Ekaterina Svanidze, Kadya Allevijah, and Rosa Kaganovich, all of them Jewesses. Interestingly Stalin passes a law during his premiership that resulted in anyone found guilty of anti-Semitism being sentenced to death.

On May 10th, J. Edgar Hoover is made Director of the Bureau Of Investigation (BOI) which will become the Federal Bureau Of Investigation (FBI) in 1935. He would remain its Director until his death in 1972. Hoover was a homosexual and during some point in his career he was photographed engaged in homosexual acts with Associate FBI Director, Clyde Tolson, his lifelong companion for more than forty years who inherited his estate upon his death. These photos were reportedly obtained through the Mafia run by Jewish Don, Meyer Lansky, for the purposes of blackmailing Hoover and keeping him in the Zionist fold.

In his book, "You Gentiles," Maurice Samuel states the following of his people, the Jews,

> "We Jews, we are the destroyers and will remain the destroyers. Nothing you can do will meet our demands and needs. We will forever destroy because we want a world of our own."

Since 1922, Maurice Samuel worked as secretary to Chaim Weizmann, the leader of the World Zionist Movement.

In the January 17th issue of "The Jewish Courier," it is stated,

> "Jews may adopt the customs and language of the countries where they live, but they will never become part of the native population."

In her book, "Secret Societies and Subversive Movements," published this year, Nesta Webster states the following of the Jewish religion,

> "The Jewish conception of the Jews as the Chosen People who must eventually rule the world forms indeed the basis of Rabbinical Judaism.... The Jewish religion now takes its stand on the Talmud rather than on the Bible."

Edmond de Rothschild establishes the Palestine Jewish Colonization Association (PICA), which acquires more than 125,000 acres of land. He goes on to establish numerous business ventures there including the founding of Israel's wine industry.

On July 1st, as he leaves the Shaarei Zedek Hospital in Jerusalem, Dr. Yaakov Yisrael Dehan is assassinated by Zionist, Avraham Tahomi. This is as a result of his organization of a meeting between a delegation of Orthodox leaders and a group of Arab leaders headed by King Abdullah. Dr. Dehan was a promoter of peace with the veteran Arab residents of the Holy Land, the direct opposite of what the Zionists wanted.

1925: This year's Jewish Encyclopaedia states of the existence of Ashkenazi Jews (who represent approximately 90% of so-called world Jewry), with the startling admission that the so called enemy of the Jews, Esau (also known as Edom, see Genesis 36:1), now actually represents the Jewish race, when on page 42 of Volume V it is stated,

> "Edom is in modern Jewry."

On March 19th, the British manufacturer, Walter Crick, is quoted in the Northampton Daily Echo as having made the following statement,

> "Jews can destroy by means of finance. Jews are International. Control of credits in this country is not in the hands of the English, but of Jews. It has become the biggest danger the British Empire ever had to face."

On April 1st, the Jew, Lord Arthur James Balfour, he of the infamous Balfour declaration, gives a speech as guest of honour at the inauguration of the Hebrew University at Mount Scopus, Jerusalem, Israel. He goes on to tour round Palestine, where he is greeted enthusiastically by the Jewish population, whilst the Arabs welcome him with black flags.

On December 3rd, in the, "London Morning Post," George Bernard Shaw, who incidentally won the Nobel Prize for Literature this year, had the following to say on the subject of the Jew,

> "This is the real enemy. The invader from the East, the Druze, the ruffian, the oriental parasite, in a word the Jew."

1926: N. M. Rothschild & Sons refinance the Underground Electric Railways Company of London Ltd which has a controlling interest in the entire London Underground transport system.

David Sarnoff, a Jew, launches the first United States radio chain in as a service of RCA. Sarnoff will go on to be heavily involved in the development of colour television and build NBC into one of the big three TV networks.

Maurice de Rothschild has a son, Edmond de Rothschild.

1927: On October 28th, the "Jewish Tribune of New York," states in an article,

> "Masonry is based on Judaism. Eliminate the teachings of Judaism from the Masonic Ritual and what is left?"

Also speaking on this subject, the well known rabbi, Isaac Wise, states,

> "Freemasonry is a Jewish establishment, whose history; grades; official appointments; pass-words; and explanations, are Jewish from beginning to end."

1928: William S. Paley, a Jew, founds CBS Radio and goes on to build it into a multi-billion-dollar TV empire.

On Page 572 of June 1st's Rothschild owned publication, "La Revue de Paris," a letter to Karl Marx from Baruch Levy is reprinted, an extract of which reads as follows,

> "The Jewish people as a whole will be its own Messiah. It will attain world dominion by the dissolution of other races, by the abolition of frontiers, the annihilation of monarchy, and by the establishment of a world republic in which the Jews will everywhere exercise the privilege of citizenship. In this "New World Order," the children of Israel will furnish all the leaders without encountering opposition.

> The Governments of the different peoples forming the world republic will fall without difficulty into the hands of the Jews. It will then be possible for the Jewish rulers to abolish private property, and everywhere to make use of the resources of the state. Thus will the promise of the Talmud be fulfilled, in which is said that when the Messianic time is come, the Jews will have all the property of the whole world in their hands."

1929: In April, Rothschild, Paul Warburg sends out a secret warning to his friends that a collapse and nationwide depression has been planned for later this year. It is certainly no coincidence that the biographies of all the Wall Street giants of that era: John D. Rockefeller; J. P. Morgan Jr.; Joseph Kennedy; Bernard Baruch; et al, all marvel at the fact these people got out of the stock-market completely, just before the crash and put their assets into cash or gold.

So, as all the bankers and their friends already knew, in August the Federal Reserve began to tighten the money supply. Then on October 24th the big New York bankers called in their 24 hour broker call loans. This meant that both the stockbrokers and their customers had to dump their stocks on the stock-market to cover their loans, irrespective of what price they had to sell them for.

As a result of this the stock-market crashed, a day that would go down in history as, "Black Thursday." In his book, "The Great Crash 1929," John Kenneth Gailbraith makes the following shocking statement,

> "At the height of the selling frenzy Bernard Baruch brought Winston Churchill into the visitors gallery of the New York Stock Exchange to witness the panic and impress him with his power over the wild events on the floor."

Republican Congressman, Louis T. McFadden, Chairman of the House Banking & Currency Committee, from 1920 to 1931, who was a staunch critic of the Jewish bankers is quite candid as to who was responsible when he states of this crash,

> "It was not accidental. It was a carefully contrived occurrence... The international bankers sought to bring about a condition of despair here so that they might emerge as rulers of us all."

Despite the claims of how the Federal Reserve would protect the country against depressions and inflation, they continued to further contract the money supply. Between 1929 and 1933, they would reduce the money supply by an additional 33%. Even, Milton Friedman, the Nobel Prize winning economist stated the following in a radio interview in January 1996,

> "The Federal Reserve definitely caused the Great Depression by contracting the amount of currency in circulation by one-third from 1929 to 1933."

In only a few weeks from the day of the crash, 3 billion dollars of wealth vanished. Within a year, 40 billion dollars of wealth vanished. However, it did not simply disappear, it just ended up consolidated in fewer and fewer hands, as was planned. An example of this is Joseph P. Kennedy, John F. Kennedy's father. In 1929 he was worth 4 million dollars, in 1935 following the greatest depression in America's history, that had increased to over 100 million dollars.

This is why depressions are caused. To take money out of the hands of the many for the benefit of a few. On this occasion the money would be largely spent overseas, as whilst this Great Depression was occurring, millions of American dollars was being spent on rebuilding Germany from damage sustained during World War 1, in preparation for the Rothschilds' next war, World War 2. Republican Louis T. McFadden, Chairman of the House Banking & Currency Committee from 1920 to 1931, would state the following in relation to this,

> "After World War 1, Germany fell into the hands of the German International Bankers. Those bankers bought her and now they own her, lock, stock, and barrel. They have purchased her industries, they have mortgages on her soil, they control her production, they control all her public utilities.
>
> The international German bankers have subsidized the present Government of Germany and they have also supplied every dollar of the money Adolf Hitler has used in his lavish campaign to build up a threat to the government of Bruening. When Bruening fails to obey the orders of the German International Bankers, Hitler is brought forth to scare the Germans into submission…

> Through the Federal Reserve Board over 30 billion of dollars of American money...has been pumped into Germany.... You have all heard of the spending that has taken place in Germany... modernistic dwellings, her great planetariums, her gymnasiums, her swimming pools, her fine public highways, her perfect factories.
>
> All this was done on our money. All this was given to Germany through the Federal Reserve Board. The Federal Reserve Board...has pumped so many billions of dollars into Germany that they dare not name the total."

Interestingly, the money pumped in to Germany to build her up in preparation for World War 2, is into the German Thyssen banks which are affiliated with the Rothschild controlled Harriman interest in New York.

1930: This year, thirty-three years after the first World Zionist Congress was held in Basel, Switzerland, the first Rothschild "World Bank," the "Bank for International Settlements (BIS)," is established in the same place, Basel, Switzerland.

It is established by Charles G. Dawes (Rothschild agent and Vice President under President Calvin Coolidge from 1925-1929), Owen D. Young (Rothschild agent, founder of RCA and Chairman of General Electric from 1922 until 1939), and Hjalmar Schacht of Germany (President of the Reichsbank).

The BIS is referred to by the bankers as the "Central

bank for the central banks." To put this bank into perspective today, whereas the International Monetary Fund (IMF) and the World Bank deal with governments, the BIS deals only with other central banks. All its meetings are held in secret and involve the top central bankers from around the world. For example the former head of the Federal Reserve, Alan Greenspan, would go to the BIS headquarters in Basel, Switzerland, ten times a year for these private meetings.

The BIS also has the status of a sovereign power and is immune from governmental control. A summary of this immunity is listed below:

> 1) Diplomatic immunity for persons and what they carry with them (i.e., diplomatic pouches).
>
> 2) No taxation on any transactions, including salaries paid to employees.
>
> 3) Embassy-type immunity for all buildings and/or offices operated by the BIS worldwide including China and Mexico.
>
> 4) No oversight or knowledge of operations by any government authority, they are not audited.
>
> 5) Freedom from immigration restrictions.
>
> 6) Freedom to encrypt any and all communications of any sort.
>
> 7) Freedom from any legal jurisdiction, they even have their own police force.

Georgetown Professor and historian, Carroll Quigley, commented on the creation of this central bank in his 1975 book, "Tragedy and Hope," as follows,

> "The powers of financial capitalism had (a) far reaching (plan), nothing less than to create a world system of financial control in private hands able to dominate the political system of each country and the economy of the world as a whole. This system was to be controlled in a feudalist fashion by the central banks of the world acting in concert, by secret agreements arrived at in frequent meetings and conferences.
>
> The apex of the system was to be the Bank For International Settlements in Basel, Switzerland, a private bank owned and controlled by the world's central banks which were themselves private corporations.
>
> Each central bank...sought to dominate its government by its ability to control treasury loans, to manipulate foreign exchanges, to influence the level of economic activity in the Country, and to influence cooperative politicians by subsequent economic rewards in the business world."

A handful of United States Senators, led by Henry Cabot Lodge, would fight to keep the United States out of the Bank for International Settlements. However, even though the United States rejected this World Central Bank, the Federal Reserve still sent members to participate in its meetings in Switzerland, right up until

1994 when the United States was, "officially," dragged into it.

1931: This year United States State Department papers come to light of the following. In 1917 during the Russian Revolution, M. Oudendyke, the Netherlands Minister in Russia at the time, informed various governments including Britain, France and the United States of the danger of communism which he identified as overtly Jewish, when he sent them a communiqué, a segment of which states,

> "The danger is now so great that I feel it my duty to call the attention of the British and all other Governments to the fact that if an end is not put to Bolshevism in Russia at once the civilization of the whole world will be threatened. This is not an exaggeration....
>
> I consider that the immediate suppression of Bolshevism is the greatest issue now before the world, not even excluding the war which is still raging and unless as above stated Bolshevism is nipped in the bud immediately it is bound to spread in one form or another over Europe and the whole world as it is organized and worked by Jews who have no nationality and whose one object is to destroy for their own ends the existing order of things."

Prominent member of the Jewish Alliance Israelite Universelle, Jean Izoulet, states this year,

> "The meaning of the history of the last century is that today 300 Jewish financiers, all Masters of Lodges, rule the world."

1933: On January 30th, Adolf Hitler becomes Chancellor of Germany. He expels the Jews and Communists out of all Governmental positions within Germany. Interestingly, at the time, the number of Jews in Germany's government was over twenty times those in their government at the end of World War 1. As a result of this expulsion, in July, the Jews hold a World Conference in Amsterdam during which they demand that Hitler re-instate every Jew back to his former position.

Hitler refuses and as a result of this, Samuel Untermyer, the Ashkenazi Jew who blackmailed President Wilson, and is now the head of the American delegation and the president of the whole conference, returns to the United States and makes a speech on radio which was transcribed in the New York Times, on, Monday, August 7th, 1933. In the speech he made the following statements,

> "...the Jews are the aristocrats of the world.... Our campaign is...the economic boycott against all German goods, shipping and services...What we are proposing...is to prosecute a purely defensive economic boycott that will undermine the Hitler regime and bring the German people to their senses by destroying their export trade on which their very existence depends...

> Each of you, Jew and Gentile alike…must refuse to deal with any merchant or shopkeeper who sells any German-made goods or who patronizes German ships or shipping."

Two thirds of Germany's food supply would have to be imported, and could only be imported with the proceeds of what they exported, so if Germany could not export, two thirds of Germany's population would starve, as there would be not enough food for more than one third of the population.

Nevertheless, Jews throughout America participate in this boycott, protesting outside and damaging any stores in which they found any products with, "Made in Germany," printed on them, causing stores to have to dump these products or risk bankruptcy.

Once the effects of this boycott began to be felt in Germany, the Germans began boycotting Jewish stores in the same way the Jews had done to stores selling German products in America.

The Nazis and the Jews in Palestine collaborate, as they would for the next seven years. This is because they essentially wanted the same thing. The Jews in Palestine wanted all the Jews to live in Palestine and the Nazis wanted all Jews out of Germany. Both sides therefore sign a transfer agreement known as "Ha'avara," which permitted the transfer of Jews and all their capital from Germany to Palestine.

As a result of this agreement, 60,000, approx 20% of

Germany's Jews, emigrate to Palestine, and make up 15% of the Jewish population there by 1939. They take with them $40 million dollars of assets (worth approximately $600 million today) with the blessing of the Nazi regime.

According to the United States Holocaust Memorial Museum,

> "By September 1939, approximately 282,000 Jews had left Germany and 117,000 from annexed Austria. Of these, some 95,000 emigrated to the United States, 60,000 to Palestine, 40,000 to Great Britain, and about 75,000 to Central and South America, with the largest numbers entering Argentina, Brazil, Chile, and Bolivia.
>
> More than 18,000 Jews from the German Reich were also able to find refuge in Shanghai, in Japanese-occupied China. At the end of 1939, about 202,000 Jews remained in Germany and 57,000 in annexed Austria, many of them elderly."

Interestingly, all of these Jews who left Germany voluntarily before the Second World War even started will go on to be known as "holocaust survivors," and be entitled to reparation payments following the end of the Second World War. This is because the definition of a holocaust survivor is as follows,

> "any Jew who lived in a country at the time when it was:

> 1) Under Nazi regime;
>
> 2) Under Nazi occupation; or
>
> 3) Under regime of Nazi collaborators as well as any Jew who fled due to the above regime or occupation."

President Franklin Delano Roosevelt, a Sephardic Crypto-Jew, real name Rosenfelt, orders the all-seeing eye to be placed upon all new dollar bills along with the motto, "Novus Ordo Seclorum." This is Latin for "A New Order of the Ages," or as more commonly stated today, "New World Order."

Furthermore, on November 16th, President Roosevelt recognizes the Bolshevik regime of Stalin in Russia without consultation with Congress whilst 8,000 Ukrainians march in protest in New York.

Roosevelt would never admit his Jewish ancestry, but he would go further than most. In the New York Times of March 14th, 1935, he is quoted with the following statement,

> "In the distant past my ancestors may have been Jews. All I know about the origin of the Roosevelt family is that they are apparently descendants of Claes Martenzen van Roosevelt who came from Holland."

In his book, "From Pharaoh to Hitler, What Is A Jew?," Jewish author Bernard Joseph Brown admits that since the Jews of today are not Israelites, they have no claim to the land of Palestine.

On May 11th, Haim Nachman Bialik, a Jewish poet, widely recognised as Israel's National Poet, in an address given to Jews at the Jewish University in Jerusalem, states,

> "Not in vain have Jews been drawn to journalism. In their hands it became a mighty weapon highly fitted to meet their needs in their war of survival."

1934: In January, staunch Zionist, Vladimir Jabotinsky, gives an update on Samuel Untermyer's boycott of Germany when he makes the following statement,

> "The fight against Germany has now been waged for months by every Jewish community, on every continent, in all labour unions and by every single Jew in the world. There are reasons for the assumption that our share of this fight is of general importance.
>
> We shall start a spiritual and material war of the whole world against Germany. Germany is striving to become once again a great nation and to recover her lost territories as well as her colonies. But our Jewish interests call for the complete destruction of Germany. Collectively and individually, the German nation is a threat to us Jews."

Swiss banking secrecy laws are reformed and it becomes an offence resulting in imprisonment for any bank employee to violate bank secrecy. This is all in preparation for the Rothschild engineered Second World War in which, as usual, they will fund both sides.

In its June 20th issue, New Britain magazine of London, publishes a statement made by former British Prime Minister David Lloyd George in which he states that,

> "Britain is the slave of an international financial bloc."

The article also contains the following words written by Lord Bryce,

> "Democracy has no more persistent and insidious foe than money power...questions regarding Bank of England, its conduct and its objects, are not allowed by the Speaker (of the House of Commons)."

In his book, "Jews Must Live," published this year, Jewish writer Samuel Roth states of the Jews,

> "Our major vice of old, as of today, is parasitism. We are a people of vultures living on the labor and the good nature of the rest of the world. But, despite our faults, we would never have done so much damage to the world if it had not been for our genius for evil leadership. Granted our parasitism!"

Edmond de Rothschild dies.

1935: Between 1930 and 1935, Elizabeth Donnan publishes her 4 volume set, "Documents Illustrative of the History of the Slave Trade to America." This shows that Jews totally dominated the trade in African slaves to America and at least 15 of the ships used to transport the slaves were owned by Jews, some of whom had clear and close ties to the Rothschilds. In order to deceive the authorities that no Jews were involved, they often would use an all Gentile crew and captain.

On November 6th, Mao Tse Tsung states,

> "All political power comes from the barrel of a gun. The Communist party must command all the guns, that way, no guns can ever be used to command the party."

Subsequently, from 1948 to 1952, 20 million political dissidents are rounded up and exterminated as they are unable to defend themselves from the Communists in China due to Mao Tse Tsung's gun control laws.

In his forty-one page pamphlet, "Race, Nation or Religion: Three Questions Jews Must Answer," Dr. Solomon Freehof states of the Jews collectively,

> "We want a world in which nationalism shall definitely diminish."

1936: With regard to the increase in anti-Semitism in Germany, Samuel Landman (at the time, secretary to the World Zionist Organisation), in his 1936 book, "Great Britain, The Jews, and Palestine," states the following of the United States entry into World War 1,

> "The fact that it was Jewish help that brought USA into the War on the side of the Allies has rankled ever since in German—especially Nazi—minds, and has contributed in no small measure to the prominence which anti-Semitism occupies in the Nazi programme."

On October 3rd, Republican Congressman, Louis T. McFadden, Chairman of the House Banking & Currency Committee from 1920 to 1931, is poisoned to death. This is the third assassination attempt on his life; he had suffered an earlier poisoning and had had shots fired at him. McFadden had been one of the staunchest critics of the Federal Reserve and the Jewish criminal cabal behind it.

1937: In his book, "Stalin, Trotsky, or Lenin," George Marlen states,

> "If the tide of history does not turn toward Communist Internationalism, then the Jewish race is doomed."

In other words he's saying that the Jews are totally in charge of Communist Internationalism, and if the world does not turn to a New World Order of Jewish

Communist Internationalism, then the Jewish race is doomed. Interestingly, Internationalism is an early incarnation of globalisation.

Another writer, William Joyce, an Englishman, so disgusted with Britain's subservience to the Jews that he would defect to Germany just before World War 2, and broadcast a radio program from there trying to wake up the British people to the enemy in their midst, stated this year,

> "Britain and Germany, particularly with the assistance of Italy, can form against Bolshevism and international finance, twin Jewish manifestations, a bulwark much too strong to invite attack.... International Finance is controlled by great Jewish moneylenders and Communism is being propagated by Jewish agitators who are at one fundamentally with the powerful capitalists of their race in desiring an international world order, which would, of course, give universal sovereignty to the only international race in existence."

Indeed, on February 4th, renowned historian, Hilaire Belloc, makes the following statement in G. K.'s Weekly,

> "The propaganda of Communism throughout the world, in organization and direction is in the hands of Jewish agents. As for anyone who does not know that the Bolshevist movement in

> Russia is Jewish, I can only say that he must be a man who is taken in by the suppression of our deplorable press."

This year, Professor A. Kulisher, a Jew, calls for the genocide of all Germans to be the priority of worldwide Jewry when he states,

> "Germany is the enemy of Judaism and must be pursued with deadly hatred. The goal of Judaism today is: a merciless campaign against all German peoples and the complete destruction of the nation. We demand a complete blockade of trade, the importation of raw materials stopped and retaliation towards every German, woman and child."

On April 28th in an article published in the Daily Express, twenty-seven year old Lord Victor Rothschild also demonstrates how prophetic he is when asked by reporter, W. Hickey, where he intended to live when the lease on his Piccadilly home ran out. He replied,

> "Nowhere probably, I just don't know. Not till after the war anyway."

It would be two and a half years before World War 2 would start, yet, naturally, he already knew the war was coming.

On October 30th, Rear Admiral Henry Hamilton

Beamish, stated the following to an assembly in New York,

> "In 1848 the word, "anti-Semitic," was invented by the Jews to prevent the use of the word, "Jew." The right word for them is, "Jew,"...I implore all of you to be accurate—call them Jews. There is no need to be delicate on this Jewish question.
>
> You must face them in this country. The Jew should be satisfied here. I was here forty-seven years ago; your doors were thrown open to the Jews and they were free. Now he has got you absolutely by the throat—that is your reward."

1938: On January 1st, Nesta Webster publishes her book, "Germany and England," in which she states,

> "England is no longer controlled by Britons. We are under the invisible Jewish dictatorship—a dictatorship that can be felt in every sphere of life."

On November 7th, a Jew, Herschel Grynszpan, assassinates Ernst vom Rath, a minor official at the German Embassy in Paris.

In December, Sir Oswald Mosley makes the following revealing statement on the allegation that the Jews are being persecuted in Germany,

> "Supposing that every allegation were true... supposing it was a fact that a minority in Germany were being treated as the papers allege, was that any reason for millions in Britain to lose their lives in a war with Germany?
>
> How many minorities had been badly treated in how many countries since the war without any protest from press or politicians?...Why was it only when Jews were the people affected that we had any demand for war with the country concerned?
>
> There was only one answer...that today Jewish finance controlled the press and political system of Britain. If you criticise a Jew at home then gaol threatens you. If others touch a Jew abroad—then war threatens them."

Rabbi Stephen Wise, the President of both the American Jewish Congress and the World Jewish Congress, puts forward his expectations of the Jew's loyalty to his country of domicile when he makes the following statement to a rally in New York,

> "I am not an American citizen of the Jewish faith. I am a Jew. I am an American. I have been an American for sixty-three sixty-fourths of my life, but I have been a Jew for four thousand years. Hitler was right in one thing. He calls the Jewish people a race and we are a race."

1939: I. G. Farben, the leading producer of chemicals in the world and largest German producer of steel dramatically increases its production. This increased production is almost exclusively used to arm Germany for World War 2.

This company is controlled by the Rothschilds and goes on to use Jews and other disaffected peoples as slave labour in concentration camps. Interestingly, I.G. Farben also created Zyklon B gas that it will be alleged was used to exterminate Jews.

In Germany, Hitler had been doing phenomenally well in turning his country around economically ever since he came to power. He did this by breaking with the Jewish international bankers, and trading by barter, thus bartering the surplus of goods Germany had, with the surplus of goods Germany needed that another country had, without debts being incurred on either side.

He, like Abraham Lincoln before him, simply issued what money was needed on the authority of the German Government, which was backed by the productivity of the German labour force, and not the empty promises of Jewish international bankers, who in a country without debt, could not function.

As a result of this policy, Germany was able to regenerate the social and spiritual life of all its citizens. Put simply, when you are able to help your people, the people in turn help you as they are of course happy because they are being respected, and are thus able to respect themselves. As a result of a Germany being run for the benefit of the Germans as opposed to for the benefit of Jewish bankers, the citizens of Germany were able to make Germany the most powerful and prosperous state in Europe in only a seven year period.

An example of how Hitler achieved this is recorded in William Gayley Simpson's 1978 book, "Which Way Western Man?" in which he states,

> "The German peasant, who had been on the verge of utter ruin, was given an honored status as the source of the nation's food supply, his land was released from the grip of the Jewish usurer and measures taken to ensure that it should, 'remain permanently in the possession of one family, handed down from father to son.'"

The Jews could not let this continue as they knew that it would spell the death of their debt driven money system and so World War 2 starts this year, in earnest. This war is about one thing, which money system would survive. This is not a war between Germany and the Allies, it is a war between Germany and the Jewish money power who are in control of the Allied leadership and use them and their media to propagandize the Allied populous into hatred of the Germans.

On May 22nd, Anthony Crossley, Conservative MP for Oldham, makes the following statement in the House of Commons in relation to the plight of the Arabs as a result of Jewish persecution of the Arabs, in Palestine,

> "I do not believe that there has ever been a

> debate in this House, when this House would have been more justified in calling to the Bar an Arab speaker to explain the Arab point of view from the viewpoint of his own countrymen and his own country…
>
> There are no Arab members of Parliament. There are no Arab constituents to bring influence to bear upon their members of Parliament. There is no Arab control of newspapers in this country. It is impossible almost to get a pro-Arab letter into the Times.
>
> There are in the City no Arab financial houses who control large amounts of finance. There is no Arab control of newspaper advertisements in this country. There are no Arab ex-Colonial Secretaries who one by one get up and thunder, as they will, at the Government during the debate, because of the mistakes they themselves have made in the past.
>
> Finally, and I want the Colonial Secretary to pay special attention to this point, tomorrow night there is to be a broadcast. There is to be himself giving the Government point of view. There is to be the honourable member for the Don Valley to advance what is obviously the Zionist point of view. There is to be the honourable member for Carnarvon Boroughs supporting the Zionist point of view. There will not be a supporter of the Arabs who can advance their point of view."

On August 15th, less than three months later, Anthony

Crossley will be killed in action off the coast of Denmark, having joined the British Armed Forces soon after the outbreak of World War 2.

1940: Hansjurgen Koehler in his book, "Inside The Gestapo," states the following, of Maria Anna Schicklgruber, Adolf Hitler's grandmother,

> "A little servant girl…came to Vienna and became a domestic servant…at the Rothschild mansion…and Hitler's unknown grandfather must be probably looked for in this magnificent house."

This is re-iterated by Walter Langer in his book, "The Mind Of Hitler," in which he states,

> "Adolf's father, Alois Hitler, was the illegitimate son of Maria Anna Schicklgruber…Maria Anna Schicklgruber was living in Vienna at the time she conceived. At that time she was employed as a servant in the home of Baron Rothschild. As soon as the family discovered her pregnancy she was sent back home…where Alois was born."

The idea that Hitler could have been a Rothschild illegitimate seems ridiculous, however it cannot be denied that one of Hitler's major successes had been the emigration of Jews to Palestine, something which was also one of the Rothschilds' main aims. The Rothschilds knew that a country without a population would be meaningless. Furthermore, the propaganda the Jews got out of the Second World War advanced the Rothschilds' program of Jewish supremacism more significantly than any other event in history.

This year William Joyce, living in self-imposed exile in Germany, publishes his book, "Twilight Over England," in which he states of the Jewish character,

> "Adamantine materialism, a flair for assuming mysticism outwardly, a supreme contempt for other races, a complete disregard for other peoples' rights, cleverness in imitation and improvisation, contempt for all labour not associated with high profits, great energy in the cause of money-making, a hatred of all nationalism but their own, a high degree of loyalty to their own family and their own community, an implicit faith in the power to corrupt gentiles, a brilliant capacity for intrigue, and a pathetic inability to keep pace with any deeper thought or higher idealism are the chief characteristics of the Jewish race. On all these attributes, volumes could be written; but it should suffice to express the resultant of these forces very simply in the following tendencies:
>
> 1) An inability to avoid forming a state within a state.
>
> 2) Complete inability to view their Gentile hosts as possessing equal rights with their own.
>
> 3) Predetermined specialisation in all those processes which bring high profit. Hence, in

> capitalism, almost exclusive preoccupation with finance, distribution, and exchange as distinct from productive industry. Professional work undertaken either for profit or for the sake of social advancement.
>
> 4) A natural tendency to utilize social and economic advancement for the purpose of gaining political power.
>
> 5) An unholy dread of nationalism as a factor which would draw attention to their racial nature and expose their operations.
>
> 6) The deliberate debasement of the standards of culture in the land of their sojourn.
>
> 7) The elimination by competition of the Aryan who merely wants to get enough for himself and not more than anybody else.
>
> These resultants seem to manifest themselves in every land that the Jew inhabits."

1941: President Roosevelt takes America into the Second World War by refusing to sell Japan any more steel scrap or oil. Japan is in the midst of a war against China and without that scrap steel and oil, Japan knows they will be unable to continue that war. Roosevelt in turn knows this economic boycott would provoke the Japanese to attack America, which they subsequently did at Pearl Harbor.

Interestingly, back in 1939, President Roosevelt tried his hardest to railroad The United States into the war in Europe to accommodate the Jews in the United States and the world, but when that failed he knew he would have to try a different tactic. That was, of course, what happened at Pearl Harbor.

Sir Josiah Stamp, director of the Bank of England during the years 1928-1941, makes the following statement with regard to banking,

> "The modern banking system manufactures money out of nothing. The process is perhaps the most astounding piece of sleight of hand that was ever invented. Banking was conceived in iniquity and born in sin. Bankers own the Earth. Take it away from them, but leave them the power to create money, and with the flick of the pen they will create enough money to buy it back again...
>
> Take this great power away from them and all great fortunes like mine will disappear, and they ought to disappear, for then this would be a better and happier world to live in. But if you want to continue to be slaves of the banks and pay the cost of your own slavery, then let bankers continue to create money and control credit."

1942: Prescott Bush, father and grandfather of future American Presidents George Herbert Walker and George W. respectively, has his company seized under the

"Trading With The Enemy" Act. He had been funding Hitler from America, whilst American soldiers were being killed by German soldiers. Interestingly the Anti-Defamation League (ADL) never criticizes any of the Bush family for this.

On May 8th, the Jewish Chronicle runs an editorial in which they state boastfully,

> "We have been at war with Hitler since the first day that he gained power."

Indeed, on December 3rd, Chaim Weizmann, President of the World Jewish Congress, makes the following statement in New York,

> "We are not denying and we are not afraid to confess, this war is our war and that it is waged for the liberation of Jewry....stronger than all fronts together is our front, that of Jewry.
>
> We are not only giving this war our financial support on which the entire war production is based.
>
> We are not only providing our full propaganda power which is the moral energy that keeps this war going.
>
> The guarantee of victory is predominantly based on weakening the enemy forces, on destroying them within their own country, within the resistance.

> And we are the Trojan horse in the enemy's fortress. Thousands of Jews living in Europe constitute the principal factor in the destruction of our enemy. There, our front is a fact and the most valuable aid for victory."

Leonard Goldenson founds the ABC television network and as President oversees ABC's success.

1943: February 18th, Zionist, Izaak Greenbaum, head of the Jewish Agency Rescue Committee, in a speech to the Zionist Executive Council states,

> "If I am asked, could you give from the UJA (United Jewish Appeal) monies to rescue Jews, I say, no and I say again no!"

He goes onto state,

> "One cow in Palestine is worth more than all the Jews in Poland!"

This is not a surprise, as Zionism and Nazism had similar aims. They both wanted the Jews out of Germany. However, the Zionists were not interested in any Jews that didn't want to go to Palestine and thought it would be more beneficial to ensure these Jews be placed in concentration camps, in order to frighten Jews worldwide into fleeing to Palestine, which they touted as the only state where they could be safe.

1944: On November 6th, Lord Moyne, British Minister Resident in the Middle East, is assassinated in Cairo by two members of the Jewish terrorist group, the Stern Gang, led by future Prime Minister of Israel, Yitzhak Shamir. He is also responsible for an assassination attempt against Harold MacMichael, the High Commissioner of the British Mandate of Palestine, this same year.

Interestingly he also masterminds another successful assassination this year against the United Nations representative in the Middle East, Count Folke Bernadotte, who, although he had secured the release of 21,000 prisoners from German camps during World War 2, was seen by Yitzak Shamir and his terrorist collaborators as an anti-Zionist.

In Bretton Woods, New Hampshire, the International Monetary Fund (IMF) and the World Bank (initially called the International Bank for Reconstruction and Development or IBRD—the name, "World Bank," was not actually adopted until 1975), are approved with full United States participation.

The principal architects of the Bretton Woods system, and hence the IMF, are Harry Dexter White and John Maynard Keynes. Interestingly Harry Dexter White who died in 1946, would be identified as a Soviet spy whose code name was "Jurist" on October 16th, 1950, in an FBI memo; and as for John Maynard Keynes, he is British.

What the IMF and World Bank essentially did was

repeat on a world scale what the Federal Reserve Act of 1913 had established in the United States. They created a banking cartel comprising the world's privately owned central banks, which gradually assumed the power to dictate credit policies to the banks of all nations.

In the same way the Federal Reserve Act authorized the creation of a new national fiat currency called, Federal Reserve Notes, the IMF has been given the authority to issue a world fiat money called, "Special Drawing Rights," or SDR's. Member nations would end up being pressured into making their currencies fully exchangeable for SDR's.

The IMF is controlled by its board of governors, which are either the heads of different central banks, or the heads of the various national treasury departments who are dominated by their central banks. Also, the voting power in the IMF gives the United States and the United Kingdom (the Federal Reserve and the Bank of England), effective overall control of it.

1945: On July 16th, the first successful test of the atomic bomb occurs at the Trinity site, two hundred miles south of Los Alamos. It's creator, J. Robert Oppenheimer, a Rothschild, states in wonder,

> "I am become Death, the Destroyer of worlds."

He is right, within the month, subsequent detonations over Hiroshima and Nagasaki in Japan, result in the deaths of 140,000 people in Hiroshima and 80,000 in Nagasaki.

The end of World War 2. It is reported that the Rothschild controlled I.G. Farben plants were specifically not targeted in the bombing raids on Germany. Interestingly, at the end of the war, whilst parts of Germany lay in ruins, I. G. Farben plants were found to have only sustained 15% damage.

The tribunals held at the end of the Second World War to investigate Nazi War Crimes censor any materials recording Western assistance to Hitler, such as that of Prescott Bush.

The Rothschilds take a giant step towards their goal of world domination when their third overt attempt at World Government, the second "League of Nations," which is called the "United Nations," is approved this year.

1946: On January 3rd, William Joyce is executed. As he awaits his execution he makes his last statement,

> "In death as in this life, I defy the Jews who caused this last war: and I defy the power of Darkness which they represent. I warn the British people against the aggressive Imperialism of the Soviet Union.
>
> May Britain be great once again; and, in the hour of the greatest danger to the West, may the standard of the Hakenkreuz (Swastika) be raised from the dust, crowned with the historic words, "Ihr habt doch gesiegt." I am proud to die for my

> ideals; and I am sorry for the sons of Britain who have died without knowing why."

On February 12th, the British Security Services receive a telegram from a reliable source in Palestine claiming that the Stern gang are,

> "Training members to go to England to assassinate members of His Majesty's Government, especially Mr Bevin (British foreign minister Ernest Bevin)."

On July 22nd, the future Prime Minister of Israel, Ashkenazi Jew, David Ben-Gurion, orders another future Prime Minister of Israel, Ashkenazi Jew, Menachem Begin, to carry out a terrorist attack on the King David Hotel in Palestine, to try and drive out the British. As a result of this, 91 people are killed, most of them civilians: 41 Arabs; 28 British; 17 Jews; and 5 others. Around 45 people are injured.

When he was asked by prominent journalist, Russell Warren Howe, if he considered himself the father of terrorism in the Middle East, Menachem Begin proudly replied,

> "No, in the entire whole world."

60 years later, on July 22nd, 2006, another future Prime Minister of Israel, Benjamin Netanyahu, together with many other Israeli government representatives, dedicate a plaque at the site of this terrorist atrocity, which cites

the bombers as freedom fighters to be admired by Israel.

Just to put the gravity of the attack on the King David Hotel into perspective, it was at the time the biggest death toll as a result of single terrorist action ever and was only surpassed nearly forty years later by the bombing of the United States barracks in Beirut in 1982.

The Bank of England is nationalised which means that the state acquired all the shares in the Bank of England, which now belong to the Treasury and are held in trust by the Treasury Solicitor.

However, as the government has no money to pay for the shares, they give the current secret shareholders of the Bank of England government stocks instead of money for their shares. This means that although the state now receives the operating profits of the bank, this gain is largely offset by the fact that the government now has to pay interest on the new stocks it has issued to pay for the shares.

So, although the Bank of England is now state-owned, the fact is that the British money supply is still almost entirely in private hands, with 97% of it being in the form of interest bearing loans of one sort or another, created by private commercial banks.

As a result of this, the bank is largely controlled and run by those from the world of commercial banking and conventional economics. The members of the Court of Directors, who set policy and oversee its functions, are drawn almost entirely from the world of banks, insurance, economists and big business, and of course a Rothschild continues to sit on its board.

Although the Bank of England is called a central bank it is now essentially a regulatory body that supports and oversees the existing system. It is sometimes referred to as "the lender of last resort," in so far as one of its functions as the bankers' bank is to support any bank or financial institution that gets into difficulties and suffers a run on its liquid assets.

Interestingly, in these circumstances, it is not obliged to disclose details of any such measures, the reason being so as to avoid a crisis in confidence.

1947: The British who, prior to World War 2, declared that there would be no more immigration of Jews to Palestine, in order to protect the Palestinians from their acts of terror against both them and British soldiers, transfer control of Palestine to the United Nations. The United Nations resolves to have Palestine partitioned into two states, one Jewish and one Arab, with Jerusalem to remain as an international zone to be enjoyed by all religious faiths.

This transfer is scheduled to take place on May 15th, 1948. However, just to put into perspective who controls the United Nations (UN), please be aware that the UN had no right to give Arab property to anyone. The Jews owned only 6% of Palestine at that time, yet UN Resolution 181 granted the Jews 57% of the land, leaving the Arabs, who at that time had 94%, with only 43%.

Terror attacks against the British in Palestine continued. In fact, during the summer, three Jewish terrorists, Jacob Weiss, Meir Nakar, and Avshalom Habib, found guilty of an attack on Acre gaol on May 4th, were to be hanged.

At the same time, the Irgun terrorist gang headed by future Prime Minister Menachem Begin were holding two British sergeants, Mervyn Paice and Clifford Martin, as hostages for the three Jewish terrorists. Indeed Begin stated,

> "We will hang the British sergeants at exactly the same time as our men die."

The executions of the Jewish terrorists took place, and the British sergeants were found executed also, hanging from two eucalyptus trees. Captain D. H. Gallatti of 23rd Field Squadron, Royal Engineers, cut down one of the bodies only to be seriously injured by an explosion. Unsatisfied with killing these British soldiers, the Jews had booby trapped their corpses.

Interestingly, a popular British newspaper, the, "Daily Express," carried as their lead story a large picture of these soldiers strung up in the trees, but this front page has now been deleted from the Daily Express archives. The owner of the Daily Express? Richard Desmond, a Jewish pornographer.

Information collected by the Anti-Defamation League (ADL) in its spy operations on United States citizens is used by the House Select Committee on Un-American Activities. Subcommittee Chair, Clare Hoffman, dismisses the ADL's reports on suspected communists as "hearsay."

In October, Ashkenazi Jew, Albert Einstein, writes an open letter to the United Nations encouraging all national governments to be destroyed to make way for a one-world government to be run by the UN.

In his diary of July 21st, President Harry S. Truman makes the following entry,

> "The Jews have no sense of proportion, nor do they have any judgement on world affairs. The Jews, I find, are very, very selfish. They care not how many Estonians, Latvians, Finns, Poles, Yugoslavs or Greeks get murdered or mistreated as (post war) Displaced Persons as long as the Jews get special treatment. Yet when they have power—physical, financial or political—neither Hitler nor Stalin has anything on them for cruelty or mistreatment to the underdog."

1948: In the spring of this year, the Rothschilds bribe President Harry S. Truman (33rd President of the United States 1945-1953) to recognise Israel as a sovereign state with $2,000,000 which they give to him on his campaign train.

At midnight on May 14th, the State of Israel is officially "proclaimed" in Tel Aviv. Eleven minutes later President Truman declares the United States as the first foreign nation to recognise it. Truman later confides to friends that he wanted to recognize the Jewish state in the "first hour of its birth," yet, when pressed by journalists on this subject, he refuses to discuss his pro-Jewish stance any further.

The Flag of Israel is unveiled. The emblem on the flag is a blue coloured version of the Rothschild "Red Hexagram." It has a blue border at the top and the bottom which represents the Nile and Euphrates rivers. This is put there to make the Jewish territorial ambitions very clear, an Israel in accordance with its biblical borders. This would of course mean the inclusion into Israel of: Iraq; Syria; Jordan; Lebanon; and parts of Saudi Arabia.

This use of the Rothschild Hexagram is disguised as it is referred to in the Rothschild media as a "Star Of David." However, it is clear to anyone with knowledge of esoteric symbolism that this Hexagram was used in the ancient mystery religions as the symbol of "Molech" (described as a demon of unwilling sacrifice and also, interestingly, the name of the stone owl the elite worship at Bohemian Grove) and, "Astaroth" (described as the Lord Treasurer of Hell). Due to the fact it is made up of six lines, has six triangular sectors and six points, it is commonly regarded as a symbol of Satan.

Interestingly, the Hexagram is also used to represent Saturn, which has been identified as the esoteric name for "Satan." Would this not indicate that anyone killed in the name of Israel is actually a sacrifice to their God, Satan? Furthermore, the Jewish Sabbath is on Saturday, which was originally known as Saturn's Day.

So, to recap, the hexagram on the Israeli flag represents the number of the beast 666, it is an ancient representation of Satan, also known as Saturn, and the Jewish weekly religious day is Saturn's Day.

In the early hours of April 19th, 132 Jewish terrorists from the Irgun gang, led by future Israeli Prime Minister Menachem Begin, and the Stern gang, led by future Israeli Prime Minister Yitzhak Shamir, brutally massacre 200 men, women and children as they are sleeping peacefully in the Arab village of Deir Yassin.

In an effort to prevent outside observers discovering the brutality of their war crimes, they try to burn some of the bodies, but when that proves unsatisfactory, they stuff some in a well to hide them from the Red Cross representatives who arrive on the scene the next day and would subsequently tell the world.

Indeed, reports from survivors can be found in the, "Report of the Criminal Investigation Division," a Palestine Government Document labelled, No. 179/110/17/GS dated April 13th, 15th, and 16th, 1948, in which British interrogating officer, Assistant Inspector General Richard Catling states,

> "The recording of statements is hampered also by the hysterical state of the women, who often break down many times, whilst the statement is being recorded. There is, however, no doubt that many sexual atrocities were committed by the attacking Jews. Many young school girls were

> raped and later slaughtered. Old women were also molested.
>
> One story is current concerning a case in which a young girl was literally torn in two. Many infants were butchered and killed.
>
> I also saw one old woman who gave her age as 104, who had been severely beaten about the head with rifle butts. Women had bracelets torn from their arms and rings from their fingers, and parts of some women's ears were severed in order to remove ear-rings."

As a result of this the Jews go on to detest the Red Cross, which is why, in the future, they always block them entering any territory in which they are involved in conflict, for as long as possible, to give them time to clean up evidence of their criminal acts.

Following the United Nations transfer of Palestine to an independent Jewish state and an independent Arab state on May 15th, the Israelis launch another military assault on the Arabs (today known as Palestinians) with blaring loudspeakers on their trucks informing the Arabs that if they do not flee immediately, they will be slaughtered.

800,000 Arabs with the recent memory of the Deir Yassin massacre at the forefront of their minds, flee in panic. They ask for help from neighbouring Arab states, but those states do not get involved as they are no match for the Israelis whose up to date military hardware had been supplied by the Jewish Stalinist regime in Russia.

Following this series of Jewish genocidal war crimes, the Jews now control 78% of the former Palestine, as opposed to the 57% that had already been given to them illegally by the Jewish controlled United Nations.

The Arabs, many of them Christians, would never be paid compensation for their homes, property and businesses stolen from them during this genocide, and as a result these people end up in slum refugee cities of tents. Furthermore, at least half of the Arabs, in a desperate hurry to flee with their lives, leave their birth certificates behind. The State of Israel then passes a law that only those Arabs who are able to prove their citizenship are allowed to return to their land, now known as Israel, which meant these 400,000 Arabs could not return and lost all the property they had left there.

Ashkenazi Jew, David Ben-Gurion, one of the father founders of Israel and its first Prime Minister, candidly describes Jewish aims in his diary entry of May 21st as follows,

> "The Achilles heel of the Arab coalition is Lebanon. Muslim supremacy in this country is artificial and can easily be overthrown. A Christian State ought to be set up there, with its southern frontier on the river Litani.
>
> We would sign a treaty of alliance with this State. Thus when we have broken the strength of the Arab Legion and bombed Amman, we could wipe out Trans-Jordan. After that, Syria would fall. And if Egypt still dared to make war on us,

> we would bomb Port Said, Alexandria and Cairo.
>
> We should thus end the war and would have put paid to Egypt, Assyria and Chaldea on behalf of our ancestors."

On October 1st, Commander Anton Muller and his second-in-command, Emil Lachout, send the following memo from Vienna to all interested parties:

> Military Police Service
> Circular Letter No. 31/48.
> Vienna, 1 Oct. 1948.
> 10th dispatch.
>
> The Allied Commissions of Inquiry have so far established that no people were killed by poison gas in the following concentration camps: Bergen-Belsen, Buchenwald, Dachau, Flossenburg, Gross-Rosen, Mauthausen and its satellite camps, Natzweiler, Neuengamme, Niederhagen (Wewelsburg), Ravensbruck, Sachsenhausen, Stutthof, Theresienstadt.
>
> In those cases, it has been possible to prove that confessions had been extracted by torture, and that testimonies were false. This must be taken into account when conducting investigations and interrogations with respect to war crimes. The result of this investigation should be brought to the cognizance of former concentration camp inmates who at the time of the hearings testified

> about the murder of people, especially Jews, with poison gas in those concentration camps. Should they insist on their statements, charges are to be brought against them for making false statements.

1949: On February 3rd, Cholly Knickerbocker, reporting in his society news column in the Hearst Press, which appeared in the N.Y. Journal-American, stated on the subject of Rothschild, Jacob Schiff,

> "Today it is estimated by Jacob's grandson, John Schiff, a prominent member of New York society, that the old man sank about $20,000,000 for the final triumph of Bolshevism in Russia."

On October 1st, Mao Tse Tsung declares the founding of the People's Republic of China in Tiananmen Square, Beijing. He is funded by Rothschild created Communism in Russia and handled by the following Rothschild agents: Solomon Adler, a former United States Treasury official who was a Soviet Spy; Israel Epstein, the son of a Jewish Bolshevik imprisoned by the Tsar in Russia for trying to foment a revolution there; and Frank Coe, a leading official of the Rothschild owned IMF.

In December 16th's Jewish Chronicle, Israeli Prime Minister, David Ben-Gurion, is quoted with the following statement,

> "Jerusalem is not only the capital of Israel and world Jewry; it aspires to become the spiritual center of the world."

1950: Figures reveal that as planned by the Rothschilds, every nation involved in World War 2 greatly multiplied their debt, bringing them further and further under Jewish control. Between 1940 and 1950, United States Federal Debt went from 43 billion dollars to 257 billion dollars, a 598% increase. During that same period Japanese debt increased by 1,348%, French debt increased by 583%, and Canadian debt increased by 417%.

James Paul Warburg, appearing before the Senate on 7th February, arrogantly states,

> "We shall have World Government, whether or not we like it. The only question is whether World Government will be achieved by conquest or consent."

Thus. the Rothschilds get to work on their plan for global government which starts with a three step plan to centralize the economic systems of the entire world. These steps are:

> 1) Central Bank domination of national economies worldwide.
>
> 2) Centralized regional economies through super-states such as the European Union, and regional trade unions such as NAFTA.

> 3) Centralization of the World Economy through a World Central Bank, a world currency and ending national independence through the abolition of all trade tariffs by treaties such as the General Agreement on Tariffs and Trade (GATT).

Israel passes their law of return, guaranteeing every person born of a Jewish mother, throughout the world, the right to dwell in the State of Israel. However, the Palestinians, who had lived there for 1,300 years, are denied that right.

John Davitt, former chief of the Justice Department's internal security section, notes that the Israeli intelligence service is the second most active in the United States after the Soviets. Both of which are of course controlled by Jews.

1951: On April 1st, the Israeli Secret Intelligence Agency, the Mossad, which will go on to terrorize the world, is formed. The Mossad works closely with the American group, the Anti-Defamation League (ADL). The motto of the Mossad is probably the most disturbing secret service motto in the world. It is,

> "By Way Of Deception, Thou Shalt Do War."

1952: Israeli Prime Minister, David Ben-Gurion oversees a project in which a generation of Sephardic

Jews in Israel are weeded out from their Ashkenazi counterparts at school and, to avoid suspicion by the parents, these Sephardic children are then taken on, "school trips." On these supposed "trips," they actually receive a radiation treatment, purportedly for ringworm infection.

At this time, the permitted maximum x-ray dose was 0.5 rad, yet these children received 350 rad directly to their heads. As a result, at least 6,000 die shortly afterwards, with those remaining developing severe conditions such as cancers, epilepsy, and psychosis. Those that are still alive today, and many of their children and grandchildren, are stricken with genetic diseases and malignant tumours.

This is an attempt to genocide the Sephardic Jews who are an underclass in Israel and are even referred to by many Ashkenazi Jews as "niggers."

On April 23rd, during a debate on immigration law, Congressman John Rankin makes the following statement to the House on the subject of the Jews, which is recorded in the Congressional Record,

> "They whine about discrimination. Do you know who is being discriminated against? The white Christian people of America, the ones who created this nation.... Communism is racial. A racial minority seized control in Russia and in all her satellite countries, such as Poland, Czechoslovakia, and many other countries I could name.

> They have been run out of practically every country in Europe in the years gone by, and if they keep stirring race trouble in this country and trying to force their Communistic program on the Christian people of America, there is no telling what will happen to them here."

1953: Dwight Eisenhower, who in the 1915 West Point U.S. Military Academy graduating class yearbook, is referred to as a "terrible Swedish Jew," is elected President of the United States.

On June 19th, Julius and Ethel Rosenberg are executed in America for espionage. They had been caught supplying secrets regarding atomic bomb manufacture to the Soviet Union, a country they had great affinity for, having met at a Young Communist League meeting in America, and also being Jewish, of course.

N. M. Rothschild & Sons found the British Newfoundland Corporation Limited to develop 60,000 square miles of land in Newfoundland, Canada, which comprises a power station to harness the power of the Hamilton (later renamed Churchill) Falls. At the time this was the largest construction project ever to be undertaken by a private company.

1954: "The Lavon Affair." Israeli agents recruit Egyptian citizens of Jewish descent to bomb Western targets in Egypt, and plant evidence to frame Arabs, in an apparent attempt to upset American/Egyptian relations. Israeli defence minister, Ashkenazi Jew, Pinhas Lavon is eventually removed from office, though many think real responsibility lies with David Ben-Gurion.

This is the first known use of Jews who look like Arabs being used by the Jews to carry out terrorist attacks that they then blame on the Arabs, and is an example of how their secret service motto, "By Way of Deception, Thou Shalt Do War," works in practice.

A hidden microphone planted by the Israelis is discovered in the Office of the United States Ambassador in Tel Aviv.

In Holland, the Bilderberg Group meets for the first time at the Bilderberg Hotel in Arnhem. The Bilderberg Group is a Rothschild founded international organization of approximately 100-200 influential people, mostly politicians and business people, who meet annually and in secret to carry out the bidding of the Jewish World Power behind the scenes. Regulars at these meetings put forward the forthcoming global policy, which delegates report back to their respective governments who then implement this policy.

Bilderberg meetings are also used so that Rothschild, David Rockefeller and Jewish front men such as Henry Kissinger can check out potential leaders of countries, and decide whether or not they want them as leaders of said countries. For example: Bill Clinton was there in

1991; Tony Blair was there in 1993; and Angela Merkel was there in 2005. Also rans, who didn't pass the Bilderberg audition, such as, future Chancellor of the Exchequer, Gordon Brown, and former leader of the Conservative party, William Hague, were there in 1991 and 1998 respectively.

1955: The Israeli government carries out the clandestine terrorist bombings of a number of American facilities in Cairo, with the aim of making the Americans believe the Egyptians are responsible for them, in order to damage relations between the United States and Egypt.

Edmond de Rothschild founds Compagnie Financiere, Paris.

1956: On October 28th, Menachem Begin, he of the infamous Deir Yassin massacre and who would go on to be a future Prime Minister of Israel, states at a Tel Aviv conference,

> "You Israelis, you should never become lenient if you kill your enemies. You shall have no pity on them until we have destroyed their so-called Arab culture, on the ruins of which we shall build our own civilization."

Telephone taps are found connected to two telephones in the residence of the United States military attaché in Tel Aviv.

1957: During a joint British, Israeli, and French invasion of the Suez Canal, Ariel Sharon commands units which murder Egyptian prisoners of war, as well as civilian Sudanese workers who the Jews had captured. A total of 273 unarmed prisoners are executed and dumped into mass graves. This story is suppressed for nearly 40 years until it breaks in the August 16th, 1995, edition of the London Daily Telegraph.

James de Rothschild dies and it is reported (by the Rothschild owned media) that he bequeaths a large sum of money to the state of Israel to pay for the construction of their parliament building, the Knesset. He states that the Knesset should be,

> "a symbol, in the eyes of all men, of the permanence of the State of Israel."

On page 219 of his book, "Tales of the British Aristocracy," L.G. Pine, the editor of "Burke's Peerage," states that the Jews,

> "...have made themselves so closely connected with the British peerage that the two classes are unlikely to suffer loss which is not mutual. So closely linked are the Jews and the lords that a blow against the Jews in this country would not be possible without injuring the aristocracy also."

Maurice de Rothschild dies in Paris.

1959: In February, Crypto-Jew, Fidel Castro, declares himself Prime Minister of Cuba, after leading a Communist Revolution there.

1960: In his book, "Impact—Essays on Ignorance and the Decline of American Civilization," published this year, Ezra Pound states,

> "A nation that will not get itself into debt drives the usurers to fury."

1962: On June 25th, prayer is banned from the American Public Schools system following a Supreme Court decision. This court decision was based upon a case brought by New York Jew named Engel in the case Engel v. Vitale. Senator Robert Byrd, a Democrat from West Virginia, states of this decision,

> "Can it be that we, too, are ready to embrace the foul concepts of atheism? Somebody is tampering with America's soul, I leave it to you who that somebody is."

Bank de Rothschild Frères establishes Imétal as an umbrella company for all their mineral mining interests.

Frederic Morton publishes his book, "The Rothschilds," in which he states,

> "Though they control scores of industrial,

> commercial, mining and tourist corporations, not one bears the name Rothschild. Being private partnerships, the family houses never need to, and never do, publish a single public balance sheet, or any other report of their financial condition."

1963: On June 4th, President John F. Kennedy (the 35th President of the United States 1961-1963) signs Executive Order 11110 which returns to the United States Government the power to issue currency, without going through the Rothschilds' owned Federal Reserve.

Less than six months later, on November 22nd, President Kennedy is assassinated by the Rothschilds for the same reason as they assassinated President Abraham Lincoln in 1865: he wanted to print American money for the American people, as opposed to for the benefit of a money grabbing war mongering foreign elite.

This Executive Order 11110 is actually rescinded by President Lyndon Baines Johnson, an alleged Crypto-Jew (the 36th President of the United States 1963-1969), in one of the first acts he carries out as United States President.

Another, and probably the primary reason for Kennedy's assassination, is, however, the fact that he made it quite clear to Israeli Prime Minister, David Ben-Gurion, that under no circumstances would he agree to Israel becoming a nuclear state. The Israeli newspaper Ha'aretz on February 5, 1999, in a review of Avner

Cohen's book, "Israel and the Bomb," states the following on this subject,

> "The murder of American President John F. Kennedy brought to an abrupt end the massive pressure being applied by the U.S. administration on the government of Israel to discontinue the nuclear program.... The book implied that, had Kennedy remained alive, it is doubtful whether Israel would today have a nuclear option."

A point of interest here is that Kennedy's wife, Jackie Kennedy, was Jewish. This is revealed by Gore Vidal in his autobiography, "Palimpsest—A Memoir." It turns out Vidal's stepfather, Hugh Auchincloss, subsequently wed Jackie Kennedy's mother, Janet Bouvier. This story was also covered in the New York Times on November 9, 1995.

Also, for those of you who saw the Oliver Stone movie, "JFK," which came up with a different conclusion with regard to the reasons for Kennedy's assassination, you may wish to know that Oliver Stone is Jewish.

Finally there is some speculation that the Kennedy family was, indeed, a Jewish family that had settled in Ireland some generations before, although this is unconfirmed.

Edmond de Rothschild establishes La Compagnie Financière Edmond de Rothschild (LCF) in Switzerland as a venture capital house. This later develops into an investment bank and asset management company with many affiliates. He also marries his wife Nadine and they have a son, Benjamin de Rothschild.

On January 10th, of this year, the 45 goals of the Communist Manifesto are stated in the United States Congress, by A. S. Herlong Jr. of Florida, and therefore form the Congressional Record of that day. Below is that list, which is important to study today to help you understand whether you live in a "democracy," a "republic," or under "Communism," which is, of course, the control of the masses by Jewish interests.

> 1) U.S. acceptance of coexistence as the only alternative to atomic war.
>
> 2) U.S. willingness to capitulate in preference to engaging in atomic war.
>
> 3) Develop the illusion that total disarmament (by) the United States would be a demonstration of moral strength.
>
> 4) Permit free trade between all nations regardless of Communist affiliation and regardless of whether or not items could be used for war.
>
> 5) Extension of long-term loans to Russia and Soviet satellites.
>
> 6) Provide American aid to all nations regardless of Communist domination.

7) Grant recognition of Red China. Admission of Red China to the U.N.

8) Set up East and West Germany as separate states in spite of Khrushchev's promise in 1955 to settle the German question by free elections under supervision of the U.N.

9) Prolong the conferences to ban atomic tests because the United States has agreed to suspend tests as long as negotiations are in progress.

10) Allow all Soviet satellites individual representation in the U.N.

11) Promote the U.N. as the only hope for mankind. If its charter is rewritten, demand that it be set up as a one-world government with its own independent armed forces.

12) Resist any attempt to outlaw the Communist Party.

13) Do away with all loyalty oaths.

14) Continue giving Russia access to the U.S. Patent Office.

15) Capture one or both of the political parties in the United States.

16) Use technical decisions of the courts to weaken basic American institutions by claiming their activities violate civil rights.

17) Get control of the schools. Use them as transmission belts for socialism and current Communist propaganda. Soften the curriculum. Get control of teachers' associations. Put the party line in textbooks.

18) Gain control of all student newspapers.

19) Use student riots to foment public protests against programs or organizations which are under Communist attack.

20) Infiltrate the press. Get control of book-review assignments, editorial writing, policymaking positions.

21) Gain control of key positions in radio, TV, and motion pictures.

22) Continue discrediting American culture by degrading all forms of artistic expression. An American Communist cell was told to "eliminate all good sculpture from parks and buildings, substitute shapeless, awkward and meaningless forms."

23) Control art critics and directors of art museums. "Our plan is to promote ugliness, repulsive, meaningless art."

24) Eliminate all laws governing obscenity by calling them, "censorship," and a violation of free speech and free press.

25) Break down cultural standards of morality by promoting pornography and obscenity in books, magazines, motion pictures, radio, and TV.

26) Present homosexuality, degeneracy and promiscuity as "normal, natural, and healthy."

27) Infiltrate the churches and replace revealed religion with "social" religion. Discredit the Bible and emphasize the need for intellectual maturity which does not need a "religious crutch."

28) Eliminate prayer or any phase of religious expression in the schools on the ground that it violates the principle of "separation of church and state."

29) Discredit the American Constitution by calling it inadequate, old-fashioned, out of step with modern needs, a hindrance to cooperation between nations on a worldwide basis.

30) Discredit the American Founding Fathers. Present them as selfish aristocrats who had no concern for the "common man."

31) Belittle all forms of American culture and discourage the teaching of American history on the ground that it was only a minor part of the "big picture." Give more emphasis to Russian history since the Communists took over.

32) Support any socialist movement to give centralized control over any part of the culture, education, social agencies, welfare programs, mental health clinics, etc.

33) Eliminate all laws or procedures which interfere with the operation of the Communist apparatus.

34) Eliminate the House Committee on Un-American Activities.

35) Discredit and eventually dismantle the FBI.

36) Infiltrate and gain control of more unions.

37) Infiltrate and gain control of big business.

38) Transfer some of the powers of arrest from the police to social agencies. Treat all behavioral problems as psychiatric disorders which no one but psychiatrists can understand (or treat).

39) Dominate the psychiatric profession and use mental health laws as a means of gaining coercive control over those who oppose Communist goals.

40) Discredit the family as an institution. Encourage promiscuity and easy divorce.

41) Emphasize the need to raise children away from the negative influence of parents. Attribute prejudices, mental blocks and retarding of

children to suppressive influence of parents.

42) Create the impression that violence and insurrection are legitimate aspects of the American tradition; that students and special-interest groups should rise up and use "united force" to solve economic, political or social problems.

43) Overthrow all colonial governments before native populations are ready for self-government.

44) Internationalize the Panama Canal.

45) Repeal the Connally reservation so the United States cannot prevent the World Court from seizing jurisdiction over domestic problems. Give the World Court jurisdiction over nations and individuals alike.

1965: Israel illegally obtains enriched uranium from NUMEC (Nuclear Materials and Equipment Corporation).

Due to friction between different races in Britain, the Race Relations Act of 1965 is introduced into parliament by the then Attorney General, Russian Jew, Frank Soskice. This act makes racial discrimination unlawful in public places.

Introduction of different races into countries is the Jews'

most effective form of warfare yet against the Western World, and is known as the "Silent War," which has taken place at various times this century, primarily in the United States and the United Kingdom.

This is generally done under the pretext of needing other races to fill a gap in the labour market in that country (although of course, in America, Jews brought Africans into the country to sell as slaves), whilst the electorate of the countries concerned are never asked whether they want immigration into their country. The Jews support immigration into countries for the following reasons:

> 1) In accordance with their most holy book, the Talmud, Jews see the world population as consisting of Jews and non-Jews (also known as goyim, goy, and gentiles). The only possible end result of immigration is the destruction of all races as they interbreed with one another and form one single race. That race will be the non-Jews.
>
> 2) The Jews have always wanted a World Government, which co-incidentally they will control. By mixing up all the races into different countries, they can argue that as every country in the world now consists of many different races, national boundaries are obsolete and should be replaced with a single World Government.
>
> 3) The Jews are fully aware of the danger a cohesive native population is to their dreams of a Jewish World Government, having had the

> experience of being kicked out of so many countries several times in history due to the natural reaction of a cohesive population against their evil and exploitative actions there.
>
> The introduction of people foreign to a country as citizens removes the threat of the native peoples acting as a single cohesive unit. This is because the different cultures and customs of both peoples, are hard for either people to accept. Whilst these two groups of people are pre-occupied sorting this out, the Jews have the benefit of invisibility to carry on as they please without question.
>
> They only ever seem to declare their race when they speak of the great benefits in diversity, and anyone who doesn't agree must be a "racist" or a "hater." Yet the plan they are promoting will result in the ethnic cleansing of specific racial types that have been on the planet for thousands of years, which they do not regard as racist or hateful.

Interestingly, the Jewish owned media throughout the world will promote diversity or political-correctness, whilst at the same time promoting the apartheid state of Israel, the only state in the world where you have to be of a particular race to emigrate to. Yes, you have to be biologically Jewish to be able to emigrate there, and it is forbidden for a Jew to marry a non-Jew.

1967: The treatment of the Palestinians by the Jews

finally ignites enough anger in the Arab world for Egypt, Jordan and Syria to mobilise on Israel's borders. All of these three countries are suddenly attacked by Israel and, as a result, the Sinai, which included Gaza, is stolen from Egypt, and the West Bank and the Jordan River stolen from Jordan.

As a result of this, on June 8th, the Israelis launch an attack on the U.S.S. Liberty with Israeli aircraft and motor torpedo boats in an effort to blame it on Egypt, to bring America into the war on their side, and of course follow to the letter, their Mossad motto,

"By Way Of Deception, Thou Shalt Do War."

As a result of their attack, 34 American servicemen are killed and 174 wounded. Israel lies as usual, claiming it mistook this warship that was flying a large United States flag, for an ancient out-of-service Egyptian horse carrier El Quseir, that is incidentally 180 feet shorter. They also claim the ship was in the war zone, when it was actually in international waters, far from any fighting. The Israelis' attack on this warship lasts for seventy-five minutes during which time they shoot up one of the United States flags, resulting in the sailors desperately raising another one. The Israelis also machine gun the lifeboats the Americans deploy in order to prevent them escaping, yet another war crime.

In the aftermath of this attack, the American sailors who survived are warned by the United States military not to discuss the matter with anyone due to "national security," a term which, when translated into plain English, means, "Jewish Security." A naval tribunal is set up to investigate the incident but it is not allowed to investigate whether the attack was deliberate, a subject which is left off their remit, and United States Senators and Congressman are warned not to raise this subject for fear of inciting anti-Semitism. The story, of course, receives no prominence in the Rothschild controlled mainstream media and as usual Israel is in no way even rebuked for their crimes by their subservient country of America.

The day after this attack, June 9th, Israel illegally occupies the Golan Heights which it seizes from Syria. This area goes on to provide Israel with one third of its fresh water.

Israeli General Matityahu Peled, is quoted in Ha'aretz (March 19th 1972) with the following statement,

> "The thesis that the danger of genocide was hanging over us in June 1967 and that Israel was fighting for its physical existence is only bluff, which was born and developed after the war."

de Rothschild Frères is renamed Banque Rothschild.

1968: Noémie Halphen, wife of Maurice de Rothschild, dies.

1970: While working for Senator Henry "Scoop" Jackson, Ashkenazi Jew, Richard Perle, is caught by the FBI giving classified information to Israel. Nothing is done.

British Prime Minister Edward Heath makes Lord Victor Rothschild the head of his policy unit. Whilst he is in that role Britain enters the European Community, a major step towards World Government.

1971: In their book, None Dare Call It Conspiracy, Gary Allen and Larry Abraham state,

> "In the reality of socialism you have a tiny oligarchial clique at the top, usually numbering no more than three percent of the total population, controlling the total wealth, total production and the very lives of the other ninety-seven percent. Certainly even the most naive observe that Mr. Brezhnev doesn't live like one of the poor peasants out on the great Russian steppes. But, according to socialist theory, he is supposed to do just that!
>
> If one understands that socialism is not a share-the-wealth program, but is in reality a method to consolidate and control the wealth, then the seeming paradox of super-rich men promoting socialism becomes no paradox at all. Instead it becomes the logical, even the perfect tool of power-seeking megalomaniacs. Communism, or more accurately, socialism, is not a movement of the downtrodden masses, but of the economic elite. The plan of the conspirator Insiders then is to socialize the United States, not to Communize it."

They go on to state,

> "One major reason for the historical blackout on the role of the international bankers in political history is the Rothschilds were Jewish...The Jewish members of the conspiracy have used an organisation called The Anti-Defamation League (ADL) as an instrument to try and convince everyone that any mention of the Rothschilds and their allies is an attack on all Jews.
>
> In this way they have stifled almost all honest scholarship on international bankers and made the subject taboo within universities. Any individual or book exploring this subject is immediately attacked by hundreds of ADL communities all over the country. The ADL has never let the truth or logic interfere with its highly professional smear jobs....Actually, nobody has a right to be more angry at the Rothschild clique than their fellow Jews....The Rothschild empire helped finance Adolf Hitler."

Author, Hank Messick, publishes his book, "Lansky," a biography of Jewish crime kingpin, Meyer Lansky. It is initially printed with the following subtitle on the cover,

> "Jews control crime in the United States."

However, as soon as the ADL got wind of this, they contacted the publishers, as they revealed in their bulletin in October of this year, and as a result of their involvement, the cover was reprinted with the following subtitle on the cover, which appears to have been translated into "Jewish English,"

> "The Mob runs America and Lansky runs the Mob."

In the Congressional Record of December 6th, Congressman John R. Rarrick quotes a speech given by Senator Jack B. Tenney of California in which he stated the following of the Anti-Defamation League (ADL),

> "The CIA and FBI are tinker toys compared to the ADL…. We are beginning to understand something of the magnitude of the ADL's operations. We are beginning to appreciate the vast spy network sprawling over the nation and throughout the whole world. Our imagination is staggered by its apparent control of the avenues of communication….
>
> Their secret agents spy upon American citizens. Extensive files and dossiers are compiled on those with whom they disagree. Through their multitudinous controls of the media of communication, they are capable of destroying reputations and silencing all rebuttal."

1972: The World Health Organization (WHO) undertakes a massive smallpox vaccination program for millions of Africans. This smallpox vaccine is laced with the HIV/AIDS virus so that the Rothschild backed population reduction program could begin amongst the poor black population which was growing at a rapid rate.

1973: In an attempt to get returned the lands stolen from them by Israel, including the Golan Heights, Gaza and the West Bank, Egypt, Jordan, Syria and Iraq attack Israel and force Israeli forces to retreat. Their initial attempts at negotiation with Israel are repeatedly met with belligerence. With Israel facing defeat, the Jewish controlled United States government sends massive amounts of United States military equipment and arms at taxpayer's expense to bolster the retreating Israeli forces. This further alienates the Arab and Palestinian victims of Jewish supremacism from America.

On top of all that, the United States government put United States forces stationed both in Germany and in Fort Bragg, North Carolina on alert, that they may be sent to Israel to assist Israeli forces in this war. This proves not to be necessary, as the Israeli forces emerge victorious following the massive infusion of military aid already given to them by the United States government, or rather, the American taxpayer.

On April 15th, Democratic Senator from Arkansas, J. William Fulbright, states the following on CBS television in relation to Jewish power in America,

> "The United States Senate is subservient to Israel.... Israel controls the Senate.... This has been demonstrated time and again, and this has made it difficult for the Government."

On October 10th, United States Vice-President, Spiro Agnew resigns. He is accused of bribery in the media, but the real reason for his removal is his knowledge and disdain for the Jewish Communist mafia in control of the United States. This is revealed in the following speech he had made,

> "The people who own and manage national impact media are Jewish and, with other influential Jews, helped create a disastrous U.S. Mideast policy. All you have to do is check the real policy makers and owners and you find a much higher concentration of Jewish people than you're going to find in the population.
>
> By national impact media I am referring to the major news wire services, pollsters, Time and Newsweek Magazines, the New York Times, Washington Post, and the International Herald Tribune. For example, CBS' Mr (William) Paley's Jewish. Mr. Julian Goodman, who runs NBC, and there's a Leonard Goldenson at ABC. Mrs. Katherine Graham owns the Washington Post and Mr Sulzberger the New York Times. They are all Jews!
>
> You go down the line in that fashion…not just with ownership but go down to the managing posts and discretionary posts…and you'll find that through their aggressiveness and their inventiveness, they now dominate the news media. Not only in the media, but in academic communities, the financial communities, in the foundations, in all sorts of highly visible and influential services that involve the public, they now have a tremendous voice.

> Our policy in the Middle East in my judgement is disastrous, because it's not even handed. I see no reason why nearly half the foreign aid this nation has to give goes to Israel, except for the influence of this Zionist lobby. I think the power of the news media is in the hands of a few people…it's not subject to control of the voters, it's subject only to the whim of the board of directors."

George J. Laurer, an employee of the Rothschilds' controlled IBM, invents the UPC (Universal Product Code) barcode which will eventually be placed upon virtually every item traded worldwide and bear the number, 666. The Book of Revelation, Chapter 13, Verse 17 through 18, states the following in relation to this number,

> "And that no man might buy or sell, save he that had the mark, or the name of the beast, or the number of his name.
>
> Here is wisdom. Let him that hath understanding count the number of the beast: for it is the number of a man; and his number is Six hundred threescore and six."

N. M. Rothschild & Sons British Newfoundland Corporation, Churchill Falls project in Newfoundland, Canada, is completed.

N. M. Rothschild & Sons also creates a new asset management part of the company which traded worldwide. This eventually became Rothschild Private Management Limited.

Edmond de Rothschild, a great-grandson of Jacob (James) Mayer Rothschild, buys the cru bourgeois estate of Château Clarke in Bordeaux.

1974: On August 8th, President Nixon resigns from office as a result of the "Watergate" scandal, which was the allegation that a group responsible for promoting the re-election of Nixon, two years prior, had broken in to the offices of the Democratic National Committee.

What the public is not told, however, is that in the year prior to that, 1971, Nixon had instructed officials to investigate the activities of the large number of Jewish IRS agents, as he had concerns they were protecting wealthy Jews in America from paying the tax they should. Isn't it interesting that following the possibility of big Jewish money being investigated, a scandal starts resulting in the only time in history a United States President has resigned from office?

A New York periodical publishes an article claiming that the Rockefeller family is manipulating the Federal Reserve for the purpose of selling off Fort Knox gold at bargain basement prices to anonymous European speculators. Three days after the publication of this story, its anonymous source, long time secretary to

Nelson Rockefeller, Louise Auchincloss Boyer, mysteriously falls to her death from the window of her ten story apartment block in New York.

On December 10th, the United States National Security Council under Henry Kissinger completes a classified 200-page study entitled, "National Security Study Memorandum 200: Implications of Worldwide Population Growth for U.S. Security and Overseas Interests," (NSSM 200). The study falsely claims that population growth in the so-called Lesser Developed Countries is a grave threat to U.S. national security and outlines a covert plan to reduce population growth in those countries through birth control, war, and famine.

1975: The United Nations passes UN Resolution 3379 which condemns Zionism as racism. In the resolution it is stated,

> "Any doctrine of racial differentiation or superiority is scientifically false, morally condemnable, socially unjust and dangerous."

This is one of those humorous situations in which the Jews' lies end up like a snake eating its own tail. This is because they promote diversity throughout the world, saying,

> "We are all equal."

Yet at the same time they promote the direct opposite in

their control of the most racist state in history, Israel, in which they claim,

> "We are God's chosen people."

This leaves the Jewish controlled United Nations in a quandary, as whichever way they rule will go against Jewish claims.

In his book, "Tragedy & Hope: A History of the World in Our Time," published this year, Carroll Quigley states,

> "There does exist…an international network whose aim is to create a world system of financial control in private hands able to dominate the political system of each country and the economy of the world."

1976: Ashkenazi Jew, Harold Rosenthal, aide to fellow Ashkenazi Jew, Senator Jacob Javits, states,

> "Most Jews do not like to admit it, but our god is Lucifer."

1977: On December 25th, the Israeli Knesset passes the anti-missionary law, 5738-1977, which decrees that if a non-Jewish Christian is apprehended giving a New Testament to an Israeli, he may face a jail term of up to 5 years.

1978: In March, as a result of an attack on Israel in which 30 bus riders were killed, Israeli forces enter South Lebanon and occupy a six mile strip of land north of their border, from where they launch indiscriminate cluster bomb attacks which result in the deaths of over 1,500 Lebanese and Palestinians, most of them civilians.

They only end their illegal occupation when threatened by President Carter that if they do not, the United States will cut off all aid to Israel. Carter pointed out to Israeli Prime Minister, Menachem Begin that the weapons the Israelis were using were subject to an agreement between the United States and Israel, which was that they were only to be used in the event of an attack on Israel.

Interestingly, it is only revealed years later that this invasion had been planned by Israel at least two years before, which questions whether the so-called terrorist attack on the bus which triggered off this invasion was not in fact an Israeli "false flag," operation. The idea behind this invasion is to seize control of the Litani river, which, amazingly, Israel was allowed access to by a United Nations Security Force after the Israelis left Southern Lebanon. So, in essence, the Israelis launch an illegal war to steal Lebanon's water supply. They withdraw, but get what they wanted anyway thanks to the United Nations.

On October 16th, Archbishop Wojtyla becomes the first non-Italian pope since Hadrian VI (455 years prior), but chooses not to reveal his mother was Jewish, which would of course also qualified him for Israeli citizenship. He is the youngest Pope in 132 years, aged only fifty-eight and he takes the name of John Paul II.

Ashkenazi Jew, Stephen Bryen, then a Senate Foreign Relations Committee staffer, is overheard in a Washington D.C. hotel offering confidential documents to top Israeli military officials.

Bryen obtains a lawyer, Nathan Lewin, and the case heads for the grand jury, but is mysteriously dropped. Bryen later goes to work for Richard Perle.

More than one thousand "promiscuous homosexual males" in the United States are targeted for an "experimental" Hepatitis B vaccination sponsored by the National Institute of Health (NIH) and Centers for Disease Control (CDC), and run by the head of the New York City Blood Bank, Dr. Wolf Schmugner, a Polish Jew born in 1919.

This vaccination is intentionally laced with the bio-weapon commonly known as the AIDS virus, and by 1981, the CDC is trying to claim only 6 percent of the Hepatitis B vaccine recipients were infected with AIDS. However, in 1984, the true figure is revealed as 64 percent, a figure which could yet increase as the complete studies remain classified.

In his book, "The Jewish Paradox," published this year, former President of the World Jewish Congress from 1948 to 1977, Nahum Goldmann, stated the following on the subject of the Jews collectively,

> "I hardly exaggerate. Jewish life consists of two elements: Extracting money and protesting."

1979: In the January issue of Playboy Magazine, Marlon Brando states the following in an interview, in relation to Jewish control over Hollywood,

> "You've seen every single race besmirched, but you never saw an unfavorable image of the Kike because the Jews were ever so watchful for that. They never allowed it to be shown on screen!"

The Egyptian-Israeli peace treaty in 1979 is underwritten by United States aid which pledges $3 billion annually to Israel from the United States taxpayer.

Shin Bet (the Israeli internal security agency) tries to penetrate the United States Consulate General in Jerusalem through a "Honey Trap," using a clerical employee who was having an affair with a Jewish girl from Jerusalem.

Baron and Baroness Phillipi de Rothschild, in a joint venture with Robert Mondavi, begin the construction of a pyramid in Napa Valley, California, where the leader/founder of the Church Of Satan, Ashkenazi Jew, Anton LaVey, is based. This is known as Opus 1 (which means, the first work), and the front for this temple is that it is a winery.

1980: The global phenomenon of privatisation increases dramatically. The Rothschilds are behind this from the very beginning in order to seize control of all state owned assets worldwide.

The, "Georgia Guidestones" are erected in Elbert County, Georgia, USA. These are engraved with 10 points, the first one being,

> "Maintain humanity under 500,000,000 in perpetual balance with nature."

Being as the world population is 6,000,000,000, this will mean a reduction of nine tenths of the world's population. Interestingly on July 24, a document called the "Global 2000 Report," written by former Secretary of State Cyrus R. Vance, is presented to President Carter. This report indicates that the resources of the planet are not sufficient enough to support the expected dramatic increase in the world population and calls for the population of the United States to be reduced by 100 million people by the year 2050.

Emigration figures from the Soviet Government in Russia reveal that in the 10 years from 1970, 246,000 Jews had been allowed to emigrate from Russia compared with only 2,000 non-Jews. What makes these figures even more staggering is that there were only

3,000,000 Jews living in the U.S.S.R. at that time compared with 255,000,000 non-Jews. This clearly shows that as late as 1980, the Soviet Government showed a far higher level of regard to the wishes of Jews as opposed to non-Jews, and would indicate that there is still a large element of Jewish control over the Soviet Government.

Interestingly, out of the 246,000 Jews who left Russia during this past decade, well over half, 157,000 in fact, emigrated to Israel. This is a greater percentage than those who left Germany for Palestine prior to the outbreak of World War 2, during the Zionist collaboration with the Nazis.

1981: On July 10th, violence once again erupts in Southern Lebanon and Israel once again bombards Beirut killing 450 people. According to Kurt Waldheim, the U.N. Secretary-General, the Israeli air force bombarded Palestinian targets in south Lebanon, and in response, later that day Palestinian elements fired artillery and rockets into northern Israel.

Banque Rothschild is nationalised by the French government. The new bank is called Compagnie Européenne de Banque. The Rothschilds subsequently set up a successor to this French bank, Rothschild & Cie Banque (RCB), which goes on to become a leading French investment house.

1982: From September 16th to 18th, future Prime Minister of Israel and then Defence Minister, Ashkenazi

Jew, Ariel Sharon, orchestrates Israel's invasion of Lebanon, which provides aerial lighting in order to facilitate the killing of between 1,000 and 2,000 men, women and children in the Sabra and Shatila massacres. They call this operation, in Jewish English, "Operation Peace for Galilee." Sharon then turns his attention to the capital, Beirut, and in a series of air strikes on civilian targets, at least 18,000 Lebanese and Palestinian civilians are killed.

Israeli Prime Minister, terrorist, Menachem Begin, arrogantly states of this massacre,

> "We do not have to answer to the world, only to ourselves."

The public are told the reason for this illegal invasion of Lebanon is to stop cross-border attacks by Palestinian guerrillas in southern Lebanon on Israel's northern settlements. Interestingly, at the time of the Israeli invasion, a truce had been in effect for more than a year and not a single settler had been killed. However, the real reason for this indiscriminate slaughter comes to light only when it ceases, once Palestinian Liberation Organisation (PLO) leader, Yasser Arafat, who was residing in Beirut, flees to Tunisia.

1983: In order that Ecuador's government be allowed a loan of one and a half billion dollars from the Rothschild controlled International Monetary Fund (IMF), it is forced to take over the unpaid private debts Ecuador's elite owed to private banks. Furthermore in order to ensure Ecuador can pay back this loan, the IMF dictate price hikes in electricity and other utilities. When that doesn't give the IMF enough cash (or rather, interest) they ordered Ecuador to sack 120,000 workers.

Ecuador is also required to do a variety of things under a timetable imposed by the IMF. These include: raising the price of cooking gas by 80% by November 1st, 2000; transferring the ownership of its biggest water system to foreign operators; granting British Petroleum (BP) the rights to build and own an oil pipeline over the Andes; and eliminating the jobs of more workers whilst reducing the wages of those remaining by 50%.

In October, Chairman Heilbrun of the Committee to Re-elect General Shlomo Lahat as mayor of Tel Aviv, states,

> "We have to kill all the Palestinians unless they are resigned to live here as slaves."

On October 23rd, in Beirut, the United States Marine barracks is blasted to shreds by a truckload of explosives resulting in the deaths of 241 servicemen. In his book, "By Way Of Deception," former Mossad agent, Victor Ostrovsky, confirms Israel had advance knowledge of the attack, yet did not bother to warn the Americans. He states,

> "The general attitude at Mossad about the Americans was: 'As far as the Yanks go, we are not here to protect them.'"

Marc Lee Raphael publishes his book, "Jews And Judaism in the United States: A Documentary History," in which he states the following in relation to the slave trade in America,

> "Jewish merchants played a major role in the slave-trade. In fact...Jewish merchants frequently dominated."

1984: The Mossad run into a problem. They are training both the Sri Lankan special-forces and the Tamil Tiger rebels from Sri Lanka at the same Mossad training school, Kfar Sirkin, in Israel. This is after selling both sides military training courses. This is a step up from the Rothschild family funding both sides in war, this time Jews are actually selling courses in how both sides can best kill each other.

It is touch and go, but the Mossad manage to keep both sides apart in their three weeks at this training camp, and both factions leave to return to Sri Lanka, none the wiser that their enemy was being trained in the same camp by the same organisation.

1985: Jack Bernstein publishes his book, "The Life of an American Jew in Racist Marxist Israel," which contains the following statement under the heading, "A Challenge,"

> "I am well aware of the tactics you, my Zionist brethren, use to quiet anyone who attempts to expose any of your subversive acts.

> If the person is a Gentile, you cry, "You're anti-Semitic," which is nothing more than a smokescreen to hide your actions.
>
> But, if a Jew is the person doing the exposing, you resort to other tactics.
>
> First, you ignore the charges, hoping the information will not be given widespread distribution.
>
> If the information starts reaching too many people, you ridicule the information and the persons giving the information.
>
> If that doesn't work, your next step is character assassination. If the author or speaker hasn't been involved in sufficient scandal you are adept at fabricating scandal against the person or persons.
>
> If none of these are effective, you are known to resort to physical attacks.
>
> But, NEVER do you try to prove the information wrong."

Jack Bernstein subsequently offers to debate the Anti-Defamation League on live television; the ADL declines and, instead, Bernstein ends up being assassinated by the Mossad.

The New York Times reports the FBI is aware of at least

a dozen incidents in which so-called American officials transferred classified information to the Israelis, quoting former Assistant Director of the F.B.I., Raymond Wannal. The Justice Department does not prosecute.

In late November, Jonathan Pollard is arrested in the United States for passing classified information to LAKAM (Lishka le Kishrei Mada), which is the Israeli Defence Ministry's Scientific Liaison Bureau, is run by Rafael Eitan, who had taken part in the 1960 abduction of Adolf Eichmann from Argentina.

Pollard worked in research at the Naval Investigative Service based just outside Washington, and this year he was transferred to the Anti-Terrorism Alert Center, which of course gave him access to extremely sensitive material. As a result of his espionage, Pollard is sentenced to life in prison.

Richard Smyth, the owner of MILCO, is indicted on charges of smuggling nuclear timing devices to Israel.

Israel conducts a "black-ops" operation on the "Achille Lauro" cruise ship as she is sailing from Alexandria to Port Said within Egypt. The ship is hijacked, and the Israelis "coup-de-grace," is when a wheelchair-bound passenger, American Jew, Leon Klinghoffer, is executed and thrown overboard, generating outrage throughout the world, especially in America. Furthermore, the Jews ensure that this is the major story of the day worldwide, in print and on the television.

This tactic is explained in the book, "Profits Of War," in which former special intelligence advisor to Israeli Prime Minister, Yitzhak Shamir, Ari Ben-Menashe, explains how Israeli intelligence had been funding Palestinian terror groups to carry out attacks on Israeli targets, in order to make the world, especially America, sympathetic to Israel and the Jews and hateful of the Palestinians.

N. M. Rothschild & Sons advises the British government on the privatisation of British Gas. They subsequently advise the British government on virtually all of their other privatisations of state owned assets including: British Steel; British Coal; all the British regional electricity boards; and all the British regional water boards. They will go on to make several billion pounds from this "advice." A British MP involved in privatisations is future Chancellor of the Exchequer, Norman Lamont, a former Rothschild banker.

It is important to illustrate that the great majority of money is not even printed these days. For proof of this, please see the following speech by the late Lord Beswick which appeared in HANSARD, 27th November 1985, vol. 468, columns 935-939, under the title, "Money Supply and the Private Banking System," which states,

> "Lord Beswick rose to call attention to the statement made by the Chancellor of the Duchy of Lancaster on 23rd July 1985 that the 96.9 per cent increase in money supply over a five-year

period has been created by the private banking system and without Government authority....

The noble Lord said, 'My Lords, on 10th June this year I asked Her Majesty's Government by what amount the money supply had increased in the five-year period to mid-April 1985. Interestingly, they gave me the answer in percentages and not in pounds. Having given him prior notice, perhaps the Minister would be good enough later to give me the answer in money terms.

The Government reply on 10th June was that the increase had been by 101.9 per cent, and that of that very large amount only 5 per cent was accounted for by the state minting of more coins and the printing of more notes. That 96.9 per cent increase represented not only an enormous sum of money but also a crucially important factor in our economy.

I wanted to know by whom it had been created, and on 23rd July I again asked Her Majesty's Government to what extent this increase had Government approval. I was told by the Chancellor of the Duchy, speaking for the Government, 'The 96.9 per cent represented new bank deposits created in the normal course of banking business and no Government authority is necessary for this.'

Had he said that some counterfeiter of coins or forger of notes had been at work there would of

> course have been an immediate and indignant outcry, yet here we have a government statement that private institutions have created this enormous amount of extra purchasing power and we are expected to accept that it is normal practice and that the government authority does not come into it.
>
> When I asked whether we ought not to consider more deeply who was benefiting from this money-creating power, the Minister said that the implications, though interesting, were maybe too far reaching for Question Time, and so I raise the matter again in debate and hope to get more enlightenment.
>
> The issues are important, they are certainly under-discussed, perhaps not adequately understood, and I hope that I am not being unduly unfair if I say that those who understand the mechanisms often do very well out of them. I make no party point; it is all much bigger and wider than that."

Notice how the Chancellor of the Duchy gives the game away when he says that, "no government authority was needed for this present system of credit creating."

1986: Sephardic Jew, Mordechai Vanunu, a technician at Dimona, Israel's nuclear installation from 1976 to 1985, discovers that the plant has been secretly producing nuclear weapons.

His cites his conversion to Christianity as his reason for

having the conscience to speak out and this year he provides the London Sunday Times with the facts and photos they used to tell the world about Israel's nuclear weapons programme. His evidence shows that Israel had stockpiled up to 200 nuclear warheads.

On September 30th, an Israeli Mossad agent, Cheryl Bentov, operating under the name of "Cindy," and masquerading as an American tourist, begins an affair with Vanunu, eventually persuading him to fly to Rome with her on a holiday. Once in Rome, the Jews, instead of going through proper channels and seeking his extradition, send Mossad agents to kidnap him, drug him, drive him to a deserted beach and smuggle him to Israel on a freighter.

After a secret trial he is sentenced to eighteen years imprisonment for "treason" and "espionage" (something Israel is very familiar with) even though he had not spied for any foreign power and had received no payment for his exposure. Throughout the trial the Israeli government refuses to admit or deny whether or not Israel has nuclear weapons.

Jews, Ivan Boesky, Dennis Levine, Martin Siegel, and Michael Milken are convicted of insider trading running into the billions of dollars. All of them subsequently receive light sentences and fines that do not reflect the fortunes they fraudulently amassed as a result of their participation. The Gordon Gekko character in the Oliver Stone film, "Wall Street," is based upon Ivan Boesky, and once again the Jew, Oliver Stone, fails to identify Gekko as Jewish.

In his book published this year, "Terrorism: How The West Can Win," future Israeli Prime Minister Benjamin Netanyahu refers to the Palestinians as,

> "A malignant cancer that must be removed."

In Britain the Public Order Act of 1986 is brought into law. This act is designed to prevent British people from discussing in any way the problems of immigration and Jewish supremacism. It also gives police the power to violently enter the homes of anyone they consider being opposed to the Race Relations Act. The Act was placed before parliament by the Home Secretary Leon Brittan, actually a Lithuanian Jew whose real name is Leon Brittanisky, with the assistance of his cousin, another Lithuanian Jew, Malcolm Rivkind, also known as Malcolm Rifkind, who would go on to become Foreign Secretary.

1987: Edmond de Rothschild creates the World Conservation Bank which is designed to transfer debts from third world countries to this bank in exchange for land those countries would give to this bank. This is designed so the Rothschilds can gain control of the Third World, which represents 30% of the land surface of the Earth.

On April 24th, the Wall Street Journal reveals the,

> "Role of Israel in Iran-Contra Scandal Won't be Explored in Detail by Panels."

1988: The three arms of the World Central Bank: the World Bank; the Bank of International Settlements (BIS); and the International Monetary Fund (IMF), now generally referred to as the World Central Bank, through their BIS arm, require the world's bankers to raise their capital and reserves to 8% of their liabilities by 1992. This increased capital requirement puts an upper limit on fractional reserve lending.

To raise the money, the world's bankers have to sell stocks which depress their individual stock-markets and cause depressions in those countries. For example in Japan, one of the countries with the lowest capital in reserve, the value of its stock-market would crash by 50%, and its commercial real estate crash by 60%, within two years.

The idea is for the IMF to create more and more of their international currency known as, "Special Drawing Rights (SDR's)," backed by nothing, in order for struggling nations to borrow them and therefore increase their cash reserves to the required BIS level. These nations will then gradually come under the control of the IMF as they struggle to pay the interest, and have to borrow more and more. The IMF will then decide which nations can borrow more and which will starve. They can also use this as leverage to take state owned assets like utilities as payment against the debt until they eventually own the nation states.

The Anti-Defamation League (ADL), initiate a nationwide competition for law students to draft anti-hate legislation designed to protect minority groups.

That competition is won by a man named, Joseph Ribakoff, whose proposals stipulate that not only must hate motivated violence be banned, but any words which stimulate: suspicion; friction; hate; and possible violence, must also be criminalised.

This ADL prize-winning paper suggests that not only should state-agencies monitor and restrict free speech in general, but they should also censor all films that criticize identifiable groups. Furthermore, even if the person making the statement can justify it, for example Christians criticizing homosexuality because the Bible expressly forbids it, Ribakoff asserts that the truth is to be no defence in court.

The only proof a court will need in order to secure a conviction of hate speech is that something has been said, and a minority group or member of such group has felt emotionally damaged as a result of such criticism. Therefore, under these proposals which the ADL will have forced into law all over the world less than 15 years later, through their bought and paid for politicians and media, Jesus Christ would have been arrested as a hate criminal.

This law is designed to protect the Rothschild conspiracy from being revealed in that if you criticize the Rothschilds' criminal cabal, you will be targeted as anti-Semitic, and thus risk imprisonment. It is also interesting to note that say, for example, a Rabbi torches his synagogue to collect insurance money because it is in need of repair, as opposed to someone else perpetrating the crime who was found to have an interest in anti-establishment media, the latter would receive a stiffer sentence for the same act.

Historian James Bacque's book, "Other Losses," reveals the shocking Allied treatment of German prisoners of war. These crimes were, of course, under the direct instructions of the Jew, Eisenhower, then Supreme Commander of Allied forces. The book features shocking revelations from a former Lieutenant in the 101st Airborne Division. This Lieutenant, who would rise to the post of Senior Historian, United States Army and would retire as Colonel Ernest F. Fisher PhD, wrote the following in his foreword to Bacque's book,

> "Starting in April 1945, the United States Army and the French Army casually annihilated about one million men, most of them in American camps...Eisenhower's hatred, passed through the lens of a compliant military bureaucracy, produced the horror of death camps unequalled by anything in American military history...an enormous war crime."

It would later be revealed that more than nine million Germans, both soldiers and civilians, had died as a result of the policies of starvation and expulsion adopted by the allied forces in the first five years following the end of the Second World War. These would include the deaths of prisoners on the road and those in allied prison camps, where food parcels were barred and children were enslaved.

One can only assume that Eisenhower was following the edicts of his beloved Jewish Talmud which is the highest religious and ethical guide for observant Jews. In this book, which to the Jews far surpasses the bible, it is repeatedly stated that non-Jews are inherently bad, and

Jews good, and furthermore, that the best among the non-Jews deserve to be killed. Jewish racial and spiritual supremacy is pre-eminent.

Unlike the Bible and Koran, which are widely available to all, it is very difficult to obtain a copy of the most holy Jewish book, the Talmud, anywhere. Maybe this is because within the Talmud it is expressly stated that it is forbidden to teach the Talmud to a non-Jew. The penalty for someone who does so is revealed in Sanhedrin 58a—Hagigah, in which it is stated,

> "Such a person deserves death."

On August 17th, the President of Pakistan, General Zia ul-Haq, is assassinated in an air crash. The United States Ambassador to India at the time, John Dean, reports to his superiors that he had evidence that the Israeli secret service, the Mossad, were behind the assassination in an effort to stop Pakistan developing the nuclear bomb. For his troubles, Dean is accused of mental imbalance and relieved of his duties at the State Department. However, he refuses to relinquish this view and comes out publicly with it in 2005 when he is 80 years old.

Philippe de Rothschild dies.

1989: Many of the satellite states in Eastern Europe, through the influence of Glasnost, become more open in their demands of freedom from Communist governance in their Republics.

Many revolutions happen in 1989, most of them involving the overthrow of their respective Communist governments and the replacement of them with Republics.

Thus, the hold the Communists had over Eastern Europe (the Iron Curtain) becomes very weak. Eventually, as a result of Perestroika (revision) and Glasnost (openness), Communism collapses, not only in the Soviet Union but also in Eastern Europe.

In Russia, Boris Yeltsin (whose wife is the daughter of Joseph Stalin's marriage to Rosa Kaganovich) and the Republican government take steps to end the power of the Communist party by suspending and banning the party and seizing all their property.

This symbolises the fall of Communism in Russia, and results in the start of a mass exodus of 700,000 Jews from the former Soviet Union to Israel.

In the Israeli Journal, Hotam (November 24th, 1989), there is a report of a speech that the then Israeli Deputy Foreign Minister, Ashkenazi Jew, Benjamin Netanyahu, gave to students at Bar Ilan University in which he states,

> "Israel should have exploited the repression of the demonstrations in China, when world attention focused on that country, to carry out mass expulsions among the Arabs of the territories."

On December 20th, the United States invades Panama as they suspect it's de facto leader, General Manuel Noriega, of drug trafficking. Early reports state that a "Mike Harari" has been captured in Panama, a man described in the wire news stories as,

> "a shadowy former officer of Israel's Mossad intelligence service who became one of Noriega's most influential advisers."

An official from the new American installed administration in Panama claims that apart from, of course, Noriega, Harari was,

> "the most important person in Panama."

However, whilst Noriega would go on to be extradited to America and jailed, Harari subsequently disappears under mysterious circumstances only to surface in Israel. Harari is not extradited to the United States to face charges, nor does it appear that his extradition was even sought by the United States.

In the former concentration camp of Auschwitz, a plaque claiming that four million people had been murdered there, mainly Jews, is replaced with a plaque stating that one and a half million had died there. Strangely, the "official" Jewish figure of six million Jews dying in the holocaust is not changed to reflect this two and a half million reduction of the stated death toll at Auschwitz. No reasons for this reduction in the death toll at Auschwitz, nor the fact the six million figure has not been reduced to reflect this reduction, are ever given.

The London and Paris Rothschilds announce the launch of a new subsidiary, Rothschild GmbH, in Frankfurt, Germany.

1990: In his book, "By Way Of Deception," published this year, former Mossad agent, Victor Ostrovsky, reveals the following:

> 1) The Mossad recruits Arab agents to carry out missions.
>
> 2) Israeli agents are skilled at impersonating Arabs.
>
> 3) Mossad has an elaborate plan to vilify Iraq and involve the US in a war against it.

He makes the following startling claims on the willingness of the worldwide Jewish community to assist the Mossad as "sayanim" (which derives from the Hebrew word lesayeah which means, "to help") over and above any loyalty they have to the nation they are citizens of or resident in. On page 86, Ostrovsky states,

> "…the sayanim, a unique and important part of the Mossad's operation. Sayanim—assistants—must be 100 percent Jewish. They live abroad, and though they are not Israeli citizens, many are reached through their relatives in Israel. An Israeli with a relative in England, for example, might be asked to write a letter saying the person bearing the letter represents an organization whose main goal is to help save Jewish people in

> the diaspora. Could the British relative help in any way?
>
> There are thousands of sayanim around the world. In London alone, there are about 2,000 who are active, and another 5,000 on the list (in his 1994 book, "The Other Side Of Deception," Ostrovsky reveals that the Mossad maintain over a hundred safe houses in London alone). They fulfil many different roles.
>
> A car sayan, for example, running a rental agency, could help the Mossad rent a car without having to complete the usual documentation. An apartment sayan would find accommodation without raising suspicions, a bank sayan could get you money if you needed it in the middle of the night, a doctor sayan would treat a bullet wound without reporting it to the police, and so on. The idea is to have a pool of people available when needed who can provide services but will keep quiet about them out of loyalty to the cause…
>
> One thing you know for sure is that even if a Jewish person knows it is the Mossad, he might not agree to work with you—but he won't turn you in. You have at your disposal a non-risk recruitment system that actually gives you a pool of millions of Jewish people to tap from outside your own borders."

And on page 292,

> "Many of the youths trained at the summer camps in Israel later become sayanim, and it certainly provides a strong group of willing helpers, well trained, undaunted by the lingo, who have already shown the ability to take chances."

This would explain the desire of the group, "Birthright Israel," to offer free holidays to Israel for Jews resident throughout the world between the ages of 18-26, in order to, according to their official website,

> "Strengthen the sense of solidarity among World Jewry."

Due to a mass panic among Jewish groups, regarding alleged discrepancies in the official version of the holocaust, they use their influence to ensure France introduces and passes the Gayssot law, making Holocaust denial a crime. The following European countries follow suit: Germany (who already had limited holocaust denial laws); Switzerland; Austria; Belgium; Romania; Czech Republic; Lithuania; Poland; and Slovakia. This is done to protect the Jews' greatest weapon against those who criticise their criminal actions: the alleged slaughter of six million Jews during World War 2. This is a weapon which they use continually to cast themselves as victims and justify their oppressive actions against other races.

1991: Following the Iraqi invasion of Kuwait on August 2nd, 1990, on January 16th of this year the United States and Britain began an aerial bombing campaign of targets within Iraq. On 24th February the ground campaign commences which lasts 100 hours until February 28th when a horrendous war crime occurs.

This crime is the slaughter of 150,000 Iraqi troops with fuel air bombs. These Iraqis are fleeing on a crowded highway from Kuwait to Basra. President George Herbert Walker Bush orders United States military aircraft and ground units to kill these surrendering troops, who are then bulldozed into mass unmarked graves in the desert.

President Bush then orders a cessation of hostilities. What was the significance of this slaughter and President Bush declaring the war over on this day? Well it was the day the "Day of Purim," fell on this year. This is the day the Jews celebrate their victory over Ancient Babylon, now based within the borders of Iraq and a day when the Jews are encouraged to get bloody revenge against their enemies, which Purim declares are basically all non-Jews.

Of approximately 697,000 American servicemen and women deployed to the Persian Gulf during Operation Desert Storm, some 40,000 end up dead and a further 400,000 end up suffering from various maladies associated with what has become known as Gulf War Syndrome.

It is subsequently discovered that the military obtained 800,000 chemical and biological protective suits from the Isratex Company of Rainelle, W.V., which were defective, and contained holes and tears, that can allow in sufficient biological or chemical material to kill the person wearing it.

Isratex, which netted $44 million in defence contracts in the late 1980's and early 1990's to make these protective suits, declared bankruptcy in 1995. For committing this genocide on American soldiers, for nothing more than financial gain.

How did the United States judicial system deal with the principals of Isratex? Abe Brin, the former president, receives four months detention, three years supervised release and a $4,000 fine. His brother, Yehudah Yoav Brin (who had been a fugitive until he was captured at JFK airport), receives six months plus one day in jail, two years supervised release and a $40,000 fine. Zvi Rosenthal, formerly the company's production manager, has to serve six months home detention, three months probation and receives a $20,000 fine.

The real reason for this war in Iraq is revealed in Victor Ostrovsky's book, "The Other Side Of Deception," in which he states on page 315,

> "What the Mossad really feared was that Iraq's gigantic army, which was being supplied by the West and financed by Saudi Arabia, would fall into the hands of a leader other than Saddam Hussein who might be more palatable to the West and still be a threat to Israel.
>
> The first step was taken in November 1988, when the Mossad told the Israeli foreign office

to stop all talks with the Iraqis regarding a peace front. At that time, secret negotiations were taking place between Israelis, Jordanians, and Iraqis under the auspices of the Egyptians and with the blessings of the French and the Americans. The Mossad manipulated it so that Iraq looked as if it were the only country unwilling to talk, thereby convincing the Americans that Iraq had a different agenda.

By January 1989, the Mossad LAP (Israeli psychological warfare) machine was busy portraying Saddam as a tyrant and a danger to the world. The Mossad activated every asset it had in every place possible, from volunteer agents in Amnesty International to fully bought members of the U.S. Congress. Saddam had been killing his own people, the cry went; what could his enemies expect? The gruesome photos of dead Kurdish mothers clutching their dead babies after a gas attack by Saddam's army were real, and the acts were horrendous. But the Kurds were entangled in an all-out guerrilla war with the regime in Baghdad and had been supported for years by the Mossad, who sent arms and advisers to the mountain camps of the Barazany family; this attack by the Iraqis could hardly be called an attack on their own people…

The media was supplied with inside information and tips from reliable sources on how the crazed leader of Iraq killed people with his bare hands and used missiles to attack Iranian cities. What they neglected to tell the media was that most of

> the targeting for the missiles was done by the Mossad with the help of American satellites. The Mossad was grooming Saddam for a fall, but not his own. They wanted the Americans to do the work of destroying that gigantic army in the Iraqi desert so that Israel would not have to face it one day on its own border. That in itself was a noble cause for an Israeli, but to endanger the world with the possibility of global war and the deaths of thousands of Americans was sheer madness."

On March 20th, under pressure from the Rabbinical Chabad Lubavitch movement, the 102nd Congress of the United States passes Public Law 102-14 to designate March 26th, 1991, as "Education Day, U.S.A," in respect of educating the public to the seven Noahide Laws from the Talmud, which are merely what the Pharisees derived from specific passages in the Torah. Furthermore they are laws that only non-Jews have to follow.

The focus of Public Law 102-14 being an "Education Day" is merely a smokescreen to fool the public into believing that the seven Noahide Laws were not actually passed into law within this act. Instead the Jews want the public to believe that this Public Law only introduced a day to educate people about this subject. However, it is rapidly obvious that a government sponsored education day does not require a law passed to ensure its implementation. Therefore, these laws were passed March 20th, in readiness for when the United States Courts wish to use them, and these seven laws are:

1) Avodah zarah—Do not worship false gods.

2) Shefichat damim—Do not murder.

3) Gezel—Do not steal (or kidnap).

4) Gilui arayot—Do not be sexually immoral (forbidden sexual acts are traditionally interpreted to include incest, bestiality, male homosexual sex acts and adultery.)

5) Birkat Hashem—Do not "bless God," euphemistically referring to blasphemy.

6) Ever min ha-chai—Do not eat any flesh that was torn from the body of a living animal (given to Noah and traditionally interpreted as a prohibition of cruelty towards animals).

7) Dinim—Do not permit oppression or anarchy to rule. Set up a system of honest, effective courts, police and laws to uphold the last six laws.

These laws are the bedrock for Jewish supremacism, as they forbid the worship of any God but their own God, Satan. This is revealed in law number one, "Do not worship false gods," which, coming from the Jewish Talmud, means any Gods the Jews don't recognize, such as Jesus Christ and the Prophet Mohammed. The Talmud states the penalty for disobedience of these laws to be as follows,

> "One additional element of greater severity is that violation of any one of the seven laws subjects the Noahide to capital punishment by decapitation—Sanhedrin 57A."

Strangely enough, these laws or the "Education Day," linked to them receive no criticism from the American Civil Liberties Union (ACLU) which one would have expected, as not only do they represent the enforcement of a particular religion's edicts upon all non-Jewish people, but they also violate the ACLU's long held belief in the separation of Church and State.

At the Bilderberg Conference on June 6th to 9th of this year, in Baden-Baden, Germany, David Rockefeller (a Rothschild) makes the following statement,

> "We are grateful to the Washington Post, the New York Times, Time Magazine, and other great publications whose directors have attended our meetings and respected their promises of discretion for almost 40 years. It would have been impossible for us to develop our plan for the world, if we had been subjected to the lights of publicity during those years.
>
> But the world is now more sophisticated and prepared to march towards a world government. The super-national sovereignty of an intellectual elite and world bankers is surely preferable to the national auto-determination practised in past centuries."

1992: In March, former Federal Reserve Board Chairman, Paul A. Volker becomes Chairman of the European banking firm, J. Rothschild, Wolfensohn and Co.

Stephen Bryen, caught offering confidential documents to Israel in 1978, is found to be serving on the board of the pro-Israeli Jewish Institute for National Security Affairs while continuing as a paid consultant, with security clearance, on exports of sensitive US technology.

"The Samson Option," by Seymour M. Hersh reports,

> "Illicitly obtained intelligence was flying so voluminously from LAKAM (a secret Israeli intelligence unit, a Hebrew acronym for Scientific Liaison Bureau) into Israeli intelligence that a special code name, JUMBO, was added to the security markings already on the documents. There were strict orders, Ari Ben-Menashe recalled, 'Anything marked JUMBO was not supposed to be discussed with your American counterparts.'"

The Wall Street Journal reports that Israeli agents apparently tried to steal Recon Optical Inc's top-secret airborne spy-camera system.

Privatisation begins in earnest in Russia. As a result of this, through corruption, the vast wealth of Russia ends up in the hands of the so-called, "Seven Oligarchs," all of them new billionaires who backed Boris Yeltsin with money and media support. The seven are, Boris Berezovsky, Vladimir Gusinsky, Mikhail Khodorkovsky, Mikhail Friedman, Alexander Smolensky, and Pyotr Aven, all Jewish, and one Russian, Vladimir Potanin. Potanin would be used as the others' public liaison to the government.

What aid Russia receives from the West goes straight to the Jewish banking cabal also. This is revealed when the Washington Times reports that Russian President, Boris Yeltsin, who was upset that most of the incoming foreign aid was being siphoned off, stated it was going,

> "Straight back into the coffers of Western Banks in debt service."

The Third World debtor nations who had borrowed from the World Bank pay 198 million dollars more to the central banks of the developed nations for World Bank funded purposes than they receive from the World Bank. This only goes to increase their permanent debt in exchange for temporary relief from poverty which is caused by the payments on prior loans, the repayments of which already exceed the amount of the new loans.

This year, Africa's external debt had reached 290 billion dollars, which is two and a half times greater than its level in 1980, and has resulted in deterioration of schools, deterioration of housing, sky-rocketing infant mortality rates, a drastic downturn in the general health of the people, and mass unemployment.

On September 16th Britain's pound collapses when currency speculators led by Rothschild agent, Ashkenazi Jew, George Soros, borrow pounds and sell them for Deutsche Marks, in the expectation of being able to repay the loan in devalued currency and to pocket the difference.

This results in the British Chancellor of the Exchequer, Norman Lamont, announcing a rise in interest rates of 5% in one day and as a result drives Britain into a recession which lasts many years as large numbers of businesses fail and the housing market crashes.

This is right on cue for the Rothschilds, as after they had privatised Britain's state owned assets during the 1980's and driven their share price up, they now took advantage of the collapse in the market so they could buy them up for pennies on the pound, a carbon copy of what Nathan Mayer Rothschild did to the British economy 180 years before, in 1812.

It cannot be overstated that the Chancellor of the Exchequer, Norman Lamont, prior to becoming a MP, was a merchant banker with N. M. Rothschild and Sons, which he joined after reading Economics at Cambridge.

1993: Norman Lamont leaves the British government to return to N. M. Rothschild and Sons as a director after his mission to collapse the British economy to profit the Rothschilds is accomplished. After Labour come to power under Tony Blair in 1997, Norman Lamont is given further recognition for his sterling work in crashing the British economy when he is made Lord Lamont of Lerwick.

Former Congressman Paul Findley publishes his seminal book, "Deliberate Deceptions: Facing the Facts About the U. S.-Israeli Relationship." In this book he lists the 65 United Nations Member Resolutions against Israel from the period 1955 to 1992, and the 30 United States vetoes on Israel's behalf which, if not made, would have seen Israel have 95 resolutions against them at this point.

No matter, even with Israel's puppet, the United States, helping them terrorise others, the 65 Resolutions passed against Israel are more than all the Resolutions passed against all other countries combined.

Not that Israel cares very much about the views of the United Nations when you consider that less than two weeks after Israel's attack on the USS Liberty (an attack designed to sink the Liberty and blame it on Egypt prompting the United States into a war with Egypt on behalf of Israeli lies, remember the Mossad motto, "By Way Of Deception, Thou Shalt Do War"), the Israeli Foreign Minister, Aba Eban, stated of the United Nations, as reported in the New York Times, June 19th 1967,

> "If the General Assembly were to vote by 121 votes to 1 in favour of Israel returning to the armistice lines (pre June 1967 borders), Israel would refuse to comply with the decision."

The Anti-Defamation League (ADL) is caught operating a massive spying operation on critics of Israel, Arab-Americans, the San Francisco Labor Council, International Longshore and Warehouse Union (ILWU) Local 10, Oakland Educational Association, National Association for the Advancement of Coloured People (NAACP), Irish Northern Aid, International Indian Treaty Council, the Asian Law Caucus and the San Francisco Police.

Data collected (which included more than 10,000 names and confidential information concerning right-wing Christians, conservatives and Moslems in America) is sent to Israel and in some cases to South Africa. Pressure from Jewish organizations forces the city to drop the criminal case, but the ADL settles a civil lawsuit for an undisclosed amount.

On July 25th, Israeli forces launch "Operation Accountability" against Southern Lebanon in response to an attack by Hezbollah forces which killed seven Israeli troops in Northern Israel. This takes the form of a week long series of air strikes in which 130 Lebanese civilians are killed and another 300,000 are forced to flee their homes.

Jewish director, Steven Spielberg, releases his Jewish propaganda "tour de force," "Schindler's List," which will go on to receive lavish praise from the Jewish controlled media, and earn him the best director Oscar from the Jewish controlled Hollywood.

It is important to note here a very interesting line that wasn't properly quoted in the film. This is where Schindler is depicted lamenting how few Jews he had been able to save from a Nazi labour camp, and then a little, old Jewish man says to him, "In our holy book, the Talmud, it says that if you save just one life, it is as if you have saved the entire world."

Wrong! What the exact wording in the Talmud actually states, is that if you save just one "Jewish" life, it is as if you have saved the entire world. It must never be forgotten that according to the Talmud, the lives of non-Jews have absolutely no value at all.

1994: In Israel, on February 25th, the Day of Purim, Dr. Baruch Kappel Goldstein, who served as a physician in the Israeli Defense Force (IDF), and is a direct descendant of Rabbi Shneur Zalman of Liadi, the founder of the Chabad Lubavitch movement, enters the Cave of the Patriachs mosque during prayers and kills 29 Muslims and wounds 125 others. He does this by shooting them with an automatic weapon. He is eventually overpowered by the survivors and beaten to death.

At the inquiry two Israeli army guards testify that Goldstein did not act alone, and even the gun found on his body did not match the gun he went into the mosque with. Nevertheless the inquiry decides that Goldstein acted alone. Almost immediately Goldstein's grave becomes a place of pilgrimage for many Jews. Indeed, the Local Religious Council of Kiryat Arba declares the gravesite a memorial and a properly constituted cemetery. Sidewalks, spotlights, streetlights, a cupboard with prayer books and pedestals with candles are installed by supporters. This is the inscription on his gravestone,

> "Here lies the saint, Dr. Baruch Kappel Goldstein, blessed be the memory of the righteous and holy man, may the Lord avenge his blood, who devoted his soul to the Jews, Jewish religion and Jewish land. His hands are innocent and his heart is pure. He was killed as a martyr of God on the 14th of Adar, Purim, in the year 5754."

Only two days after Goldstein's massacre, Rabbi Yaacov Perrin, states,

> "One million Arabs are not worth a Jewish fingernail."

Another Jewish spiritual leader, Rabbi Yitzhak Ginsburg, who is also the head of the Kever Yossev Yeshiva Talmudic school in Nablus, also sings the praises of the Goldstein massacre, which he calls,

> "a fulfillment of a number of commands of Jewish religious law....Among Goldstein's good deeds, as enumerated, are....taking revenge on non-Jews, extermination of the non-Jews who are from the seed of Amalek....and the sanctification of the Holy Name."

Poland demands the extradition of Jew, Solomon Morel, from Israel for "Crimes Against Humanity."

Morel was a brutal, vicious commandant of a concentration camp at Swietochlowice, in Poland, after World War 2. This concentration camp housed Polish men, women and children who were of German descent and had their property seized by the Jewish Communist authorities.

Among the charges that Morel is accused of are:

> 1) That he murdered babies by bashing their heads against stone walls.
>
> 2) He bludgeoned inmates to death with stools and clubs.
>
> 3) He committed torture on inmates. His preferred method was sticking objects up an inmate's anus.
>
> 4) He forced women and children to parade round naked in sub-zero temperatures.
>
> 5) He made inmates eat human faeces.
>
> 6) He starved inmates to death.

Following these charges, the Israeli government assists Morel in fleeing to Tel Aviv, and dismisses the charges as an "anti-Semitic plot." However, the Polish prosecutor in charge of pursuing the criminal Solomon Morel, Eva Kok, states of the Israeli authorities,

> "The Israelis are extremely efficient in pursuing people they have accused of such crimes, and

> they must accept that other nations want to do the same."

However, Israel refuses to extradite Morel, not that they would desire to anyway, as Israel does not extradite its citizens. In fact Israel cannot extradite its citizens as the whole basis of that racist state is that the Jews are above all other races, which is why it does not and cannot form extradition treaties with any non-Jewish nations. As a result of this, many Jewish criminals have fled to the safe haven of Israel over the years to evade prosecution for whatever crimes they have committed around the world. They live in Israel shielded.

Going back to the choice of Solomon Morel as a concentration camp commandant, interestingly, in his book, "An Eye For An Eye," author John Sack states the following of Russia's Jewish leader, Stalin,

> "Stalin deliberately picked Jews as camp commandants in the knowledge they would show little mercy to the inmates."

Former Mossad agent, Victor Ostrovsky, releases another book entitled, "The Other Side Of Deception," in which he reveals the following, on page 241,

> "Uri was on a cooling off period from the United States.
>
> 'What is the Mossad doing giving humanitarian assistance to blacks in Soweto?' I remember asking him. There was no logic to it; no short-

> term political gain (which was the way the Mossad operated) or any visible monetary advantage.
>
> 'Do you remember Nes Siyyona?' His question sent shivers up my spine. I nodded.
>
> 'This is very much the same. We're testing both new infectious diseases and new medication that can't be tested on humans in Israel, for several of the Israeli medicine manufacturers. This will tell them whether they're on the right track, saving them millions in research.'
>
> 'What do you think about all this?' I had to ask.
>
> 'It's not my job to think about it.'"

Nelson Mandela, who served 26 years in prison for, amongst other things, 193 counts of terrorism committed from 1961 to 1963 and had stated at his trial in 1964,

> "I do not deny that I planned sabotage,"

is elected President of South Africa to a fanfare of media sycophancy worldwide, as the Jewish owned media praise the historic day that a black man is elected to run South Africa.

What they fail to mention is that Mandela, who incidentally prior to his incarceration wrote the pamphlet, "How To Be A Good Communist," has simply been put there to ensure there is no disruption to the running of South Africa by the Rothschild Oppenheimer family and in particular their gold and diamond mining interests.

Indeed, the current head of the Oppenheimer family, Harry Oppenheimer, owns 95% of the world's diamond mines. Isn't it surprising that the Jewish media fail to inform their readers why, if the blacks in South Africa are getting Africa for the Africans, all the gold and diamond mines, ie. the wealth of South Africa, is still controlled by Jews.

Communism was invented for the Rothschilds by Moses Mordechai Levy, more commonly known by his Crypto-Jew name of Karl Marx, which makes it no surprise that the African National Congress (ANC) in South Africa was guided by two Communist Jews, Albie Sachs, and Yossel Mashel Slovo (Joe Slovo). Indeed, when Nelson Mandela's ANC took over South Africa, Slovo was named Minister of Housing.

Communism is designed to concentrate the wealth in the hands of the few Jews at the top (plus in this case, the odd token black man), whilst the population of the country they have usurped is left in poverty. It therefore should come as no surprise that none of the mineral wealth controlled by Rothschild front men, the Oppenheimer family, is returned to the black people and instead, South Africa, far from becoming free, experiences a dramatic decrease in living standards for the black population, and rapidly declines to the status of the world's most violent and crime-ridden country. AIDS infection soars to at least 25% of the black population. Mandela's successor, Thabo Mbeki, son of one of the terrorists jailed alongside Mandela, Govan Mbeki, after he succeeds Mandela as President, states that poverty, not HIV is the cause of AIDS.

This results in confusion to a population who, under so-called freedom, have seen crime levels and poverty soar. In their desperation in the realisation the government won't help them, they have resorted to witchdoctors who advise that sex with a virgin will cure them of AIDS. This, in a country which already boasts statistics of one rape every 26 seconds, now sees incidences of sex with babies less than six months old soar.

Interestingly, the Jewish Talmud legitimizes sex with girls under the age of three and justifies it in the Mishnah of Kethuboth 11a, because, apparently, according to the Jewish Rabbis, it is like putting your finger in the baby girl's eye, and just as tears come to the eye again and again, so does virginity come back to the baby girl.

1995: On October 21st, former Mossad agent Victor Ostrovsky, who published two books exposing the activities of the Mossad, appears on a Canadian breakfast television show, "Canada AM," with Israeli journalist Yosef Lapid, the former head of Israeli television, also on the program via satellite link. Lapid had already called for the Mossad to seek Ostrovsky out in Canada and kill him for writing his revealing books. However, this time Lapid states live on the show that as Israel's Mossad could not kill Ostrovsky in Canada without causing diplomatic incident,

> "I hope that there would be a decent Jew in Canada who would do the job for us."

Ostrovsky decides to sue in a Canadian court Yosef Lapid for inciting his murder and "Canada AM" for airing his incitement to the public. However, Ostrovsky is unable to find any lawyer in Canada who will take the case. Ostrovsky then has the last portion of his advance, $46,000, withheld by his publisher Harper Collins (owned by Jew, Rupert Murdoch), against advertising. Ostrovsky informs Harper Collins that this was not in their contract to which they reply, "Sue Us!"

The collective Jewish harassment goes on. Ostrovsky's daughter, a television producer, is denied a job she had been offered at a Vancouver television station after its Toronto head office learns of her relationship to Ostrovsky. Ostrovsky's Canadian publisher cancels the publication of his new book and some time after that, his home is burnt to the ground in an arson attack.

Former atomic energy scientist Dr. Kitty Little claims the Rothschilds now control 80% of the world's uranium supplies giving them a monopoly over nuclear power.

The Defense Investigative Service circulates a memo warning US military contractors that,

> "Israel aggressively collects (United States) military and industrial technology."

The report states that Israel obtains information using,

> "ethnic targeting, financial aggrandizement, and identification and exploitation of individual frailties," of United States citizens.

1996: A General Accounting Office report, "Defense Industrial Security: Weaknesses in US Security Arrangements With Foreign-Owned Defense Contractors," finds that according to intelligence sources, "Country A," (identified by intelligence sources as Israel, Washington Times, February 22nd 1996),

> "conducts the most aggressive espionage operation against the United States of any US ally."

The Jerusalem Post (August 30th 1996) quotes the report,

> "Classified military information and sensitive military technologies are high-priority targets for the intelligence agencies of this country."

The report describes,

> "An espionage operation run by the intelligence organization responsible for collecting scientific and technologic information for (Israel) paid a U.S. government employee to obtain U.S. classified military intelligence documents."

The Washington Report on Middle East Affairs (Shawn L. Twing, April 1996) noted that this was,

> "a reference to the 1985 arrest of Jonathan Pollard, a civilian US naval intelligence analyst who provided Israel's LAKAM espionage agency an estimated 800,000 pages of classified U.S. intelligence information."

The GAO report also notes that,

> "Several citizens of (Israel) were caught in the United States stealing sensitive technology used in manufacturing artillery gun tubes."

An Office of Naval Intelligence document, "Worldwide Challenges to Naval Strike Warfare," reports that,

> "U.S. technology has been acquired (by China) through Israel in the form of the Lavi fighter and possibly SAM (surface-to-air) missile technology."

Jane's Defense Weekly (February 28th 1996) notes that,

> "Until now, the intelligence community has not openly confirmed the transfer of U.S. technology (via Israel) to China."

The report noted that this,

> "Represents a dramatic step forward for Chinese military aviation." (Flight International, March 13th 1996).

On April 13th, in the course of Israel's military offensive

against Hezbollah forces in South Lebanon entitled, "Operation Grapes Of Wrath," Israeli forces launch a rocket attack on an ambulance in Beirut, killing six civilians, two women and four children. Israeli forces apologise, an Israeli spokesman Glyn Davies, calls it a, "terrible tragedy."

Less than a week later, on April 18th, Israelis commit another "terrible tragedy" when they deliberately shell a United Nations safe compound in the village of Qana, South Lebanon, killing 106 Lebanese civilians who had only taken refuge there on the understanding that it was an agreed non-combat area between the fighting forces of Hezbollah and Israel.

Israel makes excuses as usual, claiming it was a "mistake," but unfortunately history has by now proven that they are never able to enter into any sort of combat without committing some sort of war crime, or rather series of war crimes, which they always seem to have excuses for. Major-General Stanislaw Wozniak of the United Nations Interim Force in Lebanon (UNIFIL) clearly sees it this way, as revealed in his response to Israeli excuses in which he firmly states of the Qana massacre,

> "Simply, you do not attack civilians. You do not attack UN positions."

Amschel Rothschild, 41, is strangled with the heavy cord of his own towel robe in his hotel room in Paris. For some reason, the French Prime Minister, Jacques Chirac orders the French Police to close their investigation, and

Rupert Murdoch, born of a Jewish mother and so a Jew by Israeli immigration law, instructs his editors and news managers around the world to report it as a heart attack, if they need to report it at all.

On May 12th, United Nations Ambassador and Ashkenazi Jew, Madeleine Albright, when appearing on 60 Minutes, is asked the following by correspondent Lesley Stahl, in reference to the years of United States led economic sanctions against Iraq,

> "We have heard that half a million children have died. I mean, that is more children than died in Hiroshima. And, you know, is the price worth it?"

To which Ambassador Albright replies,

> "I think that is a very hard choice, but the price, we think, the price is worth it."

Her comments cause no public outcry. In fact, the holocaust of half a million Iraqi children is positively admired by the United States government when you consider that less than eight months later, President Clinton appointed Albright as secretary of state.

Whilst appearing before the Senate Committee considering her appointment, Albright is literally chomping at the bit for the blood of more Iraqi children when she states,

> "We will insist on maintaining tough UN sanctions against Iraq unless and until that

> regime complies with relevant Security Council resolutions."

The paper, "A Clean Break: A New Strategy for Securing the Realm," is published, which makes the following statement that will be replaced with the cock and bull story of "weapons of mass destruction" to justify the United States invasion of Iraq in 2003,

> "Israel can shape its strategic environment, in cooperation with Turkey and Jordan, by weakening, containing, and even rolling back Syria. This effort can focus on removing Saddam Hussein from power in Iraq—an important Israeli strategic objective in its own right."

The people behind this report are: Richard Perle; James Colbert; Charles Fairbanks Jr.; Douglas Feith; Robert Loewenberg; David Wurmser; and Meyrav Wurmser.

On Larry King Live in April, actor, Marlon Brando, makes the following statement,

> "Hollywood is run by Jews. It is owned by Jews, and they should have a greater sensitivity about the issue of people who are suffering because they've exploited them."

As a result of this statement, the Jewish Defense League immediately demand Brando's star be removed from the Hollywood Walk of Fame, but, fearing a public outcry, the Hollywood Chamber of Commerce refuses to do this.

1997: On February 20th, the New York Times reports that an Army mechanical engineer, Ashkenazi Jew, David A. Tenenbaum, "inadvertently" gave classified military information on missile systems and armoured vehicles to Israeli officials.

The Washington Post also reports that United States intelligence has intercepted a conversation in which two Israeli officials had discussed the possibility of getting a confidential letter that then Secretary of State, Warren Christopher had written to Palestinian leader Yasser Arafat.

One of the Israelis, identified only as, "Dov," had commented that they may get the letter from "Mega," the code name for Israel's top agent inside the United States.

United States ambassador to Israel, Martin Indyk, complains privately to the Israeli government about heavy-handed surveillance by Israeli intelligence agents.

Israeli agents place a tap on Ashkenazi Jew and daughter of a Rabbi, Monica Lewinsky's, phone at the Watergate and record phone sex sessions between her and President Bill Clinton. The Ken Starr report confirms that Clinton warned Lewinsky their conversations were being taped and ended the affair. Interestingly, at the same time, the FBI's hunt for "Mega" is called off.

Edgar Bronfman, chairman of the World Jewish Congress, effectively extorts one and a half billion dollars from Switzerland for alleged holocaust victims who he claimed had deposited their money there. He lacks sufficient proof, but the Swiss government gives in as Bronfman is one of President Clinton's largest financial backers and the Swiss fear the diplomatic consequences of their failure to do so.

Interestingly, this year a seventeen member tribunal based in Zurich set up to investigate the identities of the 5,500 foreign accounts and 10,000 Swiss accounts that have lain dormant since the end of the World War 2, subsequently discovers that only 200 accounts, containing a total of approximately ten million dollars, less than one percent of the one and a half billion dollars extorted by Bronfman, could be traced back to alleged holocaust victims.

Does Bronfman give the Swiss back the other 99% of the one and a half billion dollars? Of course not, and incidentally, some six years later, he has given almost nothing to the alleged holocaust victims he claimed the money was for. Jews allegedly misappropriated the ill gotten gains fraudulently obtained in their demands of "justice" for alleged holocaust victims.

Less than two months before Tony Blair comes to power in England, another interesting entry can be found in HANSARD, 5th March 1997, volume 578, No. 68, columns 1869-1871, in which the Earl of Caithness is recorded as having stated,

> "The next government must grasp the nettle, accept their responsibility for controlling the money supply and change from our debt-based monetary system. My Lords, will they? If they do not, our monetary system will break us and the sorry legacy we are already leaving our children will be a disaster."

On May 2nd, the British Labour Party Leader, Tony Blair, is elected as Prime Minister. Prior to his election, the man in charge of donations to Blair's "private office," donations which reached the princely sum of seven million pounds, was none other than Blair's tennis partner, a Jew, Michael Levy. Furthermore, Levy agreed to raise large sums of money for the Labour Party so long as they never became "anti-Israel," whilst Blair is leader.

Interestingly, Blair was initially introduced to Levy at a dinner party in 1994 by Gideon Meir, a senior Israeli diplomat. Levy has also acted as a fundraiser for Israeli Prime Minister Ehud Barak, and both his children live in Israel. Another Jew, David Sainsbury, becomes the Labour Party's single largest donator this year when he donated one million pounds to the party. Co-incidentally, both Levy and Sainsbury are given life peerages and become Lords, following Blair's election victory.

On May 6th, only four days after Tony Blair's election as Prime Minister, his Chancellor of the Exchequer, Gordon Brown, announces he is going to give full independence from political control to the Bank of England.

On October 29th Edmond de Rothschild dies in Geneva. On the exact same day, American Anton Szandor LaVey (real name Levy—a Crypto-Jew), the founder of the Church of Satan, also dies, who in his book, "Satan Speaks," states in relation to the Jewish blueprint for world domination, "The Protocols of the Elders of Zion,"

> "The first time I read the Protocols of the Elders of Zion, my instinctive reaction was, so what's wrong with THAT? Isn't that the way any master plan should work? Doesn't the public deserve—nay, demand—such despotism?"

Kofi Annan becomes Secretary General to the United Nations. He is married to Nane Lagergren, a Rothschild, whom he wed in 1984.

In Los Angeles, a major local, state and federal drug investigation sours. The suspects in this investigation? Israeli organized crime with operations in New York, Miami, Las Vegas, Canada, Israel and Egypt. This Israeli organized crime network was involved in cocaine and ecstasy trafficking, alongside sophisticated white-collar credit card and computer fraud. To the astonishment of the investigating officers, the Israelis under investigation had the investigators beepers, cell phones, even home phones under surveillance. Some of the network who were arrested even admitted to having hundreds of telephone numbers and using them to avoid arrest.

The investigators look at where this information may have come from and they soon stumble upon the Israeli firm AMDOCS which has a virtual monopoly in the United States on telephone billing services, and upon checking their own phone system for how they could have been wiretapped, they discover their main contractor was Converse Infosys, another Israeli firm which works closely with the Israeli government.

1998: On January 18th, Michael Specter publishes a story in The New York Times entitled, "Traffickers' New Cargo: Naive Slavic Women." The story reveals how the Jewish Russian mafia dominate the white slave trade in prostitution, with many of the unsuspecting women they deceive into this business ending up in Israel. Indeed, Specter states the following in the article,

> "The Tropicana, in Tel Aviv's bustling business district, is one of the busiest bordellos. The women who work there, like nearly all prostitutes in Israel today, are Russian. Their boss, however, is not."

President Bill Clinton receives a letter dated January 26th from a group calling themselves the "Project For A New American Century (PNAC)," which is signed by the following persons: Elliott Abrams; Richard L. Armitage; William J. Bennett; Jeffrey Bergner; John Bolton; Paula Dobriansky; Francis Fukuyama; Robert

Kagan; Zalmay Khalilzad; William Kristol; Richard Perle; Peter W. Rodman; Donald Rumsfeld; William Schneider, Jr.; Vin Weber; Paul Wolfowitz; R. James Woolsey; Robert B. Zoellick, most of which are Jews. The letter states,

> "We are writing you because we are convinced that current American policy toward Iraq is not succeeding, and that we may soon face a threat in the Middle East more serious than any we have known since the end of the Cold War. In your upcoming State of the Union Address, you have an opportunity to chart a clear and determined course for meeting this threat.
>
> We urge you to seize that opportunity, and to enunciate a new strategy that would secure the interests of the U.S. and our friends and allies around the world. That strategy should aim, above all, at the removal of Saddam Hussein's regime from power. We stand ready to offer our full support in this difficult but necessary endeavor….
>
> Given the magnitude of the threat, the current policy, which depends for its success upon the steadfastness of our coalition partners and upon the cooperation of Saddam Hussein, is dangerously inadequate. The only acceptable strategy is one that eliminates the possibility that Iraq will be able to use or threaten to use weapons of mass destruction. In the near term, this means a willingness to undertake military action as diplomacy is clearly failing. In the long

> term, it means removing Saddam Hussein and his regime from power. That now needs to become the aim of American foreign policy."

In September, with the above letter at the back of his mind perhaps, Bill Clinton whilst on a visit to Ireland, makes the following startling admission as to who really makes the decisions in the world,

> "You know, by the time you become the leader ot a country, someone else makes all the decisions. You may find you can get away with virtual Presidents, virtual Prime Ministers, virtual everything."

Indeed, rather ominously, on October 31st, as per his instructions from the PNAC group, President Clinton signs into law H.R. 4655, the, "Iraq Liberation Act," which supported the pursuit of regime change in Iraq.

However, history does tell us that the PNAC group is not actually particularly creative. Indeed, as far back as February 1990, a Mossad sayan in New York supplied a false story to ABC Television that Saddam Hussein had a uranium manufacturing plant in Iraq in order to draw attention to Saddam Hussein's so called "Weapons Of Mass Destruction," one year before America's first war with Iraq.

On February 19th, a 5-strong Mossad team is arrested in Berne, Switzerland, having been caught attempting to bug a private house.

The International Monetary Fund (IMF) eliminates food and fuel subsidies for the poor in Indonesia. At the same time the IMF soaks up tens of billions of dollars to save Indonesia's financiers, or rather the international banks from whom they had borrowed.

A document leaks out of the World Bank called, "Master Plan for Brazil." In it, it spells out five requirements to ensure a flexible public sector workforce. These are as follows:

1) Reduce Salary/Benefits.

2) Reduce Pensions.

3) Increase Work Hours.

4) Reduce Job Stability.

5) Reduce Employment.

The European Central Bank is set up in Frankfurt, the city from which the Rothschilds originate.

1999: In Brazil, Rio's privatized electric company named, "Rio Light," is responsible for repeated blackouts in neighbourhoods. The company blames the weather in the Pacific Ocean for the blackouts, when Rio is on the Atlantic. The blackouts wouldn't have anything to do with the fact that after privatization Rio Light axed 40% of the company's workorce would it? No problem for Rio Light. As a result of that drop in employees which naturally reflects their drop in standard of service, their share price goes up 33%.

The National Security Agency (NSA), headquartered in northern Maryland, issues what's called a Top Secret sensitive compartmentalized information report (TS/SCI), warning that records of calls in the United States were getting into foreign hands—to Israel, in particular. An Israeli firm named AMDOCS has a virtual monopoly on the billing records of all phone companies in the United States as all the major ones such as AT&T outsource this process to them.

2000: George W. Bush is elected President of the United States. Bush and his family claim to be descendants of the House of Plantagenet which is descended from the Royal House of Judah. He is, in fact, a Crypto-Jew. However, Bush portrays himself as a Christian for the purpose of winning the votes of evangelicals. Bush would go on to commit illegal wars in Afghanistan and Iraq and commit heinous unChristian crimes.

President of Venezuela, Hugo Chavez, prior to making an official state visit to Iraq states,

> "Imagine what the Pharisees will say when they see me with Saddam Hussein!"

The Pharisees were the Jewish leaders responsible for the crucifixion of Jesus Christ who continue to be revered by Jews today.

In April, Jacob "Cookie" Orgad, a self-confessed former Mossad agent, is arrested for running one of the biggest ecstasy smuggling operations in America on record. This operation delivered hundreds of millions of dollars in illegal drugs, manufactured in the Netherlands, to cities across the United States. One of the unique features of this operation was that orthodox Hasidic Jews acted as drug couriers, hoping their traditional black hats, black coats and locks of hair dangling around their ears, would make them appear unlikely suspects. Indeed, Commissioner of the United States Customs Service, Raymond W. Kelly, states,

> "The drug comes to us from various smuggling bases, mainly Europe, the Dominican Republic, and Canada…Israeli organized crime groups dominate the trade…"

Russian Jewish oligarch, Boris Berezovsky, flees to London to avoid arrest in Russia and transfers his business interests to his protégé, another Russian Jew, Roman Abramovich, who goes on to purchase Chelsea Football Club.

On October 1st, "The Rome Observer," runs a story of how the Italian police have broken up a paedophile ring which had been kidnapping non-Jewish children aged between two and five from orphanages, and then raping and murdering them. The paedophile ring had filmed these rapes and murders for the benefit of the global "snuff film" industry and had already sold copies to over 1,700 customers who had paid as much as $20,000 to see these two to five year old children being brutally raped and killed.

The Jews struck back. The problem is that this paedophile ring consisted of eleven Jewish gangsters, and the Italian broadcast media had been so bold as to inform their more than eleven million viewers of such, and even go so far as to broadcast footage of these Jewish gangsters' arrests! Naturally, instead of maintaining a low profile or apologising for the crimes of their brethren, the Jewish community in Italy went mad claiming, "blood libel," and demanded that the Jewish elite who sat on the board of the TV network responsible, no surprise there, fire the news executives who allowed this story to be broadcast. This was, of course done, and incidentally, none of America's news networks carried any report of this Jewish paedophile network story.

One has to wonder whether the Jews most holy book, the "Talmud," had any influence on these Jewish paedophiles. The Talmud clearly states that sex between a grown man and a girl under three years of age is "permissible," and also that the best among the non Jews "deserve to be killed." It would appear the actions of these Jewish paedophiles satisfied both of these edicts.

The International Monetary Fund (IMF) require Argentina to cut the government budget deficit from its current $5.3 billion to $4.1 billion by the following year, 2001. Argentina's unemployment is running at 20% of the working population. They then up the ante and demand an elimination of the deficit. The IMF offer Argentina some ideas of how this could be achieved. Cut the government's emergency employment program from $200 a month to $160 a month.

They also ask for an across the board 12%-15% cut in salaries for civil servants and the cutting of pensions to the elderly by 13%. By December of 2001, middle class Argentineans, sick of literally hunting the streets for garbage to eat, start to riot and burn down Buenos Aires. In January, Argentina had devalued the Peso, wiping out the value of many common people's savings accounts. Dismayed that they can't rape that country further, James Wolfensohn, the Jewish President of the World Bank, states sorrowfully,

> "Almost all major utilities have been privatized."

How do they control the unrest within the population caused by Jewish banking? An example is of an Argentinean bus driver, a thirty seven year old father of five, who lost his job as a bus driver from a company that owed him 9 months pay. During a demonstration against this and other injustices perpetrated upon him and the population, the military police shot him dead with a bullet through the head.

In Tanzania, with approximately 1.3 million people dying of AIDS, the World Bank and the IMF decide it is now necessary to require Tanzania to charge for what were previously free hospital appointments. They also order Tanzania to charge school fees for their previously free education system, then express surprise when school enrollments drop from 80% to 66%.

During the time the IMF and World Bank have been in charge of Tanzania's economy, which is since 1985, Tanzania's GDP has dropped from $309 to $210 per capita, standards of literacy have fallen and the rate of abject poverty has increased, to envelop 51% of the population. When the IMF and World Bank took charge in 1985, Tanzania was a socialist nation. In June 2000 the World Bank reported arrogantly,

> "One legacy of socialism is that most people continue to believe the State has a fundamental role in promoting development and providing social services."

There is rioting in Bolivia after the World Bank drastically increases the price of water. The World Bank claims this is necessary to provide for desperately needed repairs and expansion. This is utter nonsense but certainly not original nonsense. A British water supplier, Wessex Water, a privatized water company that was actually owned by Enron, claimed the same thing after it was privatized (England was the first country to privatize the public water supply), and like Bolivia, the quality dropped and the prices exploded. Furthermore, almost all privatized water companies in Britain have consistently failed to meet government targets on leakages, so the increase in charges is clearly not going on maintenance.

2001: On January 20th, only hours before leaving office,

President Clinton grants Marc Rich (a Crypto-Jew from Belgium, real name Marc Reich) an extremely controversial presidential pardon. In 1983, Marc Rich was indicted by United States Attorney and future mayor of New York City, Rudolph Giuliani, on charges of tax evasion and illegal trading with Iran. He fled to Switzerland before a court appearance, and remained on the FBI's "Most Wanted List" for many years.

Anti-Defamation League (ADL) National Director Abraham Foxman admits that his organization had received $250,000 in contributions from Marc Rich during a sixteen year period, including a grant of $100,000 shortly after Foxman had agreed to assist Rich in obtaining a presidential pardon from Bill Clinton. Foxman also admits it was his idea to use Rich's ex-wife, Denise, a major financial contributor to the Democratic party, as a means of influencing Clinton.

On September 10th, The Washington Times runs a story by Rowan Scarborough entitled, "U.S. Troops Would Enforce Peace Under Army Study." This article focuses on a 68-page paper by the Army School of Advanced Military Studies (SAMS), which looks at a variety of issues including different military agencies and their modus operandi. Of the Mossad, the Israeli intelligence service, the SAMS officers state,

> "Wildcard. Ruthless and cunning. Has capability to target U.S. forces and make it look like a Palestinian/Arab act."

On September 11th, the attack on the World Trade Center and the Pentagon is orchestrated by Israel with the complicity of Britain and America, under the orders of the Rothschilds, which they in turn blame on so-called Muslim terrorists. This is Stage One of getting the Western World to go to war with the Arab World, on behalf of the Jews. Another textbook Mossad false flag operation, remember their motto,

"By Way Of Deception, Thou Shalt Do War."

They also will use the attacks to gain control of the few nations in the world who don't allow Rothschild central banks, and so, less than one month after these attacks, United States forces attack Afghanistan, one of only seven nations in the world that does not have a Rothschild controlled central bank. These nations are all predominantly populated by Muslims who, unlike the majority of White Christians (see Nehemiah 5:7), obey their scripture and refuse to partake in the lending or borrowing of money, "usury," something which has riled the Jews for hundreds of years.

The Jews are also most unhappy with Muslims throughout the world. This is because the plan to destroy the Muslim faith that worked so well for the Jews with regard to the Christian faith has largely failed.

The Jews worked hard to get Muslims to migrate into many Western nations, the plan being that they would forget their religious beliefs and become nothing but consumers of Jewish owned products, services and governments, like the majority of the white Christian world.

However, the majority of Muslims maintained their religious faith and formed their own communities within these Western nations, failing to fall into the Jews trap, like the Christians. The Jews decide this means the Muslims have to be destroyed, and they decide they'll get the Christians to do the job for them.

On the day after the 9-11 attacks, in The Jerusalem Post, former Israeli Prime Minister, Benjamin Netanyahu, states,

> "Regarding what took place on September 11th, well it's very good…it will generate immediate sympathy for Israel."

Boston Logan airport, from where UAL Flight 175 and AA Flight 11 which struck the twin towers originated, and Newark airport, where UAL 93 originated from and which supposedly crashed in Pennsylvania, both had their security outsourced to a private firm named Huntleigh USA. This firm, in turn, is a wholly owned subsidiary of an Israeli company called International Consultants on Targeted Security (ICTS) International N.V., a Holland-based aviation and transportation security firm headed by former Israeli military commanding officers and veterans of government intelligence and security agencies.

The principals of ICTS include Menachem Atzmon. Atzmon was convicted in Israel in 1996 when he was treasurer of Ehud Olmert's Mayorial campaign for campaign finance fraud. His fellow defendant, Ehud Olmert, was acquitted and goes on to become Prime Minister of Israel in 2006. Another principal is Ezra

Harel, who would die of a heart attack two years later at the age of 53 on his yacht off the coast of Palestine. These two Israeli citizens took over management of security at the Boston and Newark airports when ICTS bought Huntleigh USA in 1999.

Less than a week before the 9-11 attack, on September 5th, the so-called lead hijacker Mohamed Atta and several other hijackers made a still-unexplained visit onboard one of pro-Israeli lobbyist, Ashkenazi Jew, Jack Abramoff's casino boats. No investigation is undertook as to what they were doing there. Interestingly, out of the nineteen so-called hijackers blamed for carrying out the attack on September 11th, seven would turn up still alive. Some showed up at United States embassies in Arabic countries, asking why they are being named as hijackers. Does the United States or Jewish controlled media question this? No.

On 9-11, five Israelis disguised in Arab clothing are arrested for dancing and cheering while video-taping the World Trade Center Towers collapse. Employed by Urban Moving Systems, an Israeli Mossad front, the Israelis are caught with multiple passports, a van which tested positive for explosives, and a lot of cash. As a result of this arrest, the Mayor of Jerusalem (and future Prime Minister of Israel), Ehud Olmert, personally calls New York City Mayor Rudy Giuliani, with instructions for him to intervene in this matter.

Olmert offers the following assurances that these men had nothing to do with the terrorist attack, and were just having a bit of fun, which I guess, must be something Jews do when they see two giant buildings full of non-Jews collapse, when he states,

> "That's why the five laughed at the collapse of the World Trade Center buildings, they were just being immature and irresponsible."

Two of these five Israelis are later revealed to be Mossad, negating Olmert's claims. The other three are strongly suspected of being Mossad also. As witness reports track the activity of the Israelis, it emerges that they were seen at Liberty Park at the time of the first impact, suggesting a foreknowledge of what was to come.

The Israelis are interrogated by the FBI, and then secretly sent back to Israel. The arresting officers from the local New Jersey police department are told not to discuss their arrest, so presumably if you ever want something done in New York, you're best off speaking to the Mayor of Jerusalem first.

These five Israelis who were dancing and cheering the collapse of the World Trade Center later appear on radio and television in Israel where they state they were in New York City on September 11th to "document the event," as America had never suffered an attack like this on its shores. How did they know the attack was going to take place?

The owner of the moving company used as a cover by these Mossad agents abandons his business and flees to Israel. The United States Government then classifies all of the evidence related to the Israeli agents and their connections to 9-11.

Much of this is reported to the public via a four part story on Fox News by reporter Carl Cameron. Pressure from Jewish groups, primarily AIPAC, forces Fox News to remove the story from their website.

Two hours prior to the 9-11 attacks, Odigo, an Israeli company with offices just a few blocks from the World Trade Towers, receives an advance warning of the attack via an internet instant message. The manager of the New York Office provides the FBI with the IP address of the sender of the message, but the FBI does not follow this up.

The FBI is investigating five Israeli moving companies as possible fronts for Israeli intelligence.

Approximately two hundred Israelis with ties to these moving companies, which were very active in the World Trade Center in the months prior to the attack, are subsequently arrested on suspicion of involvement when bomb residue is discovered in some of the removal vans they were using. However, under the direct orders of U.S. Justice Department official Michael Chertoff, they are deported to Israel for "visa violations." Chertoff, a dual United States/Israeli citizen whose father is a Rabbi and mother was one of the first Mossad operatives, then orders the arrest of some nine hundred Muslims with no ties to the World Trade Center incident.

On September 12th, The Jerusalem Post, tipped off about possible exposure of Israel as the perpetrator of the 911 attacks runs a story claiming that two Israelis died on the hijacked airplanes and that 4,000 were missing at the

WTC. One week later, a Beirut television station reports that 4,000 Israeli employees of the WTC were absent the day of the attack, which would appear to clarify the story in The Jerusalem Post.

Finally, on September 22nd, The New York Times states the following,

> "There were, in fact, only three Israelis who had been confirmed as dead: two on the planes and another who had been visiting the towers on business and who was identified and buried."

Between August 26th and September 11th, a group of speculators, identified by the American Securities and Exchange Commission as Israeli citizens, sold "short" a list of 38 stocks that could reasonably be expected to fall in value as a result of the pending attacks. These speculators operated out of the Toronto, Canada, and Frankfurt, Germany, stock exchanges and their profits were specifically stated to be "in the millions of dollars." The FBI never follow this up as they know it won't lead to the official line of Bin Laden, but instead, to the real perpetrator, Israel.

Also, earlier this year, Lewis Eisenberg, who was responsible for the privatisation of the World Trade Center, finds the ideal owner in former strip club owner, Larry Silverstein. Both of these men have held leadership positions with the United Jewish Appeal (UJA), a billion dollar Jewish "charity," organization. Three months prior to its destruction, Silverstein doubles the insurance on the World Trade Center. Interestingly Silverstein is very close friends with former Israeli

Prime Minister, Benjamin Netanyahu, boasting they have spoken on the phone every Sunday, at the start of the Jewish week, for years.

Following the World Trade Center attack, anonymous letters containing anthrax are sent to various politicians and media executives. As a result of exposure to anthrax within these letters five people are killed. Like the 9-11 attack this is immediately blamed on Al-Qaeda, until it is discovered that the anthrax contained within those letters is a specific type of weaponized anthrax made by a United States military laboratory.

The FBI then discovers that the main suspect for these anthrax letters is an Ashkenazi Jew, Dr. Philip Zack, who had been reprimanded several times by his employers due to offensive remarks he made about Arabs. Dr. Philip Zack was caught on camera entering the storage area where he worked at Fort Detrick which is where the Anthrax was kept. At this point, both the FBI and the mainstream media stopped making any public comments on the case.

Jewish Defence League Chairman since 1985, Ashkenazi Jew, Irv Rubin, is jailed for allegedly plotting to bomb a mosque and the offices of a Arab-American congressman. He dies shortly afterwards, allegedly slitting his own throat in a suicide attempt, before he can be brought to trial.

One week prior to the WTC attack, the Zim Shipping Company moves out of its offices in the WTC, breaking its lease and costing the company $50,000. No reason has ever been given, but Zim Shipping Company is half owned by the State of Israel.

As a result of the September 11th attack being blamed on Osama Bin Laden, the United States invades Afghanistan and topples the Taliban rulers there. Soon, the real reason for the invastion is made manifest. The real reason is that Taliban leader Mullah Omar had banned opium production in July 2000, and thus that year's opium crop was destroyed. Do you recall what happened in 1839 when the Manchu Emperor in China ordered opium destroyed, to stop the endemic addiction of the Chinese people?

The Rothschild family ordered the British Army to go over there to fight the Chinese to protect its drug running interests. Well, that is exactly what happened here with the United States Army this year. Afghanistan is the source of 75% of the world's heroin, and due to Mullah Omar's destruction of 2001's profits, there was no time to lose in ensuring he couldn't possibly be allowed to interfere in the profits of this "Synagogue of Satan" for 2002 and thus the invasion occurs in October 2001. Soon after, the media is reporting a bumper crop of opium in March 2002.

On October 3rd, Israeli Prime Minister, Ariel Sharon, makes the following statement to Ashkenazi Jew, Shimon Peres, as reported on Kol Yisrael radio.

> "Every time we do something you tell me

> America will do this and will do that...I want to tell you something very clear. Don't worry about American pressure on Israel. We, the Jewish people, control America, and the Americans know it."

At the American Friends of Lubavitch dinner, in October, Ari Fleischer, President Bush's Press Secretary, is given the group's Young Leadership award and Senator Joe Lieberman is declared the night's honoree. Both Ari Fleischer and Senator Lieberman lavish praise on the active Chabad Lubavitch effort to establish an army of young staffers in governmental and political jobs. This dinner is attended by hundreds of Washington political bigwigs, Capitol Hill staffers and Washington money people. Following Ari Fleischer's stint as President Bush's Press Secretary, he goes on to become an ordained Lubavitch Rabbi.

Former Director of National Affairs at the American Jewish Committee, Dr. Stephen Steinlight, in his October article for the Center For Immigration Studies entitled, "The Jewish Stake in America's Changing Demography—Reconsidering a Misguided Immigration Policy," under the heading, "Facing Up to the Gradual Demise of Jewish Political Power," explains how the Jews control America,

> "Not that it is the case that our disproportionate political power (pound for pound the greatest of any ethnic/cultural group in America) will erode all at once, or even quickly. We will be able to

> hang on to it for perhaps a decade or two longer. Unless and until the triumph of campaign finance reform is complete, an extremely unlikely scenario, the great material wealth of the Jewish community will continue to give it significant advantages.
>
> We will continue to court and be courted by key figures in Congress. That power is exerted within the political system from the local to national levels through soft money, and especially the provision of out-of-state funds to candidates sympathetic to Israel, a high wall of church/state separation, and social liberalism combined with selective conservatism on criminal justice and welfare issues…"

He then moves on to the power of the media which he admits is a Jewish propaganda machine,

> "It is also true that Jewish economic influence and power are disproportionately concentrated in Hollywood, television, and in the news industry, theoretically a boon in terms of the formation of favorable public images of Jews and sensitizing the American people."

He goes on to cite the absolute necessity of repeated propaganda regarding the alleged holocaust of Jews in World War 2, when talking about dual Israeli/American citizens, when he states,

> "America has largely tolerated this dual loyalty—we get a free pass, I suspect, largely

> over Christian guilt about the Holocaust…"

And he goes on to state how he believes Jewish media will benefit Muslim immigrants,

> "I confess that I suspect that MTV, for better or for worse, will prove more powerful with young Muslim immigrants…over traditional sources of religious and political authority."

Adam Goldman is appointed White House Liaison to the Jewish Community. Interestingly no other ethnic groups have a race specific White House Liaison.

Russian Jewish oligarch, Vladimir Gusinsky, flees Russia, where he was facing money-laundering charges, and hides in Israel. He is a dual Russian and Israeli citizen.

It is discovered that United States drug agents communications have been penetrated. Suspicion falls on two companies, AMDOCS and Comverse Infosys, both owned by Israelis. AMDOCS generates billing data for most United States phone companies and is able to provide detailed logs of who is talking to whom. In Israel, Comverse Infosys gets reimbursed for up to 50% of its research and development costs by the Israeli Ministry of Industry and Trade.

Comverse Infosys builds the tapping equipment used by law enforcement to eavesdrop on all American telephone calls, but suspicion forms that Comverse

Infosys, which gets half of its research and development budget from the Israeli government, has built a back door into the system that is being exploited by Israeli intelligence. The information gleaned on United States drug interdiction efforts is finding its way to Jewish drug smugglers, helping them to evade discovery.

The investigation by the FBI leads to the exposure of the largest foreign spy ring ever uncovered inside the United States, operated by Israel. Half of the suspected spies have been arrested when 9-11 happens.

Professor Joseph Stiglitz, former Chief Economist of the World Bank and former Chairman of President Clinton's Council of Economic Advisers, goes public over the World Bank's, "Four Step Strategy," which is designed to enslave nations to the bankers. I summarise this below,

> 1) Privatisation. This is actually where national leaders are offered 10% commissions to their secret Swiss bank accounts in exchange for them trimming a few billion dollars off the sale price of national assets. Bribery and corruption, pure and simple.
>
> 2) Capital Market Liberalization. This is the repealing of laws that tax money going across borders. Stiglitz calls this the, "hot money," cycle. Initially cash comes in from abroad to speculate in real estate and currency. Then, when the economy in that country starts to look promising, this outside wealth is pulled straight

out again, causing the economy to collapse. The nation then requires International Monetary Fund (IMF) help, and the IMF provides it under the pretext that they raise interest rates anywhere from 30% to 80%. This happened in Indonesia and Brazil, also in other Asian and Latin American nations. These higher interest rates consequently impoverish a country, demolishing property values, savaging industrial production and draining national treasuries.

3) Market Based Pricing. This is where the prices of food, water and domestic gas are raised which predictably leads to social unrest in the respective nation, now more commonly referred to as "IMF Riots." These riots cause the flight of capital and government bankruptcies. This benefits the foreign corporations as the nations remaining assets can be purchased at rock bottom prices.

4) Free Trade. This is where international corporations burst into Asia, Latin America and Africa, whilst at the same time Europe and America barricade their own markets against third world agriculture. They also impose extortionate tariffs which these countries have to pay for branded pharmaceuticals, causing soaring rates in death and disease.

There are a lot of losers in this system, but one winner—the Jewish owned and operated banking system. In fact the IMF and World Bank have made the sale of electricity, water, telephone and gas systems a condition of loans to every developing nation. This is estimated at 4 trillion dollars of publicly owned assets.

In September of this year, Professor Joseph Stiglitz is awarded the Nobel Prize in economics.

2002: Webster's Third New International Dictionary (Unabridged), re-printed in 2002, provides a new definition of anti-Semitism, a definition which has not been updated since 1956. The new definition reads,

> "Anti-Semitism: (1) hostility toward Jews as a religious or racial minority group, often accompanied by social, political or economic discrimination; (2) opposition to Zionism; (3) sympathy for the opponents of Israel."

Definition (2) and (3) are added in the 2002 edition, just before the USA decides to invade Iraq under orders from Israel.

Also this year, the Prime Minister of Israel, war criminal, Ariel Sharon, orders another Jewish genocide with the massacre in the Jenin refugee camp in the West Bank.

In response to this massacre, President Bush at first demands an immediate Israeli troop withdrawal from Palestinian cities, which Ariel Sharon publicly refuses to do. Bush backs down and goes on to state the following, on April 18th,

> "Ariel Sharon is a man of peace."

The DEA issues a report that Israeli spies, posing as art students, have been trying to penetrate United States Government offices. Police near the Whidbey Island Naval Air Station in southern Washington State stop a suspicious truck and detain two Israelis, one of whom is illegally in the United States. The two men were driving at high speed in a Ryder rental truck, which they claimed had been used to "deliver furniture."

The next day, police discover traces of TNT and RDX military-grade plastic explosives inside the passenger cabin and on the steering wheel of the vehicle. The FBI then announce that the tests that showed explosives were "false positived" by cigarette smoke, a claim test experts say is ridiculous.

Based on an "alibi" provided by an unidentified woman, the case is closed and the Israelis are handed over to Immigration and Naturalization Service (INS) to be sent back to Israel. One week later, the woman who provided the alibi vanishes.

On October 29th, Jewish "Project for a New American Century (PNAC)" members Robert Kagan and William Kristol state the following in a Weekly Standard article entitled, "The Gathering Storm,"

> "...what looms over the horizon...a wide ranging war in locales from Central Asia to the Middle East and, unfortunately, back again to the United States....Afghanistan will prove but an opening battle...this war will not end in Afghanistan. It is going to spread and engulf a

> number of countries in conflicts of varying intensity. It could well require the use of American military power in multiple places simultaneously. It is going to resemble the clash of civilisations that everyone has hoped to avoid."

Thomas Stauffer, a consulting economist in Washington, estimates that since 1973, Israel has cost the United States about $1.6 trillion, which, if divided by 2002's population, is more than $5,700 per person.

In his autobiography, "Memoirs," published this year, Rothschild, David Rockefeller admits his role in the World Government conspiracy when he states,

> "For more than a century, ideological extremists at either end of the political spectrum have seized upon well-publicized incidents to attack the Rockefeller family for the inordinate influence they claim we wield over American political and economic institutions. Some even believe we are part of a secret cabal working against the best interests of the United States, characterizing my family and me as "internationalists," and of conspiring with others around the world to build a more integrated global political and economic structure—one world, if you will. If that's the charge, I stand guilty, and I am proud of it."

On April 12th, every major paper in the United States runs a story that Venezuelan President Hugo Chavez had resigned as he was, "unpopular and dictatorial." In fact he had been kidnapped under a coup, where he was imprisoned on an army base. Following sympathy from the guards, the coup falls apart and President Chavez is back in his office one day later. Interestingly, he has video evidence that whilst he was wrongly imprisoned a United States military attaché supervised.

President Chavez, demonized by the Jewish media, commits the crime of giving milk and housing to the poor, and giving land not used for production by big plantation owners for more than two years, to those without land. His biggest crime, however, was in passing a petroleum law that doubled the royalty taxes from 16% to 30% on new oil discoveries, which affected Exxon Mobil, a Rothschild operation, along with many other international oil operators.

He also took full control of the state oil company, PDVSA, which before was nominally owned by the government, but in actual fact was in thrall to these international oil operators. Not only that, but President Chavez is also the President of the "Organization of Petroleum Exporting Countries" (OPEC) and vehemently rejects the World Bank's, "Four Step Strategy," and their plan to reduce wages of the common people for the benefit of the bankers.

Indeed, President Chavez has increased the minimum wage by 20%, which has increased the purchasing power of the lower paid workers and strengthened the economy. His minister, Miguel Bustamante Madriz, fully aware of the danger Venezuela poses to the bankers and aware of the conspiracy and plot against Venezuela and its president, states,

> "America can't let us stay in power. We are an exception to the new globalization order. If we succeed, we are an example to all the Americas."

Veteran filmmaker James Longley releases his documentary, "Gaza Strip," to critical acclaim. This documentary shows Israeli troops shooting Palestinian children through the head simply because they were throwing stones, and leaving booby-trapped toys on the ground to blow up curious children. It also shows Israeli helicopters dropping canisters of debilitating nerve gas on densely inhabited areas of the Gaza Strip.

2003: On March 16th, 23 year old American, Rachel Corrie, who had travelled to the Gaza Strip to defend Palestinians against Israeli war crimes being carried out there, is killed whilst trying to prevent the demolition of the home of a Palestinian pharmacist, his wife, and three young children. When she stands in front of this house to protest in front of an Israeli Defense Force (IDF) Caterpillar D9 bulldozer, she is deliberately driven over by the driver. The driver then reverses back over her for good measure. Rachel dies after saying to shocked Palestinians, who come to her aid,

> "I think my back is broken."

The United States does nothing to criticize Israel for

this, accepting their excuse that it was an "accident," even though there are several eyewitnesses that categorically say the act was deliberate and there is even photographic evidence showing Rachel was wearing a bright orange fluorescent jacket at the time it happened and that the murder occurred in broad daylight. The New York Jewish community has a lot to say about it however. When, in early 2006, a play entitled, "My Name Is Rachel Corrie," is due to premiere in New York, following two successful runs in London, it is abruptly cancelled after pressure from the Jewish community.

On March 19th, the United States, under the presidency of the Crypto-Jew, George W. Bush, announces the pending invasion of Iraq. This is the day this year when the holy "Day of Purim" falls in the Jewish calendar. This "Day of Purim" is a day the Jews celebrate their victory over all the goyim (non-Jews) in Ancient Babylon, which is now based within the borders of Iraq.

What is also revealing is that the previous United States led invasion of Iraq ended on the Day of Purim ten years earlier with the genocide of 150,000 fleeing Iraqis under the current President's father, George Herbert Walker Bush. Purim is also the time when the Jews are encouraged to get bloody revenge against the non-Jews.

Iraq is now one of six nations left in the world which do not have a Rothschild controlled central bank. However, this war is also about stealing Iraq's water supply for Israel, as Israel has always struggled for fresh water. Indeed, it had to steal the Golan Heights from Syria, which provided Israel with one third of its fresh water, 36 years before. Yet, still in Israel water extraction has surpassed replacement by 2.5 billion metres in the last 25 years. This means the water is far more precious to them than even the oil reserves of Iraq, which are the second largest reserves of oil on the planet. Indeed, less than four years ago in 1999, Israel's Environment Minister, Dalia Itzik, declared a state of emergency in relation to the country's water supply.

Not surprisingly, in June, President Bush puts a Jew, Paul Bremer, in control of Iraq when he names him the United States Administrator of Iraq. Paul Bremer had been from 1989, the managing director at Kissinger and Associates, the worldwide consulting firm founded by Jew, Henry Kissinger.

Malaysian Prime Minister Mahathir Mohamed states in a speech,

> "Jews rule the world by proxy. They get others to fight and die for them."

The Police Chief of Cloudcroft stops a truck speeding through a school zone. The drivers turn out to be Israelis with expired passports. Claiming to be movers, the truck contains junk furniture and several boxes. The Israelis are handed over to immigration. The contents of the boxes are not revealed to the public.

Israel deploys assassination squads into other countries, including the United States. The United States Government does not protest.

Russian Jewish Oligarch, Mikhail Khordorkovsy, is detained in prison in Russia facing charges of fraud, embezzlement and tax evasion.

2004: The FBI investigation continues of the American Israel Public Affairs Committee (AIPAC), the largest political lobbying group in the United States with over 65,000 members, whose job is to run the United States Government on behalf of Israel. The FBI reportedly believes AIPAC to be a spy front for Israel. Ashkenazi Jew, Larry Franklin, a mid-level Pentagon Analyst in the employ of Pentagon neo-con Jew Douglas Feith, is observed by the FBI giving classified information to two officials of AIPAC suspected of being Israeli spies. He is subsequently sentenced to 12 years in prison in 2006.

Later, Douglas Feith is fired from the United States National Security Council (NSC) in March, 1982 and loses his security clearance after he falls under suspicion of the FBI for passing classified material to Israeli embassy officials.

AIPAC hires lawyer Nathan Lewin to handle their legal defence, the same lawyer who defended suspected Israeli spy Stephen Bryen in 1978.

Spy Larry Franklin worked in the Pentagon Office of Special Plans, run by Richard Perle, at the time Perle (who was caught giving classified information to Israel back in 1970) was insisting that Iraq was riddled with weapons of mass destruction (WMDs), and the United States therefore must invade and conquer Iraq as soon as possible.

There were no WMDs, of course, and Perle dumped the blame for the, "bad intelligence" on CIA director George Tenet (real name, Cohen, another Crypto-Jew). But what does come to light is that the Pentagon Office of Special Plans was co-ordinating with a similar group in Israel, based in Ariel Sharon's office.

With two suspected Israeli spies (at least) inside the office from which the lies that launched the war in Iraq originated, it soon becomes crystal clear that the people of the United States are the victims of a deadly hoax, a hoax that started a war using the blood and money of American citizens for the purposes of Israeli oppression.

The leaking of the investigation of AIPAC by the Jewish media on August 28th this year, gives advance warning to all the other spies who had been working with Franklin. As if it couldn't get any worse, the damage to the FBI's investigation is completed when United States Attorney General John Ashcroft orders the FBI to stop all arrests in the case.

Like the Stephen Bryen case and the hunt for "Mega," this latest spy scandal seems destined to be whitewashed by officials who have their own secret allegiances to Israel and its spying apparatus to protect.

At the beginning of March, dual Israeli/American citizen and Jewish Rabbi, Dov Zakheim, resigns as the Pentagon Comptroller and Chief Financial Officer when it is revealed in an audit of the Pentagon budget that he is unable to account for the disappearance of $2.6 trillion, including defence inventory of 56 aeroplanes; 32 tanks; and 36 Javelin missile command launch units.

However, the United States government claims this cannot be investigated further because, allegedly, the records which would need to be studied to investigate this matter were destroyed in the attack on the Pentagon on September 11th 2001.

On May 20th, Senator Ernst Hollings, who is not running for a further term, decides to speak out about Israel's control of America, which he does on the floor of the Senate, firstly declaring that President Bush went to war in Iraq "to secure our friend, Israel" and, "everybody knows it." Then he makes the following statement about AIPAC's control of America,

> "You can't have an Israel policy other than what AIPAC gives you around here. I have followed them mostly in the main, but I have also resisted signing certain letters from time to time, to give the poor President a chance. I can tell you no President takes office I don't care whether it is a Republican or a Democrat....that all of a sudden AIPAC will tell him exactly what the policy is...."

In June, independent presidential candidate Ralph Nader

echoes Senator Hollings comments when he states,

> "What has been happening over the years is a predictable routine of foreign visitation from the head of the Israeli government. The Israeli puppeteer travels to Washington. The Israeli puppeteer meets with the puppet in the White House, and then moves down Pennsylvania Avenue, and meets with the puppets in Congress. And then takes back billions of taxpayer dollars."

Police near the Nuclear Fuel Services plant in Tennessee stop a truck after a three mile chase, during which the driver throws a bottle containing a strange liquid from the cab. The drivers turn out to be Israelis using fake identifications. The FBI refuses to investigate and the Israelis are released.

Two Israelis try to enter Kings Bay Naval Submarine Base, home to eight Trident submarines. The truck tests positive for explosives.

The National Director of the ADL, Abraham H. Foxman, publishes a book entitled, "Never Again? The Threat Of The New Anti-Semitism," in which he states that the New Testament's "lie," that the ancient Pharisees were responsible for the death of Christ has been responsible for anti-Semitism throughout the millennia. He suggests the New Testament writings are "hate speech" and should be censored.

On April 21st, Israeli nuclear weapons whistleblower Mordechai Vanunu is released from prison after serving eighteen years, over eleven of which were spent in a two metre by three metre cell in solitary confinement during which time he was only allowed occasional visits from his family, lawyer and a priest. Even though he is released from prison after serving his full sentence, he is not allowed to leave Israel and is not allowed to speak to foreign media.

In Northern Nigeria, Islamic leaders claim a United Nations Children's Fund (UNICEF) polio immunisation campaign is part of a United States plot to depopulate the region by spreading AIDS and sterilising agents. The Africans say their own lab tests show contaminants in the vaccine. In order to prove the vaccine is safe, the United States government sends a team of scientists, religious leaders and others abroad to witness tests on the vaccine in foreign labs; however, once the tests are completed, they refuse to release the results.

Mel Gibson releases his film, "The Passion of the Christ." To preserve its authenticity, the dialogue of the film is presented entirely in Aramaic and Latin with subtitles. However, there is one subtitle that does not appear. It is spoken but for some reason the subtitle is removed. This is of course due to pressure from Jewish media. The scene from which the subtitle was removed, was when Pilate was trying to get the Jews to stop calling for Jesus Christ's crucifixion. And what was it the Jews said in response to Pilate, that the powerful

Jewish lobby were so desperate to censor,

> "Let his blood be on us and our children."

On June 20th, according to a report in the Jerusalem Post, the Israeli Knesset has now empowered the State of Israel to criminalize anyone in the world who dares to question whether or not six million Jews died in the alleged holocaust, and request their extradition to Israel. Furthermore, the Israeli government can also seize, prosecute and imprison people who harbour such beliefs, should they ever set foot in Israel.

On September 30th, during his first Presidential debate with John Kerry, President Bush states, on the subject of Americans dying in the war in Iraq,

> "A free Iraq will help secure Israel."

On October 16th, President Bush signs into law the Global Anti-Semitism Review Act, designed to force the entire world into never being critical of the Jews, whatever their actions. This Act establishes a special department within the United States State Department to monitor global anti-Semitism, which is to report annually to Congress. This Act defines a person as being anti-Semitic if they purport any of the following beliefs:

> 1) Any assertion, "that the Jewish community controls government, the media, international business and the financial world."

2) The expression of "Strong anti-Israel sentiment."

3) Expressing "Virulent criticism" of Israel's leaders, past or present. The State Department gives an example of this occurring when a swastika is portrayed in a cartoon decrying the behaviour of a past or present Zionist leader.

4) Any criticism of the Jewish religion or its religious leaders or literature with the emphasis on the Talmud and Kabbalah.

5) Any criticism of the United States Government and Congress for being under undue influence by the Jewish-Zionist community, which would include Jewish organisations such as American-Israel Public Affairs Committee (AIPAC).

6) Any criticism of the Jewish-Zionist community for promoting globalism or what some call the "New World Order."

7) Placing any blame on Jewish leaders and their followers for inciting the Roman crucifixion of Christ.

8) Citing any facts that could in any way diminish the "six million" figure of Jewish holocaust victims.

9) Claiming that Israel is a racist state.

> 10) Making any claim that there exists a "Zionist Conspiracy."
>
> 11) Offering proof that Jews and their leaders created Communism and the Bolshevik Revolution in Russia.
>
> 12) Making "derogatory statements about Jewish persons."
>
> 13) Asserting that spiritually disobedient Jews do not have the Biblical right to re-occupy Palestine.
>
> 14) Making any allegations of Mossad involvement in the 9/11 attack.

2005: On January 20th, President Bush makes the following statement as part of his second inaugural address,

> "When our Founders declared a New Order of the Ages…"

This is not true. The founders did not declare a "New Order of the Ages," but the Jew, President Roosevelt, did when in 1933, he put the Latin translation, "Novus Ordo Seclorum," on the dollar bill.

On February 15th, Michael Chertoff is sworn in as the head of the United States Department of Homeland Security. As previously stated, Chertoff is a dual United

States/Israeli citizen, his father was a Rabbi and his mother was one of the first Mossad agents.

On February 27th, Nation of Islam leader, Louis Farrakhan, makes the following statement with regard to the Jewish domination in the trade of African Slaves to America,

> "Listen, Jewish people don't have no hands that are free of the blood of us. They owned slave ships, they bought and sold us. They raped and robbed us."

On July 7th, three stations on the London Underground Network and a London double-decker bus are bombed resulting in the deaths of 52 people. This is blamed on so-called Al-Qaeda suicide bombers. However, this is not the only parallel with the attack on September 11th 2001 in America. Here are some of the other interesting parallels:

> 1) At the times and places the separate bombings on the London Underground occur, a "crisis management," company known as Visor Consultants is carrying out terror drills of the same event. This is confirmed in separate interviews, on both Radio 5 and Britain's most popular television station ITV, with the consultancy's managing director, Peter Power. In the Radio 5 interview, he states,
>
> "At half past nine this morning we were actually

running an exercise for a company of over a thousand people in London based on simultaneous bombs going off precisely at the railway stations where it happened this morning, so I still have the hairs on the back of my neck standing up right now."

Readers may recall that the reason planes were not immediately scrambled on September 11th 2001, the day of the attack on the World Trade Center and the Pentagon, was, according to the United States government, because a drill of the same event was occurring at the same time on that day, which caused confusion to the security services, who couldn't work out if an attack on America was actually taking place or if it was a drill.

Why do people not find it suspicious when a terror drill run at the same time at three London Underground stations (it is important to note that the London Underground network consists of 274 stations, so picking 3 stations represents just over 1% of the stations they could have picked), actually becomes reality as an actual attack on the same three London Underground stations?

Unfortunately, the general public do not use their brains and instead allow their thinking to be done for them by a Jewish owned media. Why would a trained journalist not follow up such a blatant "smoking gun," especially when the man who made these claims, Peter Power, now refuses to discuss the matter any further. The answer is obvious. A journalist would not make that decision, and it can only be assumed the journalists collectively have been instructed not to investigate the matter further by the owners of the media, Jewish owners.

As for the reason for running a terror drill whilst the attacks were taking place, the most likely reason is to provide an alibi for the actual perpetrators of the attack, who knew about this drill. The way this would work is that if any of the real bombers were caught acting suspiciously, they could claim that they were only part of the drill and they would have the alibi to back that up. This would, of course, mean that the alleged perpetrators, four Muslim men, were not involved in the attack.

2) The authorities claim that personal documents relating to each of the so-called bombers were found at each of the bomb scenes. This is another strange coincidence with the attack on the World Trade Center, when authorities there claimed that although they could not find traces of bodies, a pristine paper passport belonging to one of the hijackers had been found.

3) Israel's Finance Minister, Benjamin Netanyahu, is in London on the morning of the attacks in order to attend an economic conference in a hotel near the underground station where one of the blasts occurred, but stays in his hotel room instead after he had been informed by Israeli intelligence officials attacks

> were expected. This is another similarity with the attacks on America, when 4,000 Jews were warned not to go to work in the World Trade Center that day. How come it's only Jews who get prior warning about alleged Al-Qaeda terrorism?

Following the invasions of Afghanistan and Iraq, there are now only five nations in the world left without a Rothschild owned central bank: Iran; North Korea; Sudan; Cuba; and Libya. Interestingly, the satellite state of Israel, more commonly known as the United States government, chooses to refer to these countries as "rogue nations."

Physics Professor Stephen E. Jones of Brigham Young University publishes a paper in which he proves the World Trade Center buildings could have only been brought down in the manner they were by explosives. He receives no coverage in the mainstream media for his scientifically provable claims.

On September 30th, Danish newspaper, Jyllands-Posten, publishes twelve so-called cartoons, most of which depict the Muslim Prophet Mohammed, something it is against the Islamic faith to do, regardless of what he might be doing. These cartoons are subsequently reprinted in over fifty countries resulting in large scale protests by the worldwide Muslim community.

This is exactly why they were printed. To inflame the

tensions between the western world and the Muslim community and encourage the Western world and the Muslim community to be further alienated so they can fight amongst each other until only the Jews are left. The cultural editor of Jyllands-Posten responsible for the original publication of these cartoons? Flemming Rose, a Jew.

On October 30th, the head of the Kabbalah Centre in Israel, Shaul Youdkevitch, is arrested for extracting money from a cancer patient. Over a period of a few months, the victim donated $36,000 to the Kabbalah Centre after she was told by Youdkevitch that the donation would improve her condition. When her condition did not improve, other Rabbis at the Kabbalah Centre in Tel Aviv suggested she make a "significant and painful donation."

As a result she donated a further $25,000 and also purchased some "holy water" from the Kabbalah Centre at an exorbitant price. She eventually ran out of money, so the Rabbis then suggested her husband give up work and instead work for free at the Kabbalah Centre. The victim then died and her husband went to the police to report this extortion.

Interestingly, Shaul Youdkevitch is one of the main teachers of the Kabbalah, worldwide and was directly responsible for Madonna's visit to Israel in 2004.

On November 15th, Robert Stein Jr., an American felon who was employed as a comptroller for the Coalition

Provisional Authority in Iraq, is charged with fraud and accepting kickbacks and pleads guilty to the charges. Stein, Lieutenant Colonel Michael Wheeler, and Lieutenant Colonel Debra Harrison were accused of accepting kickbacks of $200,000 per month, from Philip Bloom, in return for awarding questionable contracts.

A New York Times article, commenting on Stein's administration of reconstruction funds from Iraq's oil revenue, states,

> "For reasons that the Pentagon has so far declined to clarify, Stein was hired as a comptroller by the Coalition Provisional Authority and put in charge of $82 million for reconstruction, despite his conviction for felony fraud in the 1990's."

In November, a group of conservative to moderate Democrats called "Blue Dog Coalition" that focuses on the fiscal responsibility of government, reports that Jewish President George W. Bush has borrowed more money from banks and foreign governments than all the previous 42 United States Presidents combined. Treasury Department figures show that from 1776-2000, all the previous American Presidents borrowed a total of $1.01 trillion dollars, whereas in the past 4 years alone, the Bush administration has borrowed $1.05 trillion.

On December 5th, following accusations from holocaust revisionists that World War 2 leaders never mentioned the alleged holocaust of the Jews in gas chambers,

Richard Lynn, Professor Emeritus at the University of Ulster, reports his research into this matter as follows,

> "I've checked out Churchill's Second World War writings and speeches and the statement is quite correct—not a single mention of Nazi 'gas chambers,' a 'genocide of the Jews,' or of 'six million' Jewish victims of the war.
>
> This is astonishing. How can it be explained? Eisenhower's 'Crusade in Europe' is a book of 559 pages; the six volumes of Churchill's 'Second World War' total 4,448 pages; and de Gaulle's three-volume, 'Memoires de guerre,' is 2,054 pages.
>
> In this mass of writing which altogether totals 7,061 pages (not including the introductory parts), published from 1948 to 1959, one will find no mention either of Nazi 'gas chambers,' a 'genocide' of the Jews, or of 'six million,' Jewish victims of the war."

On December 6th, David Cameron is elected leader of the British Conservative party. Cameron is an old favourite of the Rothschilds, having been special adviser to Norman Lamont when he collapsed the British economy for them in 1993. Cameron is also related to the British royal family.

Interestingly, the organisation, "Conservative Friends of Israel," boasts proudly on their website that over two-thirds of Britain's Conservative Members of Parliament are members. Indeed, they even got David Cameron to complete a questionnaire for them prior to his election as leader, in which he stated the following,

> "Israel is in the front line in the international struggle against terrorist violence."

Another organisation, presumably in complete opposition to the "Conservative Friends of Israel," is called the "Labour Friends of Israel." They choose not to reveal how many Labour Members of Parliament are members. They do, however, state that they have sent at least fifty on expenses-paid trips to Israel since 1997.

Despite this intense political lobbying, official government figures reveal that Jews represent less than half of one percent of the British population.

Also, on December 6th, President Bush's wife, Laura Bush, is joined by Rabbi Binyomin Taub, Rabbi Hillel Baron, and Rabbi Mendy Minkowitz for the kosherization of the White House kitchen. A photo of this taking place as they stand with staff is shot by photographer Shealah Craighead and subsequently placed on the official White House website.

2006: Hamas is elected to power in the Palestinian elections in January. This is exactly what Israel wants, as it gives them the excuse to get rougher (if that's possible) with the Palestinians. Immediately following Hamas' election, Israel demands that aid be cut off to Palestine, and this is dutifully done by the United States, the European Union, and Canada. The result of this is, of course, what the Jews have always wanted, widespread suffering in Palestine, supporting Israel's long term goal of the genocide of the entire Palestinian people who refuse to leave Palestine.

It also benefits Israel's long term aims in the Middle East, as former Mossad agent Victor Ostrovsky prophetically stated on page 252 of his 1994 book, "The Other Side Of Deception,"

> "Supporting the radical elements of Muslim fundamentalism sat well with the Mossad's general plan for the region. An Arab world run by fundamentalists would not be a party to any negotiations with the West, thus leaving Israel again as the only democratic, rational country in the region. And if the Mossad could arrange for the Hamas (Palestinian fundamentalists) to take over the Palestinian streets from the PLO, then the picture would be complete."

The Edmond De Rothschild Banque, a subsidiary of Europe's Edmond De Rothschild family bank group in France, becomes the first foreign family bank that obtains approval of the China Banking Regulatory Commission and enters China's financial market.

On March 5th to 7th, the American Israel Public Affairs Committee (AIPAC) holds their annual convention in Washington D. C. More than half of all United States Senators and one third of all United States Congressmen attend.

The Anti-Defamation League (ADL) ruthlessly leans on governments throughout the world to pass hate crimes legislation. Evidently the Jews are scared that the Jewish criminal cabal is being exposed more and more on a daily basis, predominantly on the internet.

Their job is to protect this criminal network and what better way to do it than by passing so-called hate crimes laws, in which anyone who exposes a Jewish criminal, in turn becomes a criminal.

This hate crimes legislation is promoted in protecting other things, namely ethnic minorities. It is interesting that these Jewish organisations are so keen on forcing laws on countries throughout the world that might seem somewhat contradictory to their own position. Consider the following:

> 1) Israel only allows Jews to emigrate to Israel and offers them financial incentives for doing so;
>
> 2) Israeli law forbids the marriage between a Jew and a non-Jew;
>
> 3) Israel does not allow non-Jews to purchase property within the country; and most interestingly…
>
> 4) Israel does not allow non-Jews to own any media, although Jews see no problem with their owning the vast majority of the world's media.

British historian David Irving is sentenced to three years in jail in Austria, for denying the alleged holocaust of the Jews in World War 2. It is important to note that the only historical event you can be arrested for questioning is this alleged holocaust.

The Jews start to panic about being exposed and, therefore, up their attack on breaking down America by encouraging the illegal immigration of millions of Mexicans into America, and then using their lobby groups to get the government to give them all amnesty.

The idea is many fold, but it includes: using their centuries old policy of divide and conquer; getting cheap labour for the multinational companies they own; and using the social and economic problem of massive Mexican immigration to divert the Americans attention from Jewish supremacism. Why is it that Jews love mass immigration into every country, apart from their own, Israel?

On July 12th, two Israeli soldiers stray into Lebanese territory and are therefore arrested as prisoners of war by Lebanese forces. The Jewish media throughout the world screams that they have been kidnapped, yet make no reference to the fact that Israel have seized and imprisoned over 9,000 Palestinians without trial. Israel starts bombing Lebanon indiscriminately, a country in which, incidentally, 40-45% of the population are Christian.

Incidentally, in relation to the 9,000 Palestinians imprisoned without trial, Article 111 of Israeli law mandates that the government may detain any person whatsoever for an unlimited period, without trial and without declaring a charge. This was brought in with the founding of Israel, and has been gleefully adopted by other Jewish leaders such as President George W. Bush, and an attempt was made by Tony Blair to put a variation of this into British law.

When the Jewish media report this conflict between Israel and Lebanon, they make no reference to the high preponderance of Christians in Lebanon and instead portray the people of Lebanon as a bunch of evil Muslim Al-Qaeda terrorists. Within a month well over 1,000 Lebanese men, women and children have been killed, hundreds of thousands injured, and a quarter of the country's population have been displaced.

The war ends with Israel's withdrawal from Lebanon. Many Jews are not satisfied with this outcome and accuse Prime Minister Ehud Olmert, of losing this war. However when he appears before the Knesset Foreign Affairs and Defence Committee on September 5th, he states,

> "The claim that we lost is unfounded. Half of Lebanon is destroyed; is that a loss?"

To Jewish aspirations, is it indeed?

Epilogue

The Synagogue of Satan can be expected to continue its centuries-old global assault on Christian civilization. The Moslem world is also under intense attack. The plan of the Jews is to divide and conquer, to have Christians and Moslems at each others throats and thereby to destroy both.

The ultimate goal is a fasco-socialist New World Order, a Jewish Utopia, and a global system of concentration labor camps alongside wealthy Jewish enclaves.

Whether the Synagogue of Satan achieves this diabolical goal is up to you. Yes, God's will shall eventually be done. His plan shall prevail. But the question is, what does God require of you and me, now, today? Will we, with God's help, successfully fight and overcome evil, or instead, will we passively submit to the monstrous crimes of the greatest array of criminals the world has ever known—the talmudist overseers who comprise the Synagogue of Satan?

Index

60 Minutes, TV show 235
666 (the mark) 155

- A -

A Clean Break: A New Strategy for Securing the Realm (paper) 236
ABC (broadcasting company) 145, 184, 243
Abraham, Larry 180
Abramoff, Jack 253
Abramovich, Roman 246
Abrams, Elliott 241
Achille Lauro, cruise ship 198
Acre gaol 152
ADL caught operating a massive spy operation 223
Adler, Solomon 159
Afghanistan 245, 251, 258, 265, 282
Africa 220
African National Congress (ANC) 229
Africans 182
Age of the Rothschilds 46
Agnew, Vice President Spiro 183
Albright, Madeleine 235
Alexandria, Egypt 158, 198
All These Things (book) 27
Allen, Gary 180
Allevijah, Kadya 113
Allies, the 138
Almadén quicksilver mines in Spain 52
Al-Qaeda 257, 279, 282, 290
AMDOCS (telephone billing service) 241, 245, 261
American Civil Liberties Union (ACLU) 218
American Friends of Lubavitch 259
American Hebrew, The (journal) 26, 106
American Israel Public Affairs Committee (AIPAC) 255, 271, 272, 273, 277, 287
American Jewish Congress 136
amnesty 289
Amnesty International 215
An Eye For An Eye (book) 227
Annan, UN Secretary-General Kofi 240
anthrax 257
Anti-Defamation League (ADL) 56, 91, 113, 144, 152, 161, 181, 182, 197, 204, 205, 223, 250, 274, 288
anti-Semitism, defined 264
Anti-Terrorism Alert Center 198
apartheid state of Israel 177
Appomattox 69
Arab-Americans 223
Arafat, Yasser 194, 237
Argentina 127, 198, 247, 248, 268

Armenians 93
Armitage, Richard L. 241
Army School of Advanced Military Studies (SAMS) 250
Article 111 of Israeli law 289
Ashcroft, John 272
Ashkenazi Jews 24
Asian Law Caucus 223
Astaroth 154
AT&T 245
Ataturk, Mustafa Kemal 93
atheism 74, 75
atheists 74
atomic bomb 147, 163
Atta, Mohamed 253
Atzmon, Menachem 252
Auchincloss, Hugh 169
Auschwitz 209
Australia 55
Austria 49, 56, 127, 212, 289
Austro-Hungarian Blast Furnace Company 55
Aven, Pyotr 220
Aylesbury in Buckinghamshire 72

- B -

B'nai B'rith 56, 91
Bacque, James 206
Baden-Baden, Germany 218
Baghdad 215
Balfour Declaration 95, 115
Balfour, Arthur James 95, 96, 115
BIS 121, 122, 123, 204
Bank of England 27, 28, 29, 46, 53, 55, 59, 67, 130, 143, 147, 150, 151, 240
Bank of France 39
bank, de Rothschild Frères 42, 80, 167, 179
M. von Rothschild und Söhne 40, 86
bankrupt 30
Banque Rothschild 179, 193
Bar Ilan University 208
Barak, Ehud 239
Baring, Sir Francis 40
Baron, Rabbi Hillel 286
Baruch, Bernard 99, 108, 118, 119
Basle, Switzerland 82, 86, 107, 122, 123
Basra, Iraq 213
Bauer, Mayer Amschel 30, 31
Bauer, Moses Amschel 30
Bavarian government 36, 38
Beamish, Rear Admiral Henry Hamilton 84, 135
Begin, Menachem 149, 152, 155, 165, 189, 194
Beirut 193, 194, 195, 234
Belgium 212
Belloc, Hilaire 111, 133
Belmont (Schönberg), August 53, 69
Ben-Gurion, David 149, 157, 159, 161, 164, 168
Ben-ludah, Grand Rabbi Simeon 73
Ben-Menashe, Ari 199, 219
Bennett, William J. 241
Bentov, Cheryl 202
Berezovsky, Boris 220, 246
Bergner, Jeffrey 241
Berman, Matvei 103
Bernadotte, Count Folke 146
Berne, Switzerland 243
Bernstein, Jack 196, 197
Beswick, Lord 199
Bevin, Ernest, British foreign minister 149
Bialik, Haim Nachman 129
Bible 207
Bible, discredit 173
Biddles, the 76
Bilderberg Group 164, 218
Billikopf, Jacob 88

Bin Laden, Osama 256, 258
Birthright Israel 212
Bismark, Otto Von 63
black people 88
Black Thursday 118
blackmail 34
black-ops 198
Blair, Tony 165, 221, 238, 239, 290
blood libel 247
Bloom, Philip 284
Blue Dog Coalition 284
Boers 84
Boesky, Ivan 202
Bohemian Grove 154
Bolivia 127, 249
Bolshevik revolution 98, 106, 278
Bolsheviks 96, 102, 103
Bolshevism 103, 105, 124, 133, 159
Bolton, John 241
bonds 45, 48
Booth, John Wilkes 69, 70
Boston 78
Boston Logan airport 252
Bouvier, Janet 169
boycott of German goods 126, 129
Boyer, Louise Auchincloss 187
Brackman, Harold 88
Brandeis, Louis Dembitz 94, 95
Brando, Marlon 191, 236
Brazil 127, 244
Breakdown of Money, The (book) 28
morality, breakdown of 173
Bremer, Paul 270
Brezhnev 180
Brigham Young University 282
Brin, Abe 214
Brin, Yehudah Yoav 214
Britain 61, 80, 85, 86, 94, 99, 100, 124, 127, 133, 175, 180, 213, 249, 251
British Army 84
British economy 45
British Labour Leader 81
British Museum 74, 107
British Newfoundland Corporation Limited 163
British Petroleum 195
British Royal 50
British Royal family 54
British Security Services 149
Brittan (Brittanisky), Leon 203
Bronfman, Edgar 238
Brown, Bernard Joseph 128
Brown, Gordon 165, 239
Bryce, Lord 130
Bryen, Stephen 190, 219
Buchanan, President James 62
Buenos Aires, Argentina 248
Bulan, King 23, 24
Bulgaria 78, 82
Burke's Peerage 166
Bush, President George Herbert Walker 143, 213, 269
Bush, President George W. 143, 245, 264, 269, 273, 276, 284, 290
Bush, Laura 286
Bush, Prescott 143, 148
By Way Of Deception (book) 195, 210
"By Way Of Deception, Thou Shalt Do War" (Mossad motto) 161, 164, 178
Byrd, Senator Robert 167

- C -

C. M. de Rothschild e figli 68
Cairo, Egypt 146, 158, 165
California 55
Callaway, Congressman Oscar 97
Cameron, Carl 255
Cameron, David 285, 286
campaign finance reform 260

Canaan 89
Canada 65, 230, 240, 246, 256, 287
Canada AM (TV show) 230, 231
Canadian debt 160
Canadian House of Commons 70
capital market liberalization 262
capital punishment by decapitation 218
capitalism 90
Capitol Hill (Washington) 259
Carnegie, Andrew 76
Carnegies 109
Carter, President Jimmy 189, 192
Caspian and Black Sea Petroleum Company 80, 87
Castro, Fidel 167
Catling, Assisstant Inspector General Richard 155
Cause Of World Unrest, The (book) 106
Cave of the Patriachs mosque 224
CBS (broadcasting company) 117, 183, 184
censorship 172
Center For Immigration Studies (journal) 259
Centers for Disease Control (CDC) 190
Central Bank 87, 160
Central Intelligence Agency (CIA) 182
Chabad Lubavitch movement 216, 224, 259
Chancellor of the Duchy 201
Chancellor of the Exchequer 59
character assassination 197
Chase Manhattan Bank of New York 92
Chase, Salomon P. 65
Château Brane Mouton 60
Château Clarke 186
Château Lafite 72
Château Mouton Rothschild 60
Chavez, Hugo 245, 267
cheap labour 289
Chelsea Football Club 246
Chemin De Fer Du Nord railway 56, 77
Chertoff, Michael 255, 278
Chicago, Illinois 78
Chile 127
China 50, 53, 54, 59, 131, 208, 233, 258
China Banking Regulatory Commission 287
Chirac, Jacques 234
Chosen People, Jews as 114
Christian guilt 261
Christianity 75
Christopher, Warren 237
church infiltration 173
Church of Satan 240
Churchill Falls 163, 185
Churchill, Sir Winston 104, 119, 285
civil rights 171
Civil War 62, 63, 64, 68, 69, 80
Clays, Henry 51
Clinton, President Bill 164, 235, 237, 238, 241, 243, 250
Cloudcroft, Police Chief of 270
Coal industry, privitization of British 199
Coalition Provisional Authority in Iraq 283
Coe, Frank 159
Cohen, Avner 168
Cohen, Hannah Barent 40
Colbert, James 236
Cold War 242
Columbia University 88
Communism 58, 98, 180, 208, 278
Communist coup in Berlin, Germany 99

Communist Internationalism 132, 133
Communist Manifesto, The (book) 57, 170
Compagnie Européenne de Banque 193
concentration camp is invented (in 1899) 84
Confederate States of America 62, 68
Congress 72
Congress of Vienna 47, 48, 97
Congressional Record 182
Coningsby (book) 55
Conroy, George R. 90
Conservative Friends of Israel 285
Constitution, discredit 173
education, control 184
political system 136
control of the press 35, 108, 109, 111, 136
control over the Soviet Government 193
Converse Infosys 241, 261
Calvin Coolidge 121
Corrie, Rachel 268
cotton 61, 63
CFR 101, 108, 109
Craighead, Shealah 286
Crick, Walter 115
criminal justice 260
Cromwell, Oliver 25, 27
Crossley, Anthony 138
Crusade in Europe 285
Cuba 167, 282
Cush 89
Czechoslovakia 162, 212

- D -

Daily Express 134, 152
five Israelis 253, 254
Davis, Jefferson 62
Davitt, John 161
Dawes, Charles G. 121
De Beers 81
de Gaulle 285
Dean, John 207
death sentence for anyone guilty of anti-Semitism 113
debt to IMF used as leverage to take state owned assets 204
Defense Industrial Security: Weaknesses in US Security Arrangements With Foreign-Owned Defense Contractors (GAO report) 232
Defense Investigative Service 231
Dehan, Dr. Yaakov Yisrael 115
Deir Yassin massacre 155, 156, 165
Deliberate Deceptions: Facing the Facts About the U. S. Israeli Relationship 222
democracy 58
Democrat voters 78
Democratic National Committee (DNC) 186
Denmark 140
Department of Homeland Security 278
depress their individual stock-markets 204
Deputies of British Jews 38
Desmond, Richard 152
destroy religion 72
diaspora 211
Dillon, Emile Joseph 100
Dimona (Israel's nuclear installation) 201
Disraeli, Benjamin 55, 56, 77
diversity 177
divide and conquer 289
Dobriansky, Paula 241
Documents Illustrative of the History of the Slave Trade to America (4 volume set) 131

Dominican Republic 246
Donnan, Elizabeth 131
Drexels, the 76

- E -

Earl of Caithness 238
East India company 43
Eban, Aba 222
Ebb and Flow of Conflict, The: The History of Black-Jewish Relations Through 1900 88
Economics at Cambridge (book) 221
ecstasy (drug) 240, 246
Ecuador 194
Edict of Expulsion 25
Edmond De Rothschild Banque 287
Edom 115
schools 111, 172
Education Day, U.S.A, 216
Egypt 77, 157, 163, 178, 183, 222, 240
Egyptian-Israeli peace treaty 191
Eichmann, Adolf 198
Einstein, Albert 153
Eisenberg, Lewis 256
Eisenhower, Dwight 163, 206, 285
Eitan, Rafael 198
electricity 199
Encyclopaedica Judaica 109
Engel v. Vitale 167
England 67, 68, 73, 77, 94
Enron 249
entertainment industry, control of 109, 172, 184, 260
Epstein, Israel 159
Esau 115
"establishment of a central bank is 90% of communizing a nation" 102
ethnic structure of the 384
Commissars in the new Russian government 98
European Central Bank 244
European Union 160, 287
Executive Committee for Zionist Affairs 94
Executive Order 11110, is rescinded 168
Executive Order 11110, returns to the U.S. the power to issue currency 168
Exxon Mobil 267

- F -

Fairbanks Jr., Charles 236
false flag operations 189, 251
Farben, I. G. 137, 148
Farrakhan, Louis 279
Fascism 57, 74
Federal Bureau of Investigation (FBI) 113, 182, 197, 271, 274
Federal Government 72
Federal Reserve 53, 92, 118, 119, 121, 122, 123, 132, 147, 168, 186
Federal Reserve Act 92, 147
"Federal Reserve definitely caused the Great Depression..." 119
Federal Reserve Notes 147
Feith, Douglas 236, 271
Ferrières in France 59
Field, A. N. 27
financial 184
Findley, Paul 222
First Bank of the United States 37, 41
Fisher, Colonel Ernest F. 206
Flag of Israel 154
Fleischer, Ari 259
Flight International, publication 233
Force, a 75
Ford, Henry 107

Forrester, Izola 70
Fort Bragg 183
Fort Detrick 257
Fort Knox gold 186
Foundation of a New World Order, The 99
Fox News 255
Foxman, Abraham 250, 274
France 48, 61, 65, 68, 72, 77, 94, 124
Frankfurt University 57
Frankfurt, Germany 210, 256
Franklin, Larry 271
free speech 205
Free Trade 263
Freehof, Dr. Solomon 131
"Freemasonry is a Jewish establishment" 117
Freemasons, Continental Order of 33
French debt 160
French Revolution 35, 36, 38, 49, 105
Frenkel, Naftaly 103
Freud, Sigmund 60
friction 205
Friedman, Mikhail 220
Friedman, Milton 119
From Pharaoh to Hitler, What Is A Jew? (book) 128
Fukuyama, Francis 241
Fulbright, Senator J. William 183

- G -

Gailbraith, John Kenneth 118
Gallatti, Captain D. H. 152
Gapon, Georgi Apollonovich 87
Garfield, President James A. 79
gas chambers 284, 285
Gathering Storm, The (article) 265
Gayssot law 212
Gaza 178, 183
Gaza Strip 268
Gekko, Gordon 202
General Accounting Office (GAO) 232, 233
General Agreement on Tariffs and Trade (GATT) 161
General Electric 121
George II of England 32
George, Prime Minister David Lloyd 130
Georgetown University 123
Georgia Guidestones 192
German Emancipation Edict of 1822 100
German owned railway rights in Palestine 101
German prisoners of war 206
German reparations 99
Germany 87, 100, 120, 121, 126, 127, 129, 133, 135, 137, 138, 212
German 73, 74
Germany and England 135
Germany, East and West 171
Ginsburg, Rabbi Yitzhak 225
Giuliani, Rudolph 250, 253
Gladstone, William 59
Glasnost 207, 208
Global 2000 Report 192
Global Anti-Semitism Review Act 276
"goal of Judaism today is: a merciless campaign against all German peoples and the complete destruction of the nation" 134
Golan Heights 179, 183, 269
gold and diamond mines of South Africa 85, 229
Gold Standard 71
Gold, Rothschild control of 98
Goldenson, Leonard 145, 184
Goldman, Adam 261

Goldman, Emma 105
Goldman, Sachs of New York 92, 109
Goldmann, Nahum 190
Goldsmid, Abraham 40
Goldstein, Dr. Baruch Kappel 224, 225
Goodman, Julian 184
government bankruptcies 263
goyim 33
Graham, Katherine 184
grand cru estates 72
Grand Orient 33, 36
Grant, General Ulysses S. 69
Great Britain, The Jews, and Palestine (book) 132
Great Crash of 1929, The (book) 118
Great Depression 120
great social cataclysm 74
Greenbacks 66, 68, 71
Greenbaum, Izaak 145
Greenspan, Alan 122
Grynszpan, Herschel 135
Guggenheim, Untermyer, and Marshall (law firm) 91
Gulag Archipelago (book) 103
Gulf War Syndrome 213
gun control laws 131
Gusinsky, Vladimir 220, 261
Gwynne, H. A. 106

- H -

Ha'aretz (newspaper) 168, 179
Ha'avara 126
Habib, Avshalom 152
Hague, William 165
Halphen, Noémie 81, 89, 179
Ham 89
Hamas 286, 287
Hamilton Falls 163
Hamilton, Secretary of the Treasury Alexander 37
Hamitic Myth 88
Hanau, Eva 38, 58
HANSARD (report) 199, 238
Harari, Mike 209
Harel, Ezra 252
Harper Collins 231
Harriman, Edward Henry 83
Harriman, Edward R. 76
Harrington, Lord 61
Harrison, Lieutenant Colonel Debra 284
Hasidic Jews 246
hate 205
hate crimes legislation 288
hate speech 205
Havas (news agency, France) 93
Hearst Press 159
Heath, Prime Minister Edward 180
Hebrew 24
Hebrew University 116
Heilbrun, Chairman 195
Hepatitis B vaccination 190
Herlong Jr., A. S. 170
Hersh, Seymour M. 219
Herzl, Theodor 82
Hesse-Cassel 39
Hexagram 154
Hezbollah 223, 234
Hickey, W. 134
Hiroshima 147, 235
Hirsch, Rabbi Emil G. 88
History of the Jews in America, A (book) 88
Hitler could have been a Rothschild 140
Hitler, Adolf 120, 125, 137, 138, 140, 144, 148, 153, 181
Hitler, Alois 140
HIV/AIDS 182, 190, 229, 230, 248, 275
Hoffman, Clare 152
Holland 164

Hollings, Senator Ernst 273
Hollis, Christopher 28
Hollywood 236, 260
Hollywood Walk of Fame 236
Holmes, Jesse H. 26
Holocaust 261
Holocaust denial 212
homeland for the Jews 82
homosexuality 173, 205
Honey Trap 191
Hong Kong 50
Hooks, Benjamin 88
Hoover, J. Edgar 113
Hotam 208
Hotel Majestic in Paris 101, 108
House of Commons 130, 138
House of Plantagenet 245
House of Rothschild 41
House, Colonel Edward Mandell 108
How To Be A Good Communist (pamphlet) 228
Howe, Russell Warren 149
Hughes, Billy, Australian Prime Minister 104
Huntleigh USA 252
Hussein, Saddam 215, 236, 242, 243, 245
Hylan, John, Mayor of New York 110

- I -

"I am well aware of the tactics of you, my Zionist brethren" 196
IBM 185
illegal immigration of millions of Mexicans into America 289
Illuminati 32, 33, 34, 35, 49, 52, 72
Illustrated Sunday Herald 104
Imétal 167
IMF Riots 263
immigration 176
Immigration and Naturalization Service (INS) 265
Impact—Essays on Ignorance and the Decline of American Civilization 167
incest 61
independent press 79
India 60
Indonesia 244
Indyk, Martin 237
inflation 30
Inside Story of the Peace Conference, The (book) 100
Inside The Gestapo (book) 140
Institute Of International Affairs 101
International Bank for Reconstruction and Development 146
International Bankers 70, 71, 73, 110, 111, 120, 137, 181
International Consultants on Targeted Security (ICTS) 252
International Herald Tribune 184
International Indian Treaty Council 223
International Longshore and Warehouse Union (ILWU) 223
International Monetary Fund (IMF) 122, 146, 147, 159, 194, 195, 204, 244, 247, 248, 249
invisible government 110
Iran 282
Iran-Contra 203
Iraq 154, 183, 210, 213, 214, 215, 236, 242, 245, 282, 284
Iraq Liberation Act 243
Iraq's water supply 269
Iraqi invasion of Kuwait 212
Ireland 169
Irgun terrorist gang 152, 155
Irish Northern Aid 223
Iron Curtain 208

Irving, David 289
Islam 74
Israel and the Bomb (book) 169
Israel cannot extradite its' citizens 227
"Israel controls the Senate" 183
Israel Moses Seif Banks of Italy 92
Israel passes their law of return 161
Israel's nuclear weapons programme 202
Israel's wine industry 114
Israeli Defense Force (IDF) 224, 268
Israeli flag 30
Israeli government refuse to admit or deny whether or not they have nuclear weapons 202
Isratex Company 213
Italy 49, 55, 68, 94
ITV (TV station) 279
Itzik, Dalia 270
Izoulet, Jean 124

- J -

J. Rothschild, Wolfensohn and Co. 219
Jabotinsky, Vladimir 129
Jackson, President Andrew 49, 50, 51, 52, 53, 54, 56, 62
Jackson, Senator Henry "Scoop" 179
Jane's Defense Weekly 233
Japan 50, 204
Japanese debt 160
Javits, Senator Jacob 188
Jefferson, President Thomas 37, 40
Jenin refugee camp 264
Jerome (Jacobson), Jenny 104
Jerusalem 151
Jerusalem Post, The 232, 252, 255, 256, 276
Jesus Christ 217, 245, 275
Jewish Agency Rescue Committee 145
Jewish Alliance Israelite Universelle 124
Jewish Chronicle 144, 159
Jewish Courier, The 114
Jewish Defence League 257
Jewish domination in the trade of African Slaves to America 279
Jewish Encyclopaedia 42, 43, 87, 115
"Jewish financiers, all Masters of Lodges, rule the world" 125
Jewish influence made the United States just what they are—that is, American 89
Jewish Institute for National Security Affairs 219
"Jewish merchants played a major role in the slave-trade. 196
Jewish Paradox, The 190
"The Jewish people as a whole will be its own Messiah" 117
Jewish Post International Edition 102
Jewish Stake in America's Changing Demography—Reconsidering a Misguided Immigration Policy 259
Jewish Tribune of New York 117
Jewish University 129
Jews "genius for evil leadership" 130
Jews And Judaism in the United States: A Documentary History (book) 196
Jews and Modern Capitalism, The (book) 89
"Jews are the aristocrats of the world" 125
"Jews can destroy by means of finance" 115

"Jews control crime in the United States." 181
Jews in the Bolshevist movement (75%) 102
"Jews may adopt the customs and language of the countries where they live" 114
Jews Must Live (book) 130
Jews, The (book) 111
JFK, the movie 169
Johnson, President Lyndon B. 168
Jones, Stephen E. 282
Jordan 154, 178, 183, 236
Jordan River 178
Joyce, William 133, 141, 148
JUMBO (Israeli intelligence code name) 219
Jyllands-Posten 282, 283

- K -

Kabbalah 76, 206, 277
Kabbalah Centre 283
Kabbalists 75
Kagan, Robert 241, 265
Kaganovich, Rosa 113, 208
keepers of the light 32
Kelley, Raymond W. 246
Kennedy, Jackie 169
Kennedy, Joseph 118, 120
Kennedy, President John F. 120, 168, 169
Kerry, Senator John 276
Kever Yossev Yeshiva Talmudic school 225
Keynes, John Maynard 146
Kfar Sirkin 196
Khalilzad, Zalmay 242
Khazaria 23
Khordorkovsy, Mikhail 271
Khrushchev 171
killing machine 103
Kimberley diamond mines in South Africa 81
King Charles I 25
King David Hotel in Palestine 149, 150
Kings Bay Naval Submarine Base 274
Kissinger and Associates 270
Kissinger, Henry 48, 164, 187, 270
Klatzkin, Jacob 109
Klinghoffer, Leon 198
Knesset 166, 188, 276, 290
Knesset Foreign Affairs and Defence Committee 290
Knickerbocker, Cholly 159
Knodorkovsky, Mikhail 220
Koehler, Hansjurgen 140
Kogan, Lazar 103
Kok, Eva 226
Kol Yisrael radio 258
Koran 207
kosherization of the White House kitchen 286
Kristol, William 242, 265
Kruger, Stephanus Johannes Paul 85
Kuhn Loeb Bank of New York 92, 109
Kuhn, Loeb & Co. 76, 87, 90
Kulisher, Professor A. 134
Kun (Cohen), Bela 105
Kuwait 213

- L -

L'antisémitisme son histoire et ses causes 26
La Compagnie Financière Edmond de Rothschild 169
La Revue de Paris 117
Labour Friends of Israel 286
Labour Party 239
Lachout, Emil 158
Lagergren, Nane 240
Lahat, General Shlomo 195

Lamont, Norman 199, 221, 222, 285
Landman, Samuel 132
Langer, Walter 140
Lansky (book) 181
Lansky, Meyer 113, 181
Lapid, Yosef 230, 231
Larry King Live (TV show) 236
Las Vegas, Nevada 240
Laurer, George J. 185
LaVey, Anton 191, 240
Lavi fighter 233
Lavon Affair, The 163
Lavon, Pinhas 164
Lawrence, Richard 52
Lazard Brothers of Paris 92
Lazare, Bernard 26
League of Nations 101, 148
Lebanese 189
Lebanon 154, 157, 189, 193, 194, 223, 234, 289, 290
Lee, General Robert E. 69
Lehman Brothers of New York 92
Lemmy, Adrian 76
Lenin (Ulyanov), Vladimir 76, 98, 102, 105
“Let his blood be on us and our children." 276
Levine, Dennis 202
Levy, Baruch 117
Levy, Michael 239
Levy, Moses Mordechai (Karl Marx) 57, 229
Lewin, Nathan 190, 271
Lewinsky, Monica 237
Liberty Park 254
Libya 282
Lieberman, Senator Joe 259
Liebknecht, Karl 99
Life (magazine) 108
Life of an American Jew in Racist Marxist Israel, The (book) 196
Light-bearer 75
Lincoln, President Abraham 62, 65, 66, 68, 69, 70, 80, 97, 137, 168
Lindbergh, Congressman Charles 92
Lishka le Kishrei Mada (LAKAM) 198, 219, 233
Litani river 189
Lithuania 212
Little, Dr. Kitty 231
Local Religious Council of Kiryat Arba 224
Lodge, Senator Henry Cabot 123
Loeb, Solomon 76
Loeb, Teresa 76
Loewenberg, Robert 236
London Daily Telegraph 166
London Globe 103
London Morning Post 116
London Sunday Times 202
London Times 98
London Underground Network 279, 280
London, City of 59, 104
Longley, James 268
"Lords of Money and Lords of the World" 90
Los Alamos 147
Los Angeles, California 78, 240
Lucifer 75
Luxemburg, Rosa 99, 105
Lynn, Richard 285

- M -

MacMichael, Harold 146
Madonna 283
Madriz, Miguel Bustamante 267
mafia 184
"Maintain humanity under 500,000,000 in perpetual balance with nature." 192
Manchu Emperor 54
Mandela, Nelson 228

Mandelstam, Max 83
Market Based Pricing 263
Marlen, George 132
marriages 112
Martin, Clifford 152
Marx, Karl (Moses Mordechai Levy) 57, 58, 105, 117
Marxism 58
"Masonry is based on Judaism" 117
Master Plan for Brazil, World Bank document 244
Mazzini, Guiseppe 52, 73, 74, 76
Mbeki, Govan 230
Mbeki, Thabo 230
Mc Fadden, Congressman Louis T., Chairman of the House Banking & Currency Committee 119, 120, 132
McClellan, General George 69
McGeer, Gerald G. 70, 71
media corruption 40, 185
Mega (spy) 237
Meir, Gideon 239
Memoires de guerre (book) 285
Memoirs (book) 266
Mentmore in England 59
Merkel, Angela 165
Messick, Hank 181
Mexico 64, 65, 122
Meyer, Eugene 109
Miami, Florida 240
MILCO 198
Milken, Michael 202
Milner, Lord Alfred 84
Mind of Hitler, The (book) 140
Minkowitz, Rabbi Mendy 286
minority group strife 72
Mohamed, Mahathir 270
Mohammed 217, 282
Molech 154
Mondavi, Robert 191
monetary bribery 34
money is not even printed these days 199
money supply 200
Money Supply and the Private Banking System (entry in HANSARD) 199
Monroe Doctrine 64
Monroe, President James 64
Montefiore, Moses 38
Montefiores, the 104
Morals and Dogma (book) 75
Morel, Solomon 225, 227
Morgan Jr., J. P. 118
Morgan, J. P. 76, 91, 97
Mosley, Sir Oswald 135
Mossad LAP (Israeli pyschological warfare) 215
Mossad, The 161, 195, 196, 197, 202, 207, 209, 210, 214, 215, 227, 230, 243, 250, 254, 255, 278, 287
Moyne, Lord 146
MTV 261
Muller, Commander Anton 158
Munich, Germany 82
Murdoch, Rupert 231, 235
Muslim terrorists 251
Muslims to migrate 251, 261
My Name Is Rachel Corrie (play) 269

- N -

N. M. Rothschild and Sons 221
Nader, Ralph 273
Nagasaki 147
Nakar, Meir 152
Napa Valley 191
Napoleon 39, 41, 43, 44, 46
Napoleon III 64
Nation of Islam 279
National Advancement for the Association of the Coloured People (NAACP) 88, 223

National Institute of Health (NIH) 190
National Security Agency (NSA) 245
National Security Council (NSC) 271
National Security Study Memorandum 200: Implications of Worldwide Population Growth for U.S. Security and Overseas Interests 187
Naval Investigative Service 198
Nazi War Crimes 148
Nazism 57
NBC (broadcasting company) 116, 184
Negrophobic 89
Nes Siyyona 228
Netanyahu, Benjamin 149, 203, 208, 252, 257, 281
Netherlands 246
Never Again? The Threat Of The New Anti-Semitism (book) 274
new "world order, which would, of course, give universal sovereignty to the only international race in existence" 133
New Britian, magazine 130
New Testament to an Israeli 188
New World Order 117, 128, 132
New York 68, 78, 87, 240
New York City Blood Bank 190
New York Stock Exchange 119
New York Times 46, 98, 110, 125, 169, 184, 197, 218, 222, 237, 241, 256, 284
Newark airport 252
Newhouse, Samuel 108
Newsweek (magazine) 109, 184
Nietzsche, Freidrich Wilhelm 57, 58
Nietzscheanism 57
Nigeria 275
"niggers" (reference to Sephardic Jews by Ashkenazi Jews) 162
nihilists 74
Nixon, President Richard 186
"no government authority was needed for this present system of credit creating." 201
"no people were killed by poison gas in the following concentration camps" 158
Noahide Laws 216
Nobel Peace Prize 103
Nordau, Max 86
Noriega, General Manuel 209
North American Free Trade Agreement (NAFTA) 160
North Korea 282
Northampton Daily Echo 115
Novus Ordo Seclorum 128, 278
Nuclear Fuel Services plant in Tennessee 274
Nuclear Materials and Equipment Corporation 175

- O -

Oakland Educational Association 223
obscenity 173
octopus (giant) 110
Odigo 255
oil pipeline over the Andes 195
Olmert, Ehud 252, 253, 290
Omar, Mullah 258
"One cow in Palestine is worth more than all the Jews in Poland" 145
"One million Arabs are not worth a Jewish fingernail." 225
Operation Accountability 223
Operation Desert Storm 213
Operation Grapes Of Wrath 234
Operation Peace for Galilee 194

opium 53, 54, 258
Opium Wars 54
Oppenheimer, Harry 229
Oppenheimer, J. Robert 147
Opus 1 191
Order of St. George 49
Orgad, Jacob "Cookie" 246
Organization of Petroleum Exporting Countries (OPEC) 267
Original Writings of The Order and Sect of The Illuminati, The (document) 36
Ostrovsky, Victor 195, 210, 214, 227, 230, 287
Other Losses (book) 206
Other Side of Deception, The (book) 211, 214, 227, 287
Ottoman Government of Turkey 93
Oudendyke, M. 124
"our god is Lucifer" 188

- P -

paedophile 246
paedophilia 61
Paice, Mervyn 152
Palestine 78, 82, 85, 86, 94, 95, 96, 99, 100, 116, 126, 127, 138, 140, 149, 151, 156, 193, 286, 287
Palestine Jewish Colonization Association (PICA) 114
Palestinian Liberation Organisation (PLO) 194, 287
Palestinians 161, 177, 189, 199
Paley, William S. 117, 184
Palimpsest—A Memoir (book) 169
Panama 209
Panic of 1907 88
paper debits and credits 46
Pappen, David (President of Harvard University) 38
Parlament, British 139
parliamentary seat 57
Passion of the Christ, The (movie) 275
Paterson, William 28, 29
PDVSA oil company 267
Pearl Harbor 142
Peled, General Matityahu 179
Pentagon 280, 284
Peres, Shimon 258
Perestroika 208
Perle, Richard 179, 190, 236, 242, 271
Perrin, Rabbi Yaacov 225
Persian Gulf 213
pharmaceuticals 263
Philadelphia 78
physical attacks 197
Pike, Albert 73, 74, 75, 76
Pilate 275
Pine, L. G. 166
Pitter-Wilson, George 103
Playboy Magazine 191
Poland 78, 82, 162, 212
political power comes from the barrel of a gun 131
Pollard, Jonathan 198, 233
Pope Gregory XVI 49
Pope John Paul II 190
Pope Leo XIII 83
pornography 173
Port Said 158, 198
Portugal 44
possible violence 205
Potanin, Vladimir 220
Pound, Ezra 167
Power, Peter 279
"powerful international bankers virtually run the United States Government" 111
prayer is banned from the American Public Schools 167
prayer 173

Primrose, Archibald Philip 77
Primrose, Harry (Lord Dalmeny) 77
Primrose, Lady Margaret 77
Primrose, Lady Sybil 77
Primrose, Neil 77
Prince William IX of Hesse-Cassel 32
Prince William IX of Hesse-Hanau 31, 32, 39, 43
Princeton University 91
Privatisation 262
Profits Of War (book) 199
Project for a New American Century (PNAC) 241, 243, 265
promiscuity 173
Proofs of a Conspiracy Against All the Religions and Governments of Europe Carried on in the Secret Meetings of Freemasons, Illuminati and Reading Societies 38
Protocols of the Learned Elders of Zion, The (book) 107, 240
Public Law 102-14 216
Public Order Act of 1986 203
Purim, Day of 213, 224, 269

- Q -

Qana 234
Quigley, Carroll 123, 188

- R -

Race Relations Act of 1965 175, 203
Race, Nation or Religion: Three Questions Jews Must Answer (pamphet) 131
Railroad Empire 76
Rankin, Congressman John 162
Raphael, Marc Lee 196
Rappoport, Yakov 103
Rarrick, Congressman John R. 182
Rath, Ernst vom 135
RCA 116, 121
RDX plastic explosives 265
Recon Optical Inc 219
Red Cross, The 155, 156
red hexagram (sheild) 30
reduce population growth 187
Reichorn, Rabbi 73
Reichsbank 121
Report of the Criminal Investigation Division (Palestine Government document) 155
Resolution 181 151
Reuters news agency 81, 93
Revelation, Book of 185
Rhodes, Cecil 84
Ribakoff, Joseph 205
Rich (Reich), Marc 250
ridicule the information 197
Rio Light 244
Rio Tinto copper mines 76
Ritter, Karl 57, 58
Rivkind (Rifkind), Malcolm 203
Robespierre, Maximilien 35
Robison, John 38
Rockefeller, David 164, 218, 266
Rockefeller, John D. 68, 76, 108, 118
Rockefeller, Nelson 187
Rockefellers, the 111
Rodman, Peter W. 242
Romania 78, 82, 212
Rome Observer, The 246
Roosevelt (Rosenfelt), President Franklin Delano 128, 142, 278
Roosevelt, Claes Martenzen van 128
Roosevelt, President Theodore 110
Rose, Flemming 283
Rosenberg, Julius and Ethel 163
Harold Rosenthal 188
Rosenthal, Julius 88

Rosenthal, Zvi 214
Roth, Samuel 130
Rothschild & Cie Banque 193
Rothschild & Sons, N. M. 53, 77, 104, 116, 163, 185, 186, 199
Rothschild (name change) 31
Rothschild agents 62
Rothschild Bank of Berlin 92
Rothschild Bank of London 92
Rothschild GmbH 210
Rothschild Private Management Limited 186
Rothschild, Age of the 89
Rothschild, Aline Caroline de 80
Rothschild, Alphonse de 80
Rothschild, Amschel 234
Rothschild, Amschel Mayer 33, 38, 58, 60
Rothschild, Babette 35, 73
Rothschild, Benjamin de 170
Rothschild, Betty von 56, 57
Rothschild, Edmond de 57, 80, 82, 85, 86, 100, 101, 114, 131
Rothschild, Edmond de (grandson of Edmond de Rothschild) 116, 165, 169, 186, 203, 240
Rothschild, Ferdinand de 84
Rothschild, Gustave de 80
Rothschild, Hannah de 77
Rothschild, Henriette ("Jette") 37, 72
Rothschild, Isabella 35, 66
Rothschild, Jacob (James) Mayer (later as, Baron James de Rothschild 38, 42, 44, 53, 56, 57, 59, 60, 72, 80, 82, 166, 186
Rothschild, Julie 37, 48
Rothschild, Kalmann (Carl) Mayer 36, 49, 57, 60
Rothschild, Lionel de 57, 61, 77, 80
Rothschild, Lionel Nathan de 40
Rothschild, Lord Nathaniel de 43, 60, 72, 73, 80
Rothschild, Lord Victor 134, 180
Rothschild, Maurice de 80, 81, 89, 116, 166, 179
Rothschild, Mayer Amschel 31, 32, 33, 36, 37, 38, 39, 41, 42, 43, 58, 72
Rothschild, Nathan Mayer 35, 39, 40, 41, 42, 43, 44, 45, 46, 47, 53, 55, 60, 73, 97, 221
Rothschild, Philippe de 86, 191, 207
Rothschild, Salomon Mayer 33, 39, 40, 55, 57, 60
Rothschild, Schönche Jeannette 33, 61
Rothschilds as Barons 49
Rothschilds' Bank of the United States 40, 55
Rothschilds, The 91, 95, 96, 98, 99, 101, 140, 181, 231
Rothschilds, The (book) 167
Royal Dutch and Shell 87
Royal House of Judah 245
Royal Institute Of International Affairs (RIIA) 101
Rubin, Irv 257
rumours of war 81
Rumsfield, Donald 242
Russia 68, 78, 82, 98, 102, 105, 106, 124, 128, 156, 159, 162, 170, 192, 208, 219, 220, 246
Russia's oil fields 80
Russian Revolution 124
Russian takeover by Rothschild Jewish elite 102

- S -

Sabra 194
Sachar, Howard 88
Sachs, Albie 229
Sack, John 227

Said, Khedive 77
Sainsbury, David 239
Samson Option, The (book) 219
Samuel, Maurice 113, 114
San Francisco Labor Council 223
San Francisco Police 223
San Francisco, California 68
Sarnoff, David 116
Sassoon, Abdullah (Albert) 59, 115
Sassoon, David 50, 53, 54, 59, 60, 80
Sassoon, Edward Albert 60, 80
Satan 75
Satan Speaks (book) 240
Saturday Evening Post, The 104
Saturn 154
Saudi Arabia 154, 214
sayanim 210, 211, 212, 243
Scarborough, Rowan 250
Schacht, Hjalmar 121
Schicklgruber, Maria Anna 140
Schiff, Jacob (a Rothschild) 71, 76, 87, 88, 90, 91, 108, 159
Schiff, John 159
Schindler's List (movie) 223
Schmugner, Wolf 190
Schnaper, Gutle 30, 58
Schnaper, Wolf Salomon 31
Schneider Jr., William 242
Scotland Yard 103
Scott, Sir Walter 49
Scottish Rite of Freemasonry 38, 75
Second Bank of the United States 48, 49, 50, 52, 56
Secret Societies and Subversive Movements (book) 114
Securities and Exchange Commission (SEC) 256
Senate Foreign Relations Committee 190
separation of Church and State 218
Sephardic 162
Seven Oligarchs of Russia 220
sex bribery 34
shabbez goy 29
Shamir, Yitzhak 146, 155, 199
Shanghai 127
Sharon, Ariel 166, 194, 258, 264, 272
Shatila massacre 194
Shaw, George Bernard 116
Shin Bet 191
shipbuilding 97
Siegel, Martin 202
Silverstein, Larry 256
Simon Wiesenthal Center, The 88
Simpson, William Gayley 138
slaughter of 60 million in Russia 103
slavery 62, 64, 67
Slovakia 212
Slovo, Yossel Mashel (Joe) 229
smallpox vaccination program 182
Smolensky, Alexander 220
Smyth, Richard 198
snuff film industry 246
social liberalism 260
Socialism 58, 180
Sokolow, Nahum 101
Solts, Aron 103
Solzhenitsyn, Aleksandr 103
Sombart, Werner 89
Son of the Mornin 75
Soros, George 221
Soskice, Attorney General Frank 175
South Africa 228, 229
South Carolina, sesession 62, 64
Southern Pacific Railroad 83
Soviet Union 163
Spartacus-Weishaupt 105
Special Drawing Rights (SDRs) 147, 204
Specter, Michael 241

Spielberg, Steven 223
Spingarn, Professor Emeritus Joel 88
Spirit of Darkness (Lucifer) 75
Springs, A. A. (Springstein) 71
Sri Lanka 196
St. Petersburg 80
Stahl, Lesley 235
Stalin (Djugashvili), Josef 76, 113, 128, 153, 208, 227
Stalin, Trotsky, or Lenin (book) 132
Stamp, Sir Josiah, director of the Bank of England 143
Standard Oil 68, 76, 87, 90, 110, 111
Star Of David 154
Starr, Ken 237
State of Israel is officially, "proclaimed" 153
Stauffer, Thomas 266
Steel Empire 76, 97, 137, 199
Stein Jr., Robert 283
Steinlight, Stephen 259
sterilising 275
Stern Gang, The 146, 149, 155
Stern, Caroline 39, 60
Stiglitz, Professor Joseph 262, 264
Stone, Oliver 169
Sudan 282
Suez Canal 77, 166
sufferings of Jews 82
Sulzberger 184
Supreme Court 72, 111
Surface-to-air missile (SAM) 233
suspicion 205
Svanidze, Ekaterina 113
Swastika 148
Swietochlowice 226
Swinton, John 78
Switzerland 47, 212, 250
Synagogue of Satan 258
Syria 154, 157, 178, 179, 183, 236, 270

- T -

Tahomi, Avraham 115
Tales of the British Aristocracy (book) 166
Taliban 258
legitimizes sex 230
Talmud, The 24, 32, 61, 88, 89, 90, 176, 206, 207, 216, 224, 230, 247, 277
Tamil Tiger 196
Tanzania 248
Taub, Rabbi Binyomin 286
Taylor, Colonel Dick 65
Tel Aviv 195, 226, 241, 283
Tenenbaum, David A. 237
Tenet (Cohen), George 272
Tenney, Senator Jack B. 182
terror drill 281
Terrorism: How The West Can Win (book) 203
This One Mad Act (book) 70
Thyssen banks 121
Time (magazine) 108, 184, 218
Times of London, The 67, 102
TNT 265
Tolson, Clyde 113
tools and vassals of rich men 79
Torah 216
Traffickers' New Cargo: Naive Slavic Women (article) 241
Tragedy and Hope (book) 123, 188
transfer debts from third world countries 203
Transvaal Republic in South Africa, 85
Treasury Department 284
Treaty of Nanking 54
Tropicana, The (bordello) 241
Trotsky (Bronstein), Leon 76, 102, 105

Truman, President Harry S. 153, 154
Truth (magazine) 90
truth is to be no defence in court 205
Tsar Alexander I 47, 96
Tsar Alexander II 97
Tsar of Russia, Alexander II 68, 80, 87, 94
Tsar Nicholas II 96
Tse-Hsu, Lin 54
Tsung, Mao Tse 131, 159
Tunisia 194
Turkey 236
Twilight Over England (book) 141
Twing, Shawn L. 232
Tyler, John 55

- U -

U.S. Patent Office. 171
U.S. Troops Would Enforce Peace Under Army Study 250
U.S.S. Liberty 178, 222
Uganda 86
ul-Haq, President General Zia 207
Ulyanov (Lenin), Vladimir Ilyich 102
UN Resolution 3379 which condemns Zionism as racism 187
Underground Electric Railways Company of London 116
Union Pacific Railroad 83
Union States (civil war era) 62, 63, 65
United Artists (Hollywood studio) 109
United Coal Mines of Vítkovice 55
United Jewish Appeal (UJA) 145, 256
United Nations 148, 151, 153, 156, 157, 171, 188, 189, 222, 240
United Nations Children's Fund (UNICEF) 275
United Nations safe compound 234
United States Consulate General in Jerusalem 191
United States drug interdiction 262
United States Federal Debt 160
United States Holocaust Memorial Museum 127
United States military attaché 267
United States, The 124, 132, 143, 153, 161, 170, 178, 183, 189, 212, 222, 237, 265, 268, 269, 280
Universal Product Code (UPC) 185
University of Ulster 285
Untermyer, Samuel 91, 94, 125, 129
uranium supplies 231
Urban Moving Systems 253
usury 83, 84, 251

- V -

Van Hise, Charles R., President of the University of Wisconsin 99
Vance, Cyrus R. 192
Vancouver Sun 70, 71
Vanunu, Mordechai 201, 275
Vatican 49
Venezuela 245
Versailles peace conference commences 99, 100, 101
Vidal, Gore 169
Visor Consultants 279
Volker, Paul A. 219
von Estorff, General 31

- W -

Wald, Lillian 88
Waldheim, U.N. Secretary-General Kurt 193

Wall Street 76, 202
Wall Street (movie) 202
Wall Street Journal 203, 219
Wannal, Raymond 198
war of 1812 41
Warburg Bank of Amsterdam 92
Warburg Bank of Hamburg 92
Warburg, James Paul 160
Warburg, Paul 118
Warburgs, the 109
Wars 73
"Wars are the Jews' Harvest" 73
Washington Post, The 109, 184, 218, 237
Washington Report on Middle East Affairs, The 232
Washington Times 220, 232, 250
Washington, President George 37
water 199
Watergate 186
Waterloo, Battle of 45, 48
"We are God's chosen people." 188
"We do not have to answer to the world, only to ourselves." 194
"We have to kill all the Palestinians" 195
"We Jews, we are the destroyers" 114
weapons of mass destruction 236, 243, 272
Vin Weber 242
Webster, Nesta 108, 114, 135
Weekly 109, 133
Weekly Standard 265
Weishaupt, Adam 32, 33, 35, 38, 49, 58
Weiss, Jacob 152
Weizmann, Chaim 83, 114, 144
welfare 260
Wellington 43, 44, 45
Wessex Water 249
West Bank 178, 183, 264
West Point 163
Wheeler, Lieutenant Colonel 284
"When our Founders declared a, 'New Order of the Ages.'" 278
Which Way Western Man? (book) 138
Whidbey Island Naval Air Station 265
White, Harry Dexter 146
William III 28
Wilson, President Woodrow 78, 90, 94, 95, 125
Wilton, Robert 98
Wisconsin State Convention of the League to Enforce Peace 99
Wise, Rabbi Isaac 117
Wise, Rabbi Stephen 88, 136
Wolfensohn, James 248
Wolff (news agency, Germany) 93
Wolfowitz, Paul 242
Woolsey, R. James 242
World Bank 122, 146, 204, 220, 244, 248, 249, 262
World Central Bank 204
World Conservation Bank 203
World Empire 83
World Government 82, 160, 176, 180, 266
World Government conspiracy 266
World Health Organization (WHO) 182
World Jewish Congress 136, 144, 190, 238
World Revolution or the Plot Against Civilization (book) 107
World Trade Center 251, 255, 256, 257, 280, 281, 282
World War I 73, 93, 94, 120, 132
World War II 74, 120, 121, 127, 130, 134, 137, 138, 140, 142, 146, 148, 151, 160, 193, 206, 212, 238, 260, 284, 285

World War III 74
World Zionist Movement 114
World Zionist Organisation 132
Worldwide Challenges to Naval Strike Warfare 233
Worms, Benedikt Moses 33
Wozniak, Major-General Stanislaw 234
Wurmser, David 236
Wurmser, Meyrav 236

- Y -

Yagoda, Genrikh 103
Yahweh 75
Yeltsin, Boris 208, 220
Yiddish 24
Yishuv (the Jewish Settlement in Palestine) 85, 86
You Gentiles (book) 113
Youdkevitch, Shaul 283
Young Communist League 163
Young Turks 93
Young, Owen D. 121

- Z -

Zack, Dr. Philip 257
Zakheim, Dov 273
Zalman, Rabbi Shneur 224
Zim Shipping Company 257, 258
Zionism 74, 82, 264
Zionist Congress 82, 83, 86, 101, 107, 121
Zionist Federation 96
Zionist point of view 139
Zoellick, Robert B. 242
Zohar 206
Zurich 238
Zwack, Xavier 35
Zyklon B gas 137

Other Important Resources for You

Available for Order

BOOKS:

Codex Magica—Secret Signs, Mysterious Symbols and Hidden Codes of the Illuminati, by Texe Marrs (624 pages) $39.00

Circle of Intrigue—The Hidden Inner Circle of the Global Illuminati Conspiracy, by Texe Marrs (304 pages) $20.00

Dark Majesty—The Secret Brotherhood and the Magic of a Thousand Points of Light, by Texe Marrs (304 pages) $20.00

Mystery Mark of the New Age—Satan's Design for World Domination, by Texe Marrs (288 pages) $20.00

VIDEOS:

Masonic Lodge Over Jerusalem—The Hidden Rulers of Israel, the Coming World War in the Middle East, and the Rebuilding of the Temple (VHS or DVD) $27.00

Cauldron of Abaddon—"From Jerusalem and Israel Flow a Torrent of Satanic Evil and Mischief Endangering the Whole World" (VHS or DVD) $27.00

continued on next page...

Thunder Over Zion—Illuminati Bloodlines and the Secret Plan for A Jewish Utopia and a New World Messiah (VHS or DVD) $27.00

Illuminati Mystery Babylon—The Hidden Elite of Israel, America, and Russia, and Their Quest for Global Dominion (VHS or DVD) $27.00

TO ORDER

Please use your charge card and phone 1-800-234-9673, or send check or money order to:
Power of Prophecy
1708 Patterson Road
Austin, TX 78733

ALL PRICES INCLUDE SHIPPING AND HANDLING

To order online:
www.powerofprophecy.com

For Our Newsletter

Texe Marrs offers a *free* sample copy of his newsletter about Bible prophecy and world events, the global conpsiracy of the elite, secret societies, cults and false religions, and the occult challenge to Christianity. If you would like to receive this newsletter, please write to:

Power of Prophecy
1708 Patterson Road
Austin, Texas 78733

You may also e-mail your request to:
customerservice1@powerofprophecy.com

For Our Website

Texe Marrs' newsletter is published monthly on our websites. These websites have descriptions of all Texe Marrs' books, and are packed with interesting, insight-filled articles and information about prophecy and world events. You also have the opportunity to listen to Texe Marrs' radio program 24/7 and to order an exciting array of books, tapes, and videos through our online *Catalog and Sales Store*. Visit our websites at:

www.powerofprophecy.com
www.conspiracyworld.com

Our Shortwave Radio Program

Texe Marrs' international radio program, *Power of Prophecy*, is broadcast weekly on shortwave radio throughout the United States and the world. *Power of Prophecy* can be heard on WWCR at 5.070 Saturdays at 7:00 p.m. Central Time. A repeat of the program is aired on Sunday nights at 9:00 p.m. Central Time. The radio program is also aired 24/7 on streaming audio at *www.powerofprophecy.com.*

About Texe Marrs, Author of the Foreword

Author of the #1 national bestseller, ***Dark Secrets of The New Age; Circle of Intrigue;*** and the massive exposé, ***Codex Magica***, Texe Marrs has also written 37 other books for such major publishers as Simon & Schuster, John Wiley, Prentice Hall/Arco, Stein & Day, and Dow Jones-Irwin. His books have sold over two million copies.

Texe Marrs was assistant professor of aerospace studies, teaching American defense policy, strategic weapons systems, and related subjects at the University of Texas at Austin for five years. He has also taught international affairs, political science, and psychology for two other universities. A graduate *summa cum laude* from Park University, Kansas City, Missouri, he earned his Master's degree at North Carolina State University.

As a career USAF officer (now retired), he commanded communications-electronics and engineering units. He holds a number of military decorations including the Vietnam Service Medal, and has served in Germany, Italy, and throughout Asia.

President of RiverCrest Publishing in Austin, Texas, Texe Marrs is a frequent guest on radio and TV talk shows throughout the U.S.A., Canada, and Europe. His monthly newsletter, *Power of Prophecy*, is distributed around the world, and he is also heard globally on his popular shortwave radio program, *Power of Prophecy*. His website is *www.powerofprophecy.com.*

To contact the author:
Andrew Carrington Hitchcock invites you to contact him at: *andrewcarringtonhitchcock@hotmail.com*, or go to his website: *www.thesynagogueofsatan.com*